The Changing Idea of a Teachers' Union

The Stanford Series on Education and Public Policy

General Editor: **Professor Henry M. Levin**, School of Education, Stanford University

The purpose of this series is to address major issues of educational policy as they affect and are affected by political, social and economic issues. It focusses on both the consequences of education for economic, political and social outcomes as well as the influences of the economic, political and social climate on education. It is particularly concerned with addressing major educational issues and challenges within this framework, and a special effort is made to evaluate the various educational alternatives on the policy agenda or to develop new ones that might address the original research and/or competent synthesis of the available research on a topic.

The Changing Idea of a Teachers' Union

Charles Taylor Kerchner

and

Douglas E. Mitchell

The Falmer Press

(A member of the Taylor & Francis Group)
London • New York • Philadelphia

UK   The Falmer Press, Falmer House, Barcombe, Lewes, East Sussex, BN8 5DL

USA   The Falmer Press, Taylor & Francis Inc., 242 Cherry Street, Philadelphia, PA 19106-1906

First published 1988

Library of Congress Cataloging in Publication Data is available on request

ISBN 1 85000 333 5
ISBN 1 85000 334 3 (pbk.)

Jacket design by Caroline Archer

Typeset in 11/13 Bembo by
Mathematical Composition Setters Ltd, Ivy Street, Salisbury

Printed in Great Britain by Taylor & Francis (Printers) Ltd, Basingstoke

Contents

Dedication

To Our Parents
Charles Wesley Kerchner and Dorothy Taylor Kerchner
For a love that nurtures curiosity
and
the memory of Lois DeVore and David L. Mitchell
*In whom deep moral passion was always linked to open-minded inquiry, making
the search for knowledge at once a sacred obligation and a great joy*

CTK/DEM

Acknowledgements

We approach publication of this work with many debts. The largest of these cannot be properly acknowledged because it is owed to the hundreds of teachers, unionists, school administrators and school board members who talked with us during our years of field work. We approached each of these persons with the pledge that they would remain anonymous, and thus we cannot name them here, but our hope is that our hidden collaborators will find themselves in this book and will agree that we have fairly transmitted their insights.

Intellectual debts of a different sort are due to a number of scholars who came before us in the study of schools as organizations and political bodies. Laurence Iannaccone (University of California, Santa Barbara) can properly lay claim to the 'dissatisfaction theory' of school politics, with which our idea of labor relations generations is wholly consistent. Not only has he been helpful through the weight of his writing but also through his personal encouragement and advice. We have been guided by the work of a number of other scholars: Ralf Darhendorf's treatment of social conflict: Jonathan Turner's work on comparative sociological theory; Elmer Schattschneider's treatment of expanding public attention to social conflict; and Anselm Strauss' work on organizations as negotiated orders. Our work has also been enriched by the work of a large number of labor scholars whose contributions we have tried to acknowledge in the text.

The title of the book reflects a reading of Richard Hoffsteader's, *The Idea of a Party System*, which traces the status of American political parties from that of an anathema to being the bedrock of our political system.

This research would not have been possible without the financial support of the late, lamented National Institute of Education and two extraordinary program officers: Gail MaColl and Fritz Mulhauser. The lack of an agency that funds individually initiated research, such as that on which this book is built, is sorely missed. In addition, we were supported by research grants from the The Eli Lilly Endowment, the Wilbur Foundation, and the Center for Educational Policy and Management, University of Oregon.

Along the way, we have also been materially helped by Ronald Corwin (Ohio State University), Anthony Cresswell (State University of New York at Albany), Donald Bear (United Teachers Los Angeles), Joseph Weeres (The Claremont Graduate School), Ray Berry (University of California, Riverside), Michael Murphy (Utah University), Gary Sykes (Michigan State University), Lee Shulman (Stanford University), Paul Peterson (Johns Hopkins University), Robert Nielson (American Federation of Teachers (AFT)), and Albert Shanker (AFT), Susan Moore Johnson (Harvard University), Edwin Bridges (Stanford University), and Henry Levin (Stanford University) read the entire manuscript in draft, and their comments prompted substantial clarification. The above mentioned shall, of ourse, be held blameless for what you are about to read.

As graduate students, Gabrielle Pryor (now Assistant City Manager of San Dimas, California) and Wayne Erck (now Principal of Richards High School, Oak Lawn, Illinois) undertook a substantial amount of the field work, provided insights, and mediated disputes between the co-authors. Their help and good cheer was invaluable. Rhoda Baumgart acted as project secretary and organized our lives during the data collection and analysis. Special thanks are also due Ethel Parker, Fay Rulau, Marge Dokken and Helga Moore for the final manuscript preparation.

Our longest-running debt, forever unpaid and unpayable, is to Leanne Bauman Kerchner and Tedi K. Mitchell. This volume could not have seen print without their encouragement, love and continuing presence. In addition, each took time from her own doctoral studies to read and substantively comment on several chapters, and their interventions markedly improved the text.

Charles T. Kerchner
Douglas E. Mitchell
May 1988

1
The Dynamics of the Idea: An Introductory Summary

The Strike Heard 'Round the Country

A new era in American education began on the morning of 11 April 1962. The events of that day signaled a permanent change in the relationship between organized teachers and their schools. That morning *The New York Times* announced 'Teachers strike today.'[1] The day before, some 5000 members of the United Federation of Teachers — recently named bargaining agent for the city's teachers — had gathered in the St. Nicholas Arena and voted down an Executive Committee recommendation that they postpone action pending a report from Mayor Robert Wagner on the status of city-state finances. Led by what the newspapers called 'hotheads', they voted to strike.[2]

The teachers risked their jobs. New York's Condon-Wadlin Act made striking punishable by dismissal, and Max Rubin, President of the Board of Education, declared that the teachers 'themselves terminated their employment'.[3] The strike was also unpopular. Newspapers editorialized against it. The city's labor unions were either silent or hostile. The Secretary of the City Central Labor Council called the strike reckless, saying, 'It will serve no economic or social purpose'. But there they were, on strike, some 20,558 of them, more than half of the city's teachers.[4]

In twenty-four hours it was all over. Teachers returned to work the next day in the face of an injunction. No one was fired, the *Times* editorialized in favor of higher teacher salaries, and Governor Nelson Rockefeller came to the city's aid with additional finances.[5] By the next weekend education writer Fred Hechinger was to examine the social implications of strike:

> The inevitable upshot is that ... the New York teachers have put to the test not only their relationship with local school authorities, but the future of collective bargaining as a 'professional-labor' instrument for teachers elsewhere.[6]

Hechinger was perhaps more prophetic than he knew, for the New York strike marked a watershed in public school labor relations throughout the nation. While there had been a strike in New York City two years earlier — as well as teacher strikes in other cities dating back to the early part of the century — they had been regarded as extraordinary occurrences brought about by special circumstances.[7] Even the adoption of a collective bargaining statute in Wisconsin in 1959 did not galvanize the attention of the press, nor did it appear to reflect any basic shift in national attitudes toward teacher rights and responsibilities. The strike of 11 April, however, has been gradually recognized as a natural, though distasteful, correlate of a permanent change in the relationship between teachers and their school district employers.

Transformation and Idea

In the space of a quarter-century, teacher unions in the United States have changed public education — its governance, school organization, and even the nature of teaching work. The transformation has been as swift as, and more complete than, the massive industrial changes brought about by the National Labor Relations Act and the spread of industrial unionism in the 1930s. For schools, the impact rivals that caused by the municipal reform movement in the first quarter of the twentieth century that gave rise to the appointed superintendent and a belief in the legitimacy for technical expertise. Clearly, teacher unionism ranks alongside school desegregation and categorical funding as one of the three major structural changes in public education since World War II.

As teachers unionized, the idea of a teachers' union itself was also transformed. When they began, unions were nearly universally condemned as illegitimate, unnecessary and harmful — indeed, the largest of them, the National Education Association, eschewed the label 'union' for years. Now, in addition to being recognized as a permanent feature of public education, unions are generally considered legitimate, and frequently as necessary and beneficial.

The watershed marked by the 11 April strike was one of ideas, deeply-held values and long-established political interests. The strike was less important in economic terms than in the way it changed people's thinking about teacher unionism and school organizations.[8] New York's unionism had special significance because it served as a model of union organization that was to be copied or reacted to by school systems throughout the country.

In New York, and subsequently across the country, it was the *idea* of a teacher union that changed first. Before important organizational changes could be made, the idea of what it was 'supposed to be' had to change. The new idea represented a shift in the social beliefs that legitimized teachers' pursuit of self-interest, redefined their access and participation in decision-making and recast ideas about the propriety of teachers engaging in political activity. The idea of a union also had an organizational dimension which shaped decision making and the norms by which the critical sub-groups within schools related to one another. Finally, the new idea concerned itself with the conception of teachers as employees and the definition of teaching work.

Labor relations in education is shaped by a continuing dialectic between *unionism* as a normative idea and *unionization* as the social reality that results from trying to implement the idea. *Unionism* is an idea that provides the central identity which guides action and stimulates response. *Unionization* is the reality produced by labor and management, the product of conflict and accommodation as competing ideas of a union are brought together on a crowded organizational stage.

Whereas unionism has always been presented by its advocates as an utopian, definitive, and evangelical promise of future possibilities, the resulting unionization is always a pragmatic, tentative and sometimes cynically-expressed set of concrete social realities. In recounting the evolution of teacher unions, leaders of the 1960s and 1970s sometimes appear wistful or disenchanted because of the gaps between unionism's ideal and unionization's reality. Each tarnished reality serves as the seedbed for a new vision of unionism and the struggle toward reform. Unionization is not a single organizing process, but rather a continuing cycle of ideas and organization.

Defining a Union in Three Generations

In the popular mind, and to some practitioners, unions are organizations that engage in collective bargaining. But historically and functionally unions have engaged in a much broader set of activities: protective legislation, standards setting, employee education and apprenticeship, testing and certification, and electoral politics. This expansive view of union functions allows us to extend our analysis into the pre-collective bargaining days of teacher unions and find important elements of union development during a time of administrative dominance. This view also allows us to find elements of future union development in current issues and struggles surrounding unions and educational reform.

Historically, there have been three basic elements in union development: the right to organize, the establishment of binding agreements, and the expansion of employee's legitimate interests. These elements have become apparent over the last twenty-five years as teacher unionism has evolved through three distinct stages, each characterized by different core ideas. Organizing around those ideas has created what we call 'generations' of labor relations. The essence of each generation is captured in three common phrases used to describe the relationship between teachers and school managers:

— the 'Meet-and-Confer' Generation
— the 'Good Faith Bargaining' Generation, and
— the 'Negotiated Policy' Generation.

Between each of these generations there has been a highly visible period of intergenerational conflict lasting from several weeks to several years and characterized by intense social, ideological and political conflict. At its peak, the conflict virtually always becomes public, and its settlement is widely recognized as the solution to a major political crisis. At issue during the conflict period are fundamental questions about the idea of a teachers' union: What is its central purpose? How ought it behave? How should it interact with school administrators? How should the work of teachers be conceived?

First Generation labor relations — characterized by a 'meet-and-confer' relationship between teachers and managers — established the right of teachers to organize as workers. Although the establishment of meet-and-confer relationships was not greeted with the public notoriety that accompanied the onset of collective bargaining, the idea of organizing teachers presenting demands was a radical one. Both law and social custom were hostile to combinations of employees. Up until the mid-nineteenth century, unions of all types were considered to be illegal conspiracies, and as late as the second decade in this century, they were prosecuted as violations of anti-trust laws. Combinations of teachers were even more suspect: teachers were public 'servants' in an era when the word had clear class connections, and they were women for whom workplace propriety was not forwarded in active voice.

The Progressive/Urban Reform Movement, which swept the country during the first quarter of the twentieth century heralded the virtues of *bureaucracy* in education, arguing that organization should be built on a rational division of labor and driven by politically neutral technical expertise. But bureaucracy was to be joined by the new human relations school of management, which gave credibility to the idea of employee participation in organizational decisions. As these two concepts merged, it became easy to believe that educational programs and practices would be substantially improved if teachers were permitted, even encouraged, to organize and to express their views on a broad range of school policies. The right of teachers to choose representatives who would confer regularly with managers about working conditions, wages, and other matters of concern was relatively easily defended as a way of simultaneously increasing loyalty and meeting the social-psychological needs of the workers.

Before 1960, these meet-and-confer sessions were rarely thought to involve explicit bargaining between teachers and their employers.[9] The difference between conferring and bargaining is, of course, partly a matter of legal definition. But even more fundamentally, it is a matter of underlying ideology or assumption. Meet-and-confer sessions are predicated on the assumption that both sides are committed to defining and solving mutual problems using educational effectiveness as the criterion for a decision. In contrast, bargaining assumes that each side has its own interests, that each defines problems differently, and that each will pursue its own interests in dealing with the other. Teacher organizations began to discard meet-and-confer assumptions in the late 1950s, and the New York strike in 1962 gave added momentum to this change. What these organizations sought were binding contractual agreements, not just a means of airing their views.[10]

Generally, districts pass out of the First Generation prior to, or

5

with the adoption of, collective bargaining. In some districts, however, good-faith bargaining relationships were established long before they were legally supported by statute or court decision. In others, the practices and beliefs of First Generation meet-and-confer labor relations have persisted long after legal arrangements were altered. Some districts still operate within the assumptive framework of a meet-and-confer approach to labor relations long after they begin to bargain collectively and after they have signed a labor contract.

During the First Generation meet-and-confer era, the profession of education is viewed as a unitary one. School administrators are distinguished from teachers by status and job role, but their interests are seen as fundamentally the same. Both teachers and administrators are supposed to express a selfless and universal interest in 'what's good for kids', and open displays of self-interest are socially illegitimate. It is the *duty* of the institution to look after teachers' welfare. In particular, administrators are supposed to function as their advocates, and school boards, as *trustees* of the common good, are expected to see that teachers are provided for.

These relationships are, of course, normative ideals — not universal behaviors. Teachers in the First Generation do have self interests, and some of them express and act upon those interests. Some administrators openly part company with teachers and deny having a duty to represent teachers' interests. And even more frequently, school boards fail to respond disinterestedly, expressing personal or class bias in their dealings with teachers. But the idea that there are fundamental common interests is a powerful one that serves to legitimate the authority of administrators and to couch governance and organizational decision-making in terms of a unitary, shared framework of belief.

Because meet-and-confer relationships are based on the premise that all educators share a common interest in educating children, teacher organizations are seen as legitimate only so long as they recognize the ultimate authority of the administration and school board and do not challenge it publicly. Teachers can form organizations, participate in a broad range of discussions, and bring their special knowledge to bear. But they must interpret their special interests in terms of the whole school system. And when their conception of the common goals diverges from those of administrators and school boards members, they are expected to defer and acquiesce.

Sometimes First Generation teacher organizations exert substantial influence; more often they do not. The inclusive nature of their relationship to management is revealed by the use of words like 'clublike' or 'family', but it is always clear that the family has a 'head of the house' in the person of district superintendent or an influential board member.

In due time, social and political conditions change, ending the idea that teacher interests can be incorporated into school policy through First Generation meet-and-confer procedures. Conflict erupts — often quite suddenly — and a new system of labor relations becomes dominant.

The *Second Generation* is epitomized by the phrase 'good faith bargaining' because it becomes legitimate for teachers to represent their own welfare interests, and to explicitly bargain with management over economic and procedural due process questions.

Establishing a right to contract represented a second important milestone in history: for unions generally, for teacher unions, and for each group of teachers and their school district employers. Collective contracts replace administratively determined civil service salary schedules, and grievance adjudication replaces board policy or administrative discretion as the basis for settling disagreements over negotiated work rules.

Second Generation norms include a very strong belief that conflict is endemic to the workplace and that effective conflict management is a vitally important aspect of labor relations. When strikes and other forms of public conflict occur, they are generally viewed as breakdown of the system, the result of bad faith or lack of expertise on the part of either labor leaders or managers. Second Generation labor relations values expertise and eschews amateurism. Labor relations experts emerge quickly. Once they are established, experts view as meddlers any outsiders (citizen groups, students, or politicians) who want to use labor relations for other than the intended purpose of codifying the welfare interests of teachers.

The participants in Second Generation labor relations generally adopt the beliefs of private sector industrial unionism that labor relations can and should be separated from organizational policy: 'Boards govern, superintendents administer, teachers teach.' This belief disappears during the transition to the Third Generation. More importantly, however, a close examination of school systems reveals that this belief is fundamentally inaccurate. Changes in labor relations do transform both policy and practice in the schools; this, despite the fact that labor laws almost universally forbid bargaining over educational or organizational policy. While managers and unionists often perceive that bargaining is largely limited to wages and working conditions, the evidence from our study suggests that many important issues of school policy and program are directly affected. To a surprising extent, negotiators for both sides heatedly deny that their actions affect the flow of educational services to children. And when they do think about such effects it is usually to claim that they are helping to keep labor strife from interfering with the educational mission of the schools. As a result, the very substantial policy effects that have resulted from the adoption of Second Generation, good faith bargaining, approaches to labor relations are often *accidental by-products* rather than the intended results of the new labor relations system.

Good faith bargaining is not, however, the end of the line for public school labor relations. After some years of trying to make Second Generation labor relations work, an increasing number of school districts are finding that new tensions and conflicts have surfaced around the legitimacy of teachers engaging in substantive agreements about school policy. The essence of conflict and the subsequent movement to *Third Generation* labor relations is an explicit attempt to shape school district policy through the contract and the union rather than attempting to manage 'around the contract' or through informal accommodation with the union. Sometimes the union is the moving party pressing for a new relationship, but in other cases external school reformers — citizens groups, board candidates — are the sources of renewed political tension. Two symbolic issues surface during this second period of labor conflict. In some cases, the union's informal role in educational matters becomes an issue, the perception being that the bilateral bargaining relationship has frozen out other participants, particularly school board members. School boards and managers set out to 'win back the keys to the store' usually by attacking the work rule clauses in the contract. In other cases, school reformers target school performance itself: declining test scores, lax discipline, and flimsy curriculum. Sometimes with strong union backing, sometimes with opposition, the reformers perceive that collective bargaining is a means toward educational reform.

The result of this renewed tension and conflict is a *Third Generation* of labor relations, the essence of which is conveyed in the phrase 'negotiated policy'. During this generation, all parties, including the public, acknowledge that teacher negotiations are substantially and directly concerned with the ways in which schools will be run; the patterns of authority and social interaction in the buildings; the definition of what will be taught, for how long, and to whom; and the determinations of who has the right to decide how planning, evaluation and supervision of instruction will be carried out. Typically, the era of negotiated policy begins with the recognition by management and the school board that they have a genuine interest in negotiating an effective and workable evaluation clause in the contract. Their affirmative interest in having particular issues placed in a written agreement represents a fundamental departure from the Second Generation ideology, in which management asserts that 'the best contract is the shortest one'.

There is no reason to expect that the Third Generation is to last forever. Like the two generations that preceded it, the Third Generation is a period of relatively broad agreement about the conduct and meaning of labor relations, a period of implementing an idea and solving real problems. Beliefs about what is right are strong in the Third Generation, but no stronger than they were in the First and Second Generations. And, because beliefs change, careful attention must be given to how the belief system that create each generation are created, and how they are changed.

The New Idea and Generational Change

Changes in labor generations are driven by changes in belief. The instigators of change are radicals, in the dictionary sense of the word, people who attack the root belief system, who break away from prevailing norms, who challenge the status quo, and who embrace and articulate new social arrangements. Radicals are noisy. By definition they are also outsiders, estranged from the school districts even though they may have been employed by or lived within the district for decades. The conflicts they create cannot be settled by smoothing and compromise within the recognized elite of a school district, for the root of the conflict is over whether these same radicals should become part of the ruling elite. As a result, generational conflicts tend to be highly public and, as one would expect, they most often involve decisions

9

about replacing persons who were considered part of the ruling establishment — particularly union leaders, school board members and superintendents.

To understand the social and political conflict which drives the movement from one labor relations generation to the next, it is important to differentiate it from other types of conflict. Conflict is a normal, some would say, healthy organizational function. It does not necessarily imply violence or personal nastiness. In fact, much of the structural apparatus of labor relations is designed to prevent intensification of conflict and to control disputes when they occur. These structures are designed to deal with normal *economic or frictional* conflicts which are resolved win-lose-or-draw without changing the organization's basic authority structure. At an interpersonal level, a disagreement between teacher and principal can be settled either by easy compromise or by vigorous disagreement, but when the conflict is over both stand in approximately the same social relationship as before.

Economic or frictional conflicts sharply contrast with *structural or sociopolitical conflicts* that have as their purpose a challenge to existing authority structures or organizational leaders. Sociopolitical conflict occurs in cycles and begins with diffuse feelings of dissatisfaction by individuals who are not part of a school district's current ruling elite. Dissatisfaction results largely from a sense that the norms of fair treatment or fair play have been violated. Even though they involve disagreements over the distribution of status and resources, these disagreements generally serve to symbolize deeper value-based conflicts. Thus, it is not administrative power or influence that causes teacher dissatisfaction and the end of the First Generation. Rather it is the perceived *illegitimacy* of administrative actions which transforms frictional interpersonal conflict into structural sociopolitical conflict. When leaders violate important norms of their subordinates, those offended turn to new, radical outsiders who are willing to claim that they, rather than the current elite, represent the true values of the institution and that the elite has forfeited its right to position.

Dissatisfaction spreads through the use of symbols. Abstract, value laden, and attractive images such as dignity, protection, efficiency, and impropriety are used to mobilize support for new leaders. In order to be politically effective, these symbols must somehow get onto the public agenda. They must be attached to specific events in which decisions are made. Sometimes there is sufficient political mobilization to create an event. Recall or referendum campaigns, or agitation for a superintendent's dismissal, are examples of events which force their way onto the political agenda. More frequently, however, the symbols are attached to relatively routine, scheduled decisions. In school districts the most common of these events is the election of school board members or the settlement of a labor contract. Usually, these scheduled events result in decisions that do not challenge the social order. Even when there is a dispute, a hotly contested election or a strike, the event can be decided in such a way that no fundamental value is at issue. When the symbols of dissatisfaction are attached to decision-making events, however, they create changes in the lines of political cleavage within a school district.

The lines of political cleavage dividing a community separate the populace into two groups. Individuals are challenged to choose one side or the other. Once the lines have been drawn, say between 'good schools' and 'responsible taxation', enormous political energy is invested in attracting others to the fight. Thus, in the struggle to gain a recognition agreement or a substantive contract, teachers generally find it necessary to make direct appeals for public support. Existing community groups are activated, brought into functional coalitions on one side or the other around the line of cleavage created by teacher union demands. The winner is determined by which group succeeds in attracting the most powerful elements of the public. For that reason, changes in labor relations generations generally are controlled by opinions of parents and citizens.

With remarkable frequency, generational changes involve changes in school district office-holders. School board incumbents are defeated, superintendents are fired, union presidents or executives are driven from office. When office-holders stay, they change the way they behave, and sometimes they sack underlings as a gesture of change and conciliation. 'Better him than me', remarked the superintendent in one of our districts as he canned the district's labor attorney following a difficult collective bargaining season and a fractious board election.

The new or reformed elite then tries to consolidate its position. Peace, normalcy and the legitimacy of the new rules of fair play become the initial tasks of a new generation.

Perhaps the least surprising finding from our work is that life during periods of labor crisis is not at all like life during periods of labor peace. Ideologically based, norm challenging labor conflict, the kind involved in generational changes, is clearly a crisis to school districts. Communication is disrupted. Established behavior and authority patterns are altered and the organization ceases to function normally. It is surprising, however, to discover just how much conflict periods vary in duration. Some intergenerational conflicts last only a few days; others drag on for years.

Three Levels of Impact

Interpretation of union impacts on schools begins with the recognition that teacher unions are large, complex, and (even though unions face substantial financial strain) wealthy. By the mid-1980s membership in the two major teacher's unions — the American Federation of Teachers and the National Education Association — approached two million. The NEA's membership alone is about 1.65 million, making it the second largest labor union in the country, behind the Teamsters. The United Federation of Teachers in New York City is the largest local within the AFL-CIO. Education, in comparison with other industries, is highly unionized. As early as 1975, approximately 90 per cent of the teachers in districts with more than 1000 students worked under a collective bargaining contract. [11]

Teachers rank among the largest political contributors in some states. The California Teachers Association, for example, ranked tenth in lobbying activity in 1984 and was thirteenth among campaign contributors. [12] The Michigan Education Association outspent the United Autoworkers in Michigan's 1978 state legislative elections, and the NEA's Political Action Committee raised more than $3 million for 1976 state and federal elections. [13]

We expect large and potent organizations to have large effects, and this is the case with teacher unions. They have substantially altered the way in which schools are governed, the way in which they operate as organizations, and ultimately, the nature of the work teachers do. However, as the history of labor generations shows, the impact of teacher unions on schools is likely to vary, depending on where a particular school district finds itself in the generational process. A First Generation union that emphasizes participation will have a very different impact than a First Intergenerational Conflict Period union whose emphasis is on ideological struggle. In the sections that follow, we discuss unionization's impact in terms of Second Generation union-ism. We do this because the Second Generation is the most common, and because collective bargaining and the practices of Second Generation unionism are widely believed, understood and accepted within the American tradition of labor relations. Most of the school districts we studied displayed Second Generation characteristics, and we feel it important to capture what Thomas Kuhn would call the 'normal science' of labor relations. [14]

Impacts on Governance

Schools governance involves two primary issues: fair representation or democracy in decision-making; and acceptable quality of public services. Most public discussion of union impacts has centered around the first question: 'Have unions caused schools to become less democratic'? Our answer is no; the political dynamic that surrounds evolving labor generations actually provides a self-correcting mechanism that revitalizes democratic governance. Because other authors have come to different conclusions, we will develop the argument for unions as democratizing influences as carefully as possible.

One reason for these differences of opinion about the relationship between unions and school democracy is that there are at least three, sharply different, views about what constitutes democracy in school districts. Each of the three looks to different indicators for the presence or absence of democracy. *Dissatisfaction theory* looks for critical turning points in the political process: are fundamental realignments in direction and governance taking place? Dissatisfaction theorists assume that popular influence over public policy is, and probably ought to be, *episodic* rather than continuous. *Informed competition theory* looks for the presence of multiple candidates for school offices and an informed electorate. *Issue responsiveness theory* is less concerned with who makes policy decisions and more concerned with what decisions are made — whether they reflect the wishes of the community.

Most analyses of school democracy hew to one theory or another, but our analysis of the movement from one labor relations generation to the next shows how each of the three basic mechanisms of democratic control is brought into play *in sequence*. The transition from one generation to the next begins with the accumulation of *dissatisfaction* over the established mode of unionism and a concomitant impetus toward reform. Once new labor relations structures have been established, attention shifts to creating mechanisms for *informed* access to the policy process. When these mechanisms are in place and routinized, attention shifts to narrower concerns about whether the schools are *responsive* to specific issues about which different publics have interests. The process is not perfect. It does, however, produce a dynamic for attending to the need for democratic control of school service delivery.

Maintaining democratic control is only half of the school governance problem. A school governance system needs to maintain public support and confidence in the institution of public education, and Second Generation unionism has largely failed to do this. Unionization has not increased the public perception that schools are competent in their delivery of services or that teachers are dedicated to the tasks that the public values. We suggest that the problem lies in the underlying assumption of Second Generation unionism, the split between conception and execution of work. Unions become empowered to represent the self-interests of their members, but are legally, functionally and psychologically distanced from responsibility for the institution of education.

Impacts on School Organization

As with school governance, the effects of Second Generation unionization on school organizations fall into two categories, one of which is adequately addressed and attended to and the other of which is not. Second Generation labor relations begin with an overriding concern about managing conflict and maintaining stable organizational relationships. Union leaders and school district labor relations managers are attentive and diligent in their efforts to control labor conflict. The norms of labor professionals impress the importance of carefully orchestrating conflict when it cannot be prevented altogether. Strikes are often considered a sign of failure.

The net effect of this attention to conflict management and organizational maintenance is to draw attention away from the relationship between labor relations and organizational effectiveness or productivity. For example, wage settlements are almost always analyzed according to the fiscal capacity of the school district and their 'fairness' in comparison with wages paid to other teachers and workers in industries outside public education. They are almost never evaluated according to how the changes in wages will affect the delivery of educational services. Will program cutbacks be the result? Will specialist services be available? Will the mixture of teachers and aides be changed by the way the school reacts to the fiscal implications of a new contract?

Strikes and the policy impact of labor relations are similarly interpreted. Strikes are condemned for their disruptiveness, but the long grinding impasses, which characterize much school collective bargaining, are hardly noticed. Yet strikes, which usually last only a few days, are frequently less damaging to school effectiveness than are the ongoing stress, truncated communications, psychological alienation, and work minimization associated with protracted disagreement. The policy effects of school labor relations are frequently not perceived at all. While we found negotiators could talk with great precision about bargaining strategies and their effects on teachers or managers, they gave little indication of understanding the chain of organizational dynamics they were setting in motion.

Substantial changes result in organizational structures, which become more formalized, standardized, centralized and specialized — in a word more bureaucratized. School administration becomes more explicitly managerial as authority comes to rest on one's formal work role rather than one's expertise. The tendency to inspect teachers and teaching increases.

Decision-making also changes, becoming more complex as new arenas for deciding questions are introduced. This tendency toward decisional complexity is further exaggerated as new participants, particularly labor relations professionals, enter the scene, bringing their unique values and beliefs to bear on decision-making and, thereby, altering the agenda of what is decided. Finally, decisions become more complex because decisions are linked with one another. Little is ever finally decided because each decision is subject to appeal or requires further approval.

The net effect of these organizational changes is to make school organizations more dependent on bureaucratic controls and to draw attention away from establishing a productive organizational culture.

Impact on Teaching Work Roles

The most frequent assertion about the relationship between teacher unionization and teaching is that there has been no impact. Teaching is an isolated activity, and when the teacher closes the classroom door, these influences — so apparent in the political and organizational structures — cease to have an effect. We assert the contrary: *that the most important impact of teacher unionization lies in its potential to shape the nature of teaching work.*

Teaching work, like all work, can be described according to how the *tasks are defined* and *how the quality of work performance is overseen.* The definition of teaching tasks and the monitoring of their execution deeply affect the kind of education delivered by the school. There are, we argue, four fundamental types of work in our society: labor, craft, art, and profession. Which type of work is performed by teachers (or anyone else) depends on how their task responsibilities are defined and what provisions are made to monitor the effectiveness with which they execute those tasks.

In general, tasks are defined in one of two ways. Some tasks are preplanned: Their content and goals are specified, and the specific activities that lead to their accomplishment are defined. Other tasks cannot be preplanned but emerge in the context of the work itself. These tasks are adaptive, arising from the diagnosis of situational variables and the development of adaptive responses to specific working conditions. The work of laborers and craft workers generally involves preplanned tasks. Artistic and professional work, in contrast, cannot be fully planned in advance but must be defined by the workers themselves as they attend to the unique characteristics of each particular occasion.

Just as there are two different approaches to task definition, so oversight of task performance is typically approached through one of two fundamentally different mechanisms. Some work efforts are directly inspected. In other cases, the work itself goes unexamined but workers are screened and *licensed* to perform particular tasks. In inspected work settings, a superior either monitors workers while workers execute particular tasks or else critically appraises the products that result from completion of the tasks. Some aspects of teaching, like many other jobs, are not amenable to direct inspection. This is true, in part due to the requirement of trust and privacy between teachers and students and the fact that direct inspection of classroom instruction is simply too complex and expensive. Other aspects of teaching can and are directly inspected: arrival and departure times, written lesson plans. In other work settings, inspection is typically used in oversight of *laboring* and *artistic* work activities while licensure is characteristic of craft and professional work.

The task definition and oversight elements just described are ideal types. All real jobs involve a mixture of preplanning and adaptive task definitions as well as a combination of inspection and licensure approaches to oversight. Most jobs, however, are characterized by a predominance of one task and of one type of oversight mechanism. The archetypal professions of law and medicine, for example, have stringent licensure requirements that must be met before one is admitted to practice. They also give special recognition to the importance of adaptive task definition. Practitioners are expected to recognize new problems as they occur and to alter the course of treatment accordingly. Those who do this very well are held in great esteem by their colleagues. This type of work stands in stark contrast to that of laborers, in agriculture or manufacturing assembly work, for example. For these workers, tasks are defined and preplanned by their supervisors who generally are physically present to oversee their work activities. To some extent, however, classic professionals and common laborers face overlapping task definition and oversight mechanisms. Early in their careers, most doctors and lawyers find themselves under the direct supervision of other members of their profession. By the same token, laborers who earn the trust of their supervisors are sometimes given substantial latitude in defining their own work schedules and activities. In effect, they are informally certified to work without direct supervision.

Teaching, more than most lines of work, is a mixture of labor, craft, art, and professional approaches to task definition and supervision. During the Second Generation or good faith bargaining era, school districts tend to give increased emphasis to direct supervision and to rationalizing teaching tasks. 'Teacher — proofing' the curriculum, emphasizing time-on-task schedules, and engaging in clinical supervision are all symptoms that teaching is increasingly regarded as laboring work.

Second Generation unionization fuels this tendency. The labor contract, changed social relations in schools, and alterations in school politics all operate to encourage increased rationalization and direct inspection of teaching work. We do not mean to suggest that teaching has lost all its professional elements, as some critics of unions contend or that teaching was a 'true profession' in some earlier time. Rather, the purpose of our paradigm is to provide a means of creating a linkage between labor relations and the nature of work. Our data indicate that there is a connection between what teachers do collectively and who they are occupationally.

Professional Unionism

In considering the prospects for labor relations in the third and subsequent generations, we conclude that fundamental changes are both possible and necessary. We suggest a new idea of teacher unionism — one we call *Professional Unionism*. Professional unionism is contrasted with industrial unionism, which has guided teacher unionization during the Second Generation. We also describe several basic legal and organizational changes needed to support professional unionism.

Professional unionism retains collective bargaining and expands on its uses. Professional unionism recognizes the need for individual autonomy and latitude in the workplace, and it recognizes the need for corporate self-governance by teachers. Concurrently, it requires teacher unions to address the difficult problems of school productivity and effectiveness. Partly this is a question of standards for controlling entry of novices into teaching, for assurance of job performance, and for discipline and dismissal of incompetents. Partly it is a question of decisions about how resources can be applied to achieve student gains.

Three changes are needed if teacher organizations are to become professional unions. First, the scope of negotiations will need to expand. Rather than trying to legally narrow the scope of bargaining to economic issues and related terms and conditions of employment, professional unions need to be encouraged to discuss all issues related to the quality of their work. Professional unions need to negotiate frankly and openly about such issues as curriculum, teaching methods, student assignments, criteria for assessment of student achievement, and teacher responsibility for non-instructional duties.

However, contracts as a form of agreement are inherently rigid. A prudent person will never agree in a contract to that which cannot, with certainty, be delivered. Intentions, goals, dreams, and strategies are not well expressed in legal contracts. Contracts are explicit, and if the decisions made under a broadened scope of bargaining have the same contractual character as those currently being negotiated they will lead to sharply increased rationalization and routinization of teaching work — taking it further and further away from the professional ideal we are seeking to support. To prevent this, the negotiated agreement between teachers and school districts needs to be restructured. We propose augmenting the conventional collective contract with a new form of agreement that we call an Educational Policy Trust Agreement. The new form of agreement, modeled after the assumptions of trust law, will allow teachers and school managers to form agreements that are properly flexible in application.

Finally, professional workers need a different approach to the problem of unit determination: which employees are grouped together for the purposes of bargaining. Existing statutes form bargaining units by grouping all employees with similar job titles across an entire school district. As a result, the employee bargaining units seldom have much in common with functional work integration. Integrated work groups usually develop around particular school sites or departments frequently including employees other than classroom teachers. Professional unionism needs to recognize the importance of functional groupings and to create units that can effectively address the integration of workers and educational services

Our Study of Labor Relations in Education

In preparing this book, we studied labor relations in more than 100 school districts in Illinois and California and reviewed scores of studies conducted by others. Four field research projects were involved. The first, supported by a grant from the Eli Lilly Endowment to Charles Kerchner, was a study of teacher labor relations in big cities.[15] The second, supported by the National Institute of Education in a grant to Douglas Mitchell, was a study of teacher work incentives.[16] The third, a study of the diffusion of labor relations policy in school districts, was undertaken by Kerchner for the Center for Education Policy and Management at the University of Oregon.[17]

The fourth project, also supported by NIE, involved collaboration between Kerchner and Mitchell in a two-year study of seventy-three districts in Illinois and California.[18] The technical reports on each study have appeared earlier. Here, our intent is to synthesize what we have learned and to place it in social and organizational context.

The Plan of This Book

This chapter has provided an overview of the analysis developed throughout this volume, as well as a brief introduction to the key concepts. The following chapters provide detail in roughly the same order and following the same logic as does this introduction. In chapter 2 we develop a theoretical perspective on union dynamics: one rooted both in conflict and interactionist thought. We then show how these dynamics logically lead to the periods that we call generations of labor relations. Using this theoretical perspective, we describe labor relations in generational perspective. Chapter 3 contains a review of labor and teacher union history showing the changes in central organizing idea that have marked the generations in unions as *institutions*. In chapter 4, we look to the *organizational* aspects of generational change and to an evaluation of evidence that the generational concept represents an accurate depiction of change in school labor relations.

Beginning in chapter 5, we follow the course of labor relations during the generations, and in this chapter we show the pattern of behavior in First Generation districts and how those behaviors break down in the First Generational Conflict Period. Chapter 6 includes the description of Second Generation good-faith bargaining: the relationship found in most school districts and most of our study districts. Here, the normal science of labor relations — accommodation and conflict resolution — can be seen at work. However comfortable this relationship may be, we believe that it eventually dissolves, and in chapter 7 we show process of movement toward a Second Intergenerational Conflict Period and the outlines of a Third Generation of labor relations.

The next three chapters describe the impacts of good faith bargaining, expanding on the summary given earlier in this chapter. Chapter 8 contains the description of governance impacts, chapter 9 the organizational impacts, and chapter 10 the impacts on teacher work lives.

In the book's conclusion, chapter 11 we present the idea of

professional unionism and why we think it a logical and likely form for labor relations in the Third Generation.

Notes

1 'Teachers Strike Today', *New York Times*, 11 April 1962, p. 1.
2 *Ibid.*,. p. 34.
3 *New York Times*, 12 April 1962, pp. 1 and 31.
4 *New York Times*, 11 April 1962, p. 42.
5 *New York Times*, 12 April 1962, and 13 April 1962, p. 1.
6 *New York Times* 15 April 1962, p. E9.
7 There were 105 teacher strikes between 1941 and 1961, the most notable of them in Norwalk, Connecticut, St. Paul, Minnesota (1946) and Buffalo, New York (1947). For background on early teacher strikes see: STINNETT T.M. (1968) *Turmoil in Teaching*, New York, Macmillan, p. 33; and COLE, S. (1969) *The Unionization of Teachers: A Case Study of the UFT*, New York, Praeger, p. 51.
8 KLAUS, I. (1967) 'The evolution of a collective bargaining relationship in public education: New York city's changing seven-year history' *Michigan Law Review*, 67, pp. 1033–66.
9 In 1960 only one state had legislation permitting collective bargaining by teachers. NEA executives had drafted a document dealing with 'collective negotiations' but the organization had not adopted it, and the AFT had not yet renounced its prohibition on strikes.
10 Some states, such as California, had statutes that gave a legal structure to the words 'meet and confer', but here we are concerned with the common generic description of behaviors. These were widespread and not dependent on statutes.
11 CRESSWELL M. and MURPHY M.J. with KERCHNER, C.T. (1981) *Teachers, Unions and Collective Bargaining in Public Education*, Berkeley, CA, McCutchan, pp. 31 and 105.
12 Fair Political Practices Commission, State of California, telephone query, JAMES, P. and GILLAM, J. (1985) '$36-million buys clout in capitol', *Los Angeles Times*, 21 October, Part I, p. 3, 15.
13 HERNDON, T. (1979) 'Annotating a Reader's Digest article: The NEA a Washington lobby run rampant', *Phi Delta Kappa*, February, 60, pp. 420–3.
14 KUHN, T. (1970) *The Structure of Scientific Revolutions*, 2nd ed, Chicago, IL, University of Chicago Press.
15 KERCHNER, C.T. (1980) 'More than contract: The changing relationship of teachers to the governance and operation of American schools', Report to the Eli Lilly Endowment, May.
16 MITCHELL, D.E., ORTIZ F.I. and MITCHELL T.K. (1980) *Final Report: Controlling the Impact of Rewards and Incentives on Teacher Task Performance*,

Report G-80-0154 to the National Institute of Education. Washington, NIE.

17 KERCHNER, C. (1986) *Labor Policy in School Districts: Its Diffusion and Impact on Work Structures*, final report to Center for Educational Policy and Management, Division of Educational Policy and Management, University of Oregon, Eugene, OR, CEPM.

18 KERCHNER, C.T. and MITCHELL, D.E. (1981) *The Dynamics of Public School Collective Bargaining and its Impacts on Governance, Administration and Teaching*, Report G-79-0036 to the National Institute of Education. Washington, D.C. NIE, (ERIC Document Reproduction Services No. ED 211-925.)

2
Idea and Reality: The Theory of Teacher Labor Relations

Labor relations in education are best understood by examining the dynamic tension between *unionism* as an ideal and *unionization* as the concrete attempt to realize those ideals. This tension produces episodic conflict which redefines the central idea or belief system surrounding unionism and reorganizes the structures of unionization.

As we asserted in chapter 1, we believe that teacher labor relations have evolved through two central belief systems and two concrete realities — meet-and-confer and good-faith bargaining — and that negotiated policy is emerging as a third. As a belief system, each generation of unionism guides aspirations and expectations and thus provides the basis for organizational mobilization and political debate. As social reality, unionization is what actually happens: organization of teachers, formulation of proposals, negotiation of contracts, development of informal relations. These two processes interact to reshape educational governance, alter school structures, and redefine the work roles of teachers and administrators into what we call 'generations'.

The word 'generation' is both an appropriate and significant description of school labor relations. Generations differ from periods, which are merely historical times with different characteristics but with no necessary sequence or causal relationship one to another. The term 'generation' implies the sort of relationship that exists between parents and their offspring. Children mix the heritage of their parents with their own aspirations and needs to create a lifestyle of their own. And they usually pass through a period of conflict with their parents in order to establish the right to be different. But after the conflict is over, and independence is won, it is easy to see that the children's lives embody both the aspirations and the problems of their parents. So it is with teacher unions. Each school district's labor relations is colored by its own history, and long after arrangements have changed, participants remember and carry forward a portion of their past.

A Contrasting Perspective

Our multigenerational view contrasts sharply with the more common view of labor relations as movement from conflict to social accommodation. Perhaps the most graphic expression of this view can be found in a commemorative stamp issued by the Postal Service in 1975 which bore the legend, 'Out of conflict: Accord'. In this view, labor relations are a process whereby 'conflicts over ends are reduced to conflicts over means'.[1] In other words, the practice of labor relations is fine tuned until it becomes 'not quite routine'.[2] Unions slowly come to share in the process of rationalizing labor relations by substituting rules and organization for revolt and revolution.[3] The implications of this view are that, once established, the *unionism* idea changes only incrementally and that the *unionization* process gradually makes this single idea work better as labor, management, and other interested parties learn how to make the process more productive and less disruptive.

In contrast, our study indicates that, for teacher unions at least, the periods of accommodation within a system of shared beliefs may be quite short, lasting no more than five to ten years. Thus, it is just as important to understand the recurring ideological revolutions in labor relations as it is to understand the techniques of so-called normal labor relations.

Although there are other examples of 'stages' in labor relations literature[4] most studies of union dynamics embrace or imply a 'diversity thesis'. These studies suggest that variation between firms, governmental agencies or schools is so large that there are only very weak general trends in the development of labor relations and no 'uniform pattern of evolution exists'.[5] This conclusion is present in Slichter, Healy and Livernash's monumental study of private sector unionism, in Lewin, Horton and Kuhn's study of big city municipal unions and in various studies of teacher unions, including our own earlier work.[6]

Our data led us to believe that the diversity thesis has been overstated. While we recognize diversity full well, we also see central tendencies and, more importantly, common patterns of development over time which partly explain the enormous diversity that appears when one does cross-sectional analysis of union behaviors or impacts.

In sum, we believe that generations are a good way to describe labor relations in school districts. Generational development is a good way to describe the process of change. Taking a generational view of change has a substantial impact on how one views teacher unions and their future potential.

Interaction and Conflict as Social Change Processes

Generations of labor relations, in which unions and management largely agree about their relative roles and functions, are separated by intergenerational periods in which common understandings fall apart. The most apparent difference between the generations and the inter-generational periods is that the former appear stable and quiet while the later appear chaotic and conflictual. Appearances are deceiving. Change takes place *both* during the generations and during the intergenerational periods, but the changes utilize quite different social processes. Normal labor relations, as practiced during the generations, are designed and structured to produce change though interaction — those processes recognized as accommodation, mutual learning, and socialization. Even in situations of overt conflict, such as strikes, the parties are conscious of the practical limits to which they can push the conflict and still maintain the relationship. Revolutionary labor relations as practiced during the intergenerational periods, attacks these underlying relation-ships and follows the path of change suggested by conflict theorists — separation of in-groups and out-groups, the organization of the dispossessed and disgruntled, overt conflict and the replacement of elites. Conflict theory explains how labor relations makes large discon-tinuous changes and how the events of each generation eventually lead to its breakdown.

In its most basic representation, conflict theory involves recogni-tion of fundamental ill-distribution of power and resources within a social institution, the organization of opposition, and the replacement of an old social order with a new one.[7] It is fundamentally revolution-ary in character although not necessarily violent. In schools, as with

25

other organizations, the challenge to the existing order often is focused on the leadership of that order — school board members, superintendents, teacher leaders. And quite often leaders are replaced during the conflict. But the significance of the conflict is much larger. As Dahrendorf observed in the industrial revolution, the change does not just replace an old elite with a new one. It involves, above all, the 'simultaneous abolition of the system of norms and values which guaranteed and legitimized the [old] order'.[8]

In contrast, an interactionist theory of social change places deep emphasis on social processes rather than structural alteration in explaining change. Heavily identified with George Herbert Mead, Robert Park, Herbert Blumer, Anselm Strauss, and 'the Chicago school of sociology', interactionism holds that social structures are difficult to understand without attaching meaning to group and individual behavior.

Thus, behavior is symbolic, and organizations change because different symbols are attached to the same behavior. For example, a principal's tours of a school building may carry with them the symbols of distrust and pettiness, or they may be taken as an interest in the work of teachers and the problems they face. A labor grievance arbitration may represent a simple adjudication of rights, or it may represent a rearrangement of the symbols of control and authority.

It is through the rearrangement of these symbols that organizations can be changed without altering their structures or acknowledging that a transformation has taken place. Ordinary 'interactions, agreements, temporary refusals, and changing definitions of the situation at hand are of paramount importance', as day-to-day events shape the social order.[9]

The interactionist and conflict perspectives produce quite different interpretations of how organizations change, and consequently each theoretical perspective suggests a different pattern of historical development for teacher unions, as figure 1 suggests. Perhaps the most vivid image within the interactionist perspective is the role episode: the means by which individuals attach meaning to action and engage in self-regulation because of their relations with others in the social system. The emphasis of this perspective is on what makes things come together. Repetition of role cycles produces mutual learning, and the parties engage in conflict-reducing techniques such as smoothing, avoidance, and compromise. While there may be periodic outbursts of

Figure 1: Causal imagery of change in labor relations and resultant patterns of labor conflict

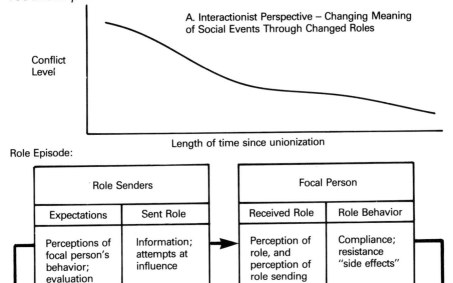

A. Interactionist Perspective – Changing Meaning of Social Events Through Changed Roles

Conflict Level

Length of time since unionization

Role Episode:

Role Senders		Focal Person	
Expectations	Sent Role	Received Role	Role Behavior
Perceptions of focal person's behavior; evaluation	Information; attempts at influence	Perception of role, and perception of role sending	Compliance; resistance "side effects"

Source: Adapted from Katz and Kahn, (1966) *The Social Psychology of Organizations,* New York, Wiley, p. 182.

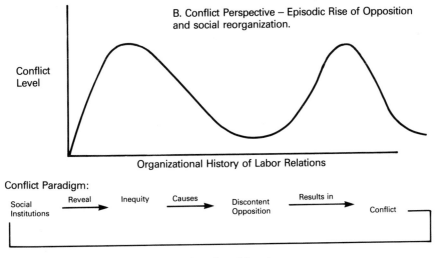

B. Conflict Perspective – Episodic Rise of Opposition and social reorganization.

Conflict Level

Organizational History of Labor Relations

Conflict Paradigm:

Social Institutions → Reveal → Inequity → Causes → Discontent Opposition → Results in → Conflict

Reorganization of social system

conflict, these are taken as abnormalities within the larger context of increasing accommodation.

The system image from the conflict perspective is quite different. Change is discontinuous and relatively abrupt. It occurs through the *organization* of discontent, confrontation, and overt conflict that ultimately leads to restructuring. Social systems operate to produce repeated episodes of conflict, and as figure 1 suggests, each conflict period produces a reorganized social system.

If viewed at their poles, conflict and social interactionist perspectives are incompatible. The interactionist perspective sees all change as incremental and all disagreements negotiable within the existing social system. Conflict theory argues that important changes are never solved through negotiation and interaction, but always require overthrow of the ruling elite. Those who have advanced either conflict or interaction theory have, understandably, ignored or glossed over the importance of the other. But actually the theories nest rather well. An interactionist, such as Anselm Strauss, speaks of the *structural context* 'within which negotiations take place in the largest sense'.[10] These are the systemic properties of an institution that tend to have substantial permanence, and to the extent that these properties embody the social acceptance of an idea, they are like our notion of generations or like Kuhn's idea of a scientific paradigm. Conflict theorists, such as Dahrendorf, recognize permanence of elite ruling structures, that which he calls 'the problem of inertia'.[11] Within the permanent structure there exists a tendency toward marginal adjustment and taking on of new roles as the dominant and dominated interact.[12]

In terms of our generational framework, active organization for conflict and overt conflict take place at the end of each generation and during the relatively short intergenerational period. They are represented by a sharp upswing in the conflict level (figure 2). Conflict regeneration takes place during the generations when overt conflict is low.

The conflict process, which peaks during the intergenerational period, basically determines:

— who rules, that is, what organizations or individuals will be established as an elite leadership that gains authoritative control of schools.[13]

— what normative idea of a teacher's union will define the goals and practices of labor relations.

Figure 2: Conflict levels and generations of labor relations

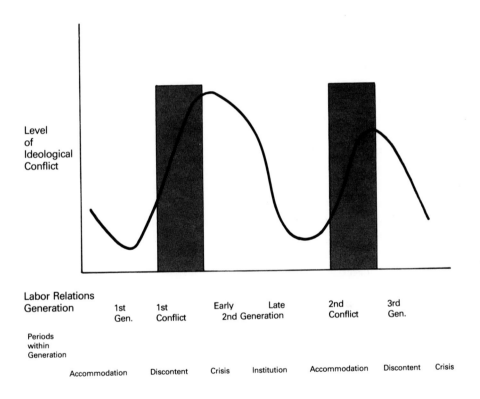

The conflict process involves polar decisions — yes or no, in or out, up or down — and can be seen in the electoral process, in ideologically-based strikes or negotiations, or in the passage of statutes that alter the legal framework of unionism. Conflict involves long-lasting changes in the way people or factions line up politically and in the issues over which the polity splits.

The interaction process, operating during the generations, controls:

— how fiscal and other resources are divided among those whose interests are considered legitimate;
— how organization will be adjusted to pursue established goals.

These decisions are incremental; they result from repeated interactions between, teachers and principals, unionists and superintendents, board members and community leaders. These daily interactions focus on the inherent ambiguities and imperfections left by structural reforms, and they gradually adjust organizational practices to personal needs and practical requirements. They determine the social roles of the participants, each taking and modifying a position and a set of behaviors in relationship to the other. Representatives of both labor and management become expert at what they do, they develop norms and expectations about the behavior of others, and they regulate their own behavior on the basis of the behavior they have learned to expect from the opposite party. Grievance handlers engage in similar patterns of learning, and they approach their jobs with the expectation that they will have repeated interactions. Interaction driven change is not limited to the special settings initiated by collective bargaining. Social interaction spreads the process of change throughout the organization, altering relations through the daily interaction between superior and subordinate in the work place, through fractional bargaining within work groups, and through side payments and rule making which serve to limit conflict.

Generational Dynamics in Teacher Unions

The forces of conflict and the forces of social interaction combine to produce the periods that we call labor relations generations. The process involves four approximately chronological stages shown in figure 2:

(a) Discontent — when flaws in the existing system of labor relations become obvious, new ideas are advocated and gain support. They are also strongly opposed, setting the stage for conflict and political crisis.

(b) Crisis — when intense, and sometimes sustained, conflict is experienced between those who support the old order and those committed to the new idea. The crisis is resolved when advocates for one belief system win a symbolic political victory — often one accompanied by leadership changes on one or both sides.

(c) Institutionalization — when the representatives of the new unionism idea establish their right to shape the labor relations agenda. They redefine roles and responsibilities and develop new decision-making and resource allocation procedures.

(d) Accommodation — when the leaders of both labor and management routinize with the new arrangement and engage in practical problem solving. As accommodation proceeds, new sources of discontent also develop initiating the possibility of a new change cycle.

These stages are often not clearly bounded. Discontent, for instance, continues on through the crisis stage and lingers into the institutionalization of new leaders, and accommodation is still being attempted even when growing discontent is apparent.

Discontent: Making Dissatisfaction Clear

Our studies repeatedly demonstrate that the comfortable, steady, 'not quite routine' order developed during the mature Late Generational Period does not last forever. Even as labor and management leaders are making accommodations and mutual adaptations, there is an increase in the number of disappointed people whose interests and desires are traded away in the pursuit of harmonious labor relations. As time goes by, these dissatisfactions accumulate and are expressed in more aggressive ways. New leaders emerge to initiate a search for different means to protect basic interests, and they begin to explore new ideas about the appropriate form for labor relations.

While accommodation may provide an antidote to conflict and a solution to practical problems, it also encourages organizational processes to drift farther and farther away from the original intent of those who fought for its establishment. In the case of the First Generation, meet-and-confer procedures laid the foundations for the 'good faith bargaining' that has replaced them in most school districts. Meet-and-confer procedures provided a means for teacher self-expression. But because they are based on the assumption that teacher interests do not differ fundamentally from the interests of management, they do not give teachers legitimate right to express serious demands for change. First Generation labor relations, ruled by this assumption of common purpose, encourages the belief that differences result from 'misunderstanding', not from any divergence of fundamental interests. As the NEA put it in one of their last defenses of the meet-and-confer era: 'Teachers and boards of education can perform their indispensable functions only if they act in terms of identity of purpose'.[14] Under this conception of unionism — a unionism supporting organization division but unable to recognize fundamental differences in interest — discontent is almost inevitable. Teachers who do not like the results of the meet-and-confer process say, 'We can express our views but they will be politely deferred.'[15] They soon start looking for more powerful mechanisms of self-expression.

Discontent is most intense among those excluded from the dominant generation's conception of unionism. As the First Generation of school labor relations ends, discontent is concentrated among teacher groups, who increasingly come to believe that they are not being treated with dignity or respect. Especially, in large urban school systems, the popular literature characterized school management as preoccupied with personal ambition or petty bureaucratic procedures rather than with the real interests of teachers or students. In the case of the Second Generation, dissatisfaction tends to mount in citizen groups and school board members, who increasingly feel locked out of an elite process controlled by labor professionals.

Discontent by itself is not enough to create the intense political conflict and public crisis that marks the onset of an intergenerational conflict period. Discontent must first turn into explicit debate over established ideas of labor relations. Spokespersons for the old order typically react with shock. They charge that the newly converted followers are the victims of 'irresponsible radicals' or 'outside agitators' primarily interested in 'making trouble' rather than exposing or solving real problems.

Defenders of the established order proclaim the virtues of the *status quo*. Their radical critics formulate a new idea and transform it into a secular gospel to be preached to all who will listen. The result is a moralization of politics, a challenge to the legitimacy of the compromise and accommodation that are the hallmarks of late generation labor relations. This moralism is exemplified in First Generation education practices by the militant declaration that workers have a right to organize for mutual protection. By contrast, Second Generation school labor relations are being challenged by lay boards, citizens groups, and maverick educators and unionists who have taken a hard look at school effectiveness, the union's 'undue influence' over school policy, and the school system's protection of 'deadwood' teachers and administrators.

Within each intergenerational conflict period, radical leaders exaggerate the contrast between their own idea of a union and the prevailing system of labor relations, thereby laying the foundation for a realignment of political forces. They attract converts by painting an idyllic picture of a future characterized by dignity, justice, and an end to conflict. The early converts to the new ideas search out stories of favoritism, insensitivity or abuse within the prevailing system. They use these stories to broaden their political base and persuade others to join in proclaiming the present system unworkable and its leaders corrupt.

A 'liberation theology' develops in which opposition to the old order is not pursued out of self-interest but because the existing system has become inherently unfair and unworkable. This perceptual shift was documented in Corwin's study of militant teachers in Ohio during the 1960s.[16] He found that their desire for increased power within the schools sprang not from a concern with having too little power but from a belief that they were being treated unfairly by those who were responsible for managing the schools and that they had to gain power in order to protect themselves from this unfair treatment. As teachers share these stories of unfair treatment, they also begin to adopt an ideology which, as Peter Blau put it, 'further justifies and reinforces hostility against existing powers'.[17]

In summary, the militancy and rising conflict that characterize the period of discontent begin with concrete, usually personalistic, stories of arbitrary, biased, insensitive, or downright abusive treatment on the part of those who have the most power under the existing labor relations system. Overt tension and conflict do not increase significantly, however, until two other developments occur: (i) the formulation of an ideological justification for rebellion against the established system; and (ii) the emergence of new leaders willing to press demands consistent with the new ideology. Thus, the organizer, the radical who is willing to break with the prevailing ideological belief system, is the catalyst for turning unhappiness into militant action. For, as Shorter and Tilley remind us,

> Individuals are not magically mobilized for participation in some group enterprise, regardless of how angry, sullen, hostile or frustrated they may feel. Their aggression may be channeled into collective ends only through the coordinating, directing functions of an organization, be it formal or informal.[18]

Crisis: Making Change Happen

Once new leaders have emerged and the leaders of the existing order have been declared illegitimate, political cleavage is inevitable. Gradually the new leaders shift their attention away from clarifying what is wrong with the existing order and articulating their utopian vision for the future, and instead begin to concentrate on making change happen. The rebels seek power through political coalition building and through judicial, administrative, and electoral battles with established leaders. They do not always win, but they always organize and try.

The aim of overt conflict is, of course, to overpower (or at least exhaust) the other side. A victory is signaled by the acceptance of the new ideas. The organizers advance their cause by spreading the conflict, by gathering strength from those not previously involved who can be persuaded to support them in the battle. They are especially sensitive to Elmer Schattschneider's sage advice to, 'watch the crowd, because the crowd plays the decisive role'.[19] Established leaders try to keep the conflict private, and those who want to 'go public' with their complaints are branded disloyal and subversive. Usually the established leaders have the power and prestige to monopolize virtually all public communication channels (not only the mass media but also meeting calendars, agendas, speakers' platforms, mimeograph machines, offices and sometimes even telephones). In union organizing campaigns, access to employee mailboxes and workplace bulletin boards is often a matter of bitter controversy.

The initially less powerful rebels use organization as a means to attract the crowd, and to build their political potency. Issues are magnified and couched in the most provocative (but not necessarily the most accurate) symbols available.[20] Through organization the rebels convert the alienated, the timid and the uninformed into active foot-soldiers for their cause. They do so by convincing their audience that a critical choice has to be made and that their own futures depend upon joining in the struggle.

In the school districts we studied, the political crises associated with the two intergenerational conflict periods display quite different characteristics. Organizational activities and political debates in those districts undergoing the First Intergenerational Conflict are characterized by the use of 'teacher dignity' and 'protection from abuse' as the central symbols of dissatisfaction with the meet-and-confer process of First Generation labor relations. School board and administrative leaders respond with symbols linking insurgent teachers with 'protectionism' and an 'irresponsible or undemocratic grab for power'. In each case, the symbols encourage new actors to become active in the fight to control labor relations policy.

Broad, moralistic, emotional and ambiguous symbols are more useful in activating a broad constituency than are narrow economic or pragmatic issues. Issues are more attractive to bystanders and more likely to win their support if they are not overly concrete. Issues of great social significance are more likely to attract support than those that are not. But social movements have to appeal to personal interests before truly widespread support can be garnered. Even prohibition did not gain strength as a political movement until its moral appeal was combined with arguments that it would reduce taxes for the middle class, which would no longer have to support jails and asylums filled with drunkards.[21]

The crisis comes to a head in a particular event — a strike, an election, a court decision, the dismissal of a superintendent. In some ways the form of the decisive event is incidental, an accident of time and circumstance. The critical event is needed to test the strength of the movement toward change and to allow large numbers of people to rationalize changing their beliefs and commitments. In the process, 'friends become enemies and enemies become friends in a general reshuffle of relations'.[22] Among players who know each other and have established patterns of friendship and rivalry, the conflict 'can become dominant only if [old friendships are] subordinated, or obscured, or forgotten ... or become irrelevant.[23]

Whatever the form of the conflict, it tends to expand rapidly when it becomes public. Established groups appeal for support and dissidents search for needed leverage to force accommodation to their demands. In addition, the conflict itself becomes a public issue. Political leaders and ordinary citizens urge the opposing parties to settle their differences so as not to damage the stability of the schools. Often, the victorious side consolidates support by pledging to put an end to the conflict.

Not all challenges to an existing order are successful. In fact, most dissident groups are not able to attract enough attention and support to start a public campaign or to challenge overtly the old order. Nor do all overt conflicts end in a victory for the challengers. Without a convincing argument that the existing system is unworkable or obviously unfair, the insurgents usually lose their following and run out of steam. When the challengers are successful, however, they quickly replace the machinery of decision-making and bring new actors into the day-to-day processes of governance and organizational administration. In the schools, the victory of Second Generation labor leaders produced carefully structured collective bargaining procedures, new mechanisms for handling grievances, and a wide variety of new forms for consultative decision-making between teachers and administrators.

Institutionalizing A New Idea: The Early Generational Phase

Once the political crisis is past and a new ideology has established its legitimacy, it is necessary to institutionalize the new idea into a new 'web of rules', which spells out clearly the powers and responsibilities of all the participants. Institutionalization is necessary because, as Dahrendorf puts it, 'one cannot negotiate with unorganized, loosely-connected 'rebels'.[24]

The movement from crisis to institutionalization is successful only if all parties are willing and able to move away from public posturing and political organizing into the relative privacy afforded by newly — established conflict resolution structures. As this happens, continued overt conflict comes to be viewed as an indication of bad faith, poor organization or badly applied techniques for handling conflict. Conflict is not so much suppressed as channeled. Negotiations, mediation, grievance arbitration, consultation, even contract ratification or rejection are means for resolving and controlling conflict in such a way that the existing labor relations system is not threatened.

In addition to the creation of new institutional structures, the early generational prose is characterized by gradual changes in attitudes and beliefs. Skepticism and lingering resistance gradually give way to the belief that the new ideology is 'here to stay' and that it 'can work'. As this acceptance grows, managers and workers start to act in more routinized and predictable ways. They engage in what Mead aptly described as 'role taking' — reacting with a conscious regard for the expectations and presuppositions of other actors.[25] They express support for the new institutional structures and adjust their behavior in accordance with the responses of others. Roles become generalized — labor negotiators are expected to act like labor negotiators, principals like principals — and strong professional subgroup pressures develop. These expectations are present in each labor relations generation, but they differ from one generation to the next. Teacher leaders during the First Generation expect to 'participate', but they do not challenge the right of school board members and administrators to control the time, place, manner and outcomes of that participation. Teacher leaders in the Second Generation expect to 'bargain'. They expect contractual agreements to embody the outcomes of their bargaining.

The identification of important 'role senders' shapes the character of each generation. When Early Second Generation teachers adopt collective bargaining, attorneys and other experienced labor practitioners tend to react with benevolent dismay over school district deviation from the standard conventions of negotiations. One prominent labor lawyer remarked, after trying to negotiate his first public school agreement, 'The curse of amateurism is rampant'.[26] Labor professionals become powerful role senders for both teachers and administrators during the Early Second Generation. While these professionals differ in their specific orientations and expectations, virtually all of them support the second generation idea that collective bargaining modeled after industrial unionism is the most appropriate mechanism for solving fundamental organizational (and even broad societal) problems in education.[27] Much of labor relations research has been shaped by a desire to facilitate early second generation institutionalization processes in order to 'make collective bargaining work'.[28]

The dark side of the role taking and role sending process is that all those who fail to play the roles in which they are cast are subject to strong social pressures and sanctions. Among those assigned active roles, a fairly tight feedback loop is utilized to evaluate their performances. Negotiators, for example, are told rather quickly whether they have followed expected bargaining norms and settled on acceptable contractual language. Just as soon as they can possibly do so, Early Generation leaders brand anyone who resists the institutionalization of the new ideology as 'illegitimate' pretenders to leadership, to be shunned and ignored. By using the sanction of illegitimacy on dissenters and hold-outs, a newly-institutionalized social order can eliminate potential resistance and disruptiveness. Progressives used this tactic during the Early First Generation to get politicians out of personnel decision-making. And in the Early Second Generation it is used to keep parents and citizen groups away from the bargaining table.

The Early Generation focus eventually shifts to the development of pragmatic routines for handling the school problems: too little money, the wrong people in the wrong places, a lack of appreciation for either the benefits or the costs of a quality education among the political agencies responsible for its support. This confrontation with reality eventually brings the idealists down to earth, forcing them to adjust their aspirations to the pragmatics of a world where compromise and accommodation are the order of the day. As this starts to happen, the Early Generation phase of high tension and moralized action gives way to the routinization and pragmatic accommodation of Late Generation labor relations.

Accommodation: The Late Generational Phase

As the practical problems of running a school system gradually come to be seen as more important, or at least more pressing, than maintaining fidelity to any particular ideal of unionism, labor relations move into a new phase. This Late Generational phase involves routinization, accommodation and compromise as everyone tries to make the institutionalized structures of the Early Generation phase work more smoothly and effectively. Typically, this phase is the longest one, providing several years — sometimes even decades — of relatively peaceful and productive labor relations. Working relationships can still be contentious, but each party unquestioningly accepts the legitimacy and utility of the other. Trust in the motives and essential good faith of the other party is built up, leading both sides to prefer working with the established leadership group. As one administrator commented about the aggressive teacher union president in his district 'We know he's a bastard, but he's our bastard!'

Politically, this phase is characterized by the successful privatization of labor conflicts through mutual accommodation and pluralistic bargaining. Each side invests heavily in keeping just within the bounds of toleration of the other. Agreements take on the flavor of 'log rolling' or 'back scratching' as each side tries to keep the other side at least minimally satisfied.

Paradoxically, both the use of labor professionals for bargaining and grievance adjudication and the use of informal labor-management contracts for day-to-day problem solving expand rapidly in the Late Second Generation. The professionalization of contract negotiations, district personnel procedures, grievance arbitration, and other key functions in the good faith bargaining era facilitate the development of trust and raises everyone's expectations for smoother and more productive working relationships. This, in turn, facilitates the development of informal decisionmaking procedures. For example, when teachers believe that their chief negotiator is a thoroughgoing professional whose management counterpart has an equally professional orientation, they are much more likely to accept 'side bar' agreements and other informal, pragmatic approaches to solving potential labor problems.

This accommodative phase gives full expression to the interactionist's vision of social change as shared meaning in a 'negotiated order'. Ongoing negotiations produce a 'blur of conflict, cooperation and compromise'. As research on workers in hospitals, psychiatric wards, industrial plants, and law enforcement agencies long ago recognized, workers — including teachers — use both formal and informal negotiating arrangements to generate new work rules and personal relationships which alter the social order and culture of the work place. Teachers, in particular, bargain daily to adapt their work places to new circumstances.

In both professional and scholarly circles, this phase of labor relations is looked upon as 'mature' and generally beneficial. Stability is seen as self-reinforcing because the parties realize the relative agree-ableness of the institutionalized relationship. They can be expected to make great efforts to make it permanent and stable. Our data suggest, however, that the very techniques used to ensure stability gradually become the seeds of a new round of discontent. Stability in the Late Generation is maintained by distributional equity, a fair shake for each recognized interest group. The cost of satisfying all constituents tends to grow until it becomes the object of overt discontent. Stability is also maintained by persuading the less powerful groups that their problems are simply not capable of solution. When tough issues threaten to offend an important constituency, they are dropped from the agenda. Sometimes these issues reflect employee problems, such as transfer policy. Sometimes they are organizational ones, such as improving reading test scores, but the existence of problems that seem insolvable invites discontent and active opposition.

Finally, stability is maintained through limiting access to decision-making arenas to the proper elected and appointed persons and by branding anyone who seeks to violate these restrictions as a 'malcon-tent' or a 'troublemaker' and thus outside the protection of the system. Thus, the cycle edges toward repeating itself.

From A Theoretical To An Empirical Question

Thus far we have described labor relations generations in terms which, though theoretically plausible, lack a clear empirical foundation. It remains to provide a suitable measure of the proposition that genera-tional development accurately captures the idea and dynamics of public school labor relations in the United States. This book, and the research that undergirds it, was undertaken to generate hypotheses rather than to formally test them. However, straightforwardness demands that we indicate the evidence that we would expect to exist if our definition of labor dynamics is correct and where in the remainder of the book such evidence may be found. If the generational view of labor relations is correct, we would expect the following four conditions to exist:

First, we would expect ideological conflict over labor relations to re-emerge in districts which have well established patterns of conduct and a substantial history of stable harmonious labor relations. Ideo-logical conflict involving issues of authority of governance is to be distinguished from ordinary, frictional conflict such as that which might occur in a strike over economic issues. The generational concept developed in this book suggests that ideological conflict is the basic mechanism of change, and that the ideological meaning of conflict will be recognizable to participants.

Second, we would expect that recurrent ideological conflict would not be over reactionary efforts to disestablish unions, but rather that the conflict be directed toward reforming the central idea of unionism. Examples of districts which have passed through more than one cycle of discontent-crisis-institutionalization-accommodation would prove particularly convincing. Conversely, if no districts are found that have undergone conflict at the time collective bargaining was initially adopted and subsequently developed a new conflict cycle, it could be argued that the conflict-to-accommodation vision of labor dynamics was a more accurate depiction than generational development.

Third, we would expect ideological conflicts to be accompanied by abrupt turnover in the key leadership positions in either labor or management. Leadership turnover, especially involuntary turnover, is a central element in conflict theory. If periods of high stress and conflict are closely associated with the departure of key leaders, the generational scheme would gain credence. Conversely, if frequent dismissals occur with little or no linkage to labor strife, or if strife does not affect leadership tenure, we should begin to doubt the generational interpretation.

Fourth, we would expect to find changes in basic belief about labor relations among key actors in school districts. Since generational development is seen as the vehicle for changing beliefs and attitudes about acceptable and desirable forms of labor relations, we would expect to be able to identify particular ideas with each ideological change cycle. New and more positive attitudes about the union, the administration, and the school board should follow once a clear victory for one side has been achieved and conflict subsides. Conversely, if we found little difference in belief among individuals whose school districts had the earmarks of different labor relations generations, we would come to question the robustness of the generational idea.

In the following chapters we present four different kinds of data which led us to the argument in this book. The historical record of unions in general and teacher unions in particular, which is the subject of chapter 3, appears to us to fall in the approximate pattern of generations. The variables that are important to the concept of generational development ought to be useful for categorizing schools that display similar histories and similar patterns of belief. As we have suggested in the previous pages, the level of labor conflict and the extent to which the union is recognized as representative of the teachers are of central importance in understanding each labor relations generation and the conflict periods that separate them. If we use these two variables to classify our districts according to labor relations generations, then the districts should display similar kinds of events in their labor histories. In chapter 4 we examine this record. In the same chapter, we examine changes in belief across generations and show that the patterns of belief change represents that which the conflict change cycle would lead us to expect. In chapter 8, which describes the governance impacts of unionism, we present data on perceptual changes among different groups active in school politics. These data, we believe, highlight the unique pivotal role of parents and citizens in generational change. The organizational histories of our study districts, particularly the eight districts we studied most closely, should also demonstrate the stages of development we have outlined. These data are woven into chapters 5, 6 and 7, which illustrate each generational period.

Implications of the Generational View

Generational development through cycles of conflict and accommodation substantially alter how we understand unionism and the unionization. The first, and most obvious, conclusion is that nothing is settled once and for all. Not only will the daily working relationships between labor and management change, but the underlying assumptions and beliefs about the nature and purpose of the relationship change. This conclusion implies that unions are a much more dynamic force than is usually suggested. It is frequently asserted that established unions become conservative and inflexible. The generational view of union dynamics also implies that they do so at their own peril.

Generational change implies that a labor relations strategy built solely around conflict avoidance is doomed. Effective long-term labor relations requires distinguishing between ideological and frictional conflict.

The second, and derivative conclusion is that characterizing opposition is both important and difficult for those who engage in unionization. Opposition comes both from the 'laggards' who are mentally fixed in the previous generation or intergenerational period and the 'leaders' who want to go further.[29] Laggards are equally troublesome to unions and management because they are unable to recognize or celebrate the closure of one period and the opening of another. They tend to garner a great deal of attention by threatening to refight past battles. Their threats to 'go non-union' or campaigns against the collective bargaining law are very real. In actuality, however, the greater threat to the status quo is created by the leaders, those radicals and visionaries who attempted to organize the future. Not all radical threats will be successful, but some will.

The third conclusion of the generational thesis is that ideology is very important. American labor relations is thought of as being fundamentally pragmatic because it is not revolutionary or Marxian in the societal sense, and that holds for teacher unions, too. But teacher unions *are* revolutionary in their changing views about school organizations and about the roles of teachers as workers.

Fourth and perhaps most important, accepting the generational thesis dramatically alters one's thinking about the overall impact of second generation good-faith bargaining on education. Most studies of labor relations in public schools consider the primary impact to be on the way schools are governed — a more-or-less serious threat to the public's right to govern their schools. But the generational perspective on labor relations recognizes multiple opportunities for the governance system to correct itself, or at least for the public to intervene. As a consequence, throughout this book, our attention is drawn to the impacts of unionism on organizational processes and particularly on the work lives and work role identification of teachers.

Notes

1 KERR, C., DUNLOP, J.T., HARBISON, F.H. and MYERS, C.A. (1964) *Industrialism and Industrial Man*, New York, Oxford University Press, pp. 166–220.
2 BARBASH, J. (1969) 'Rationalization in the American union', in SOMMERS, G.G. (Ed.) *Essays in Industrial Relations Theory*, Ames, IA, Iowa State University Press, p. 154.
3 *Ibid.*, p. 147.

4 CARLTON, P. W. (1969), 'Educator attitudes and value differences in collective negotiation', in CARLTON, P.W. and GOODWIN, H.I. (Eds) *The Collective Dilemma: Negotiations in Education*, Worthington, OH, Jones.

5 LESTER, R.A. (1958) *As Unions Mature: An Analysis of the Evolution of American Unionism*, Princeton, NJ, Princeton University Press, p. 98.

6 SLICHTER, S.H., HEALY, J.J. and LIVERNASH, E.R. (1960) *The Impact of Collective Bargaining on Management*, Washington, DC, Brookings Institution; D. LEWIN, R.D. HORTON and J.W. KUHN (1979) *Collective Bargaining and Manpower Utilization in Big City Governments*, Montclair, NJ, Allanhead Osmun and Co.; PERRY C. (1979) 'Teacher bargaining: The experience in nine systems', *Industrial and Labor Relations Review*, 33, 1, pp 3–17; JOHNSON, S.M. (1984) *Teachers Unions in Schools*, Philadelphia PA, Temple University Press; JESSUP, D. (1985) *Teachers Unions and Change*, New York, Praeger.

7 TURNER, J.H. (1978) *The Structure of Sociological Theory*, rev. edn, Homewood, IL, Dorsey Press. See particularly chapter 6, pp. 121–42.

8 DAHRENDORF, R. (1959) *Class and Class Conflict in Industrial Society*, Stanford, CA, Stanford University Press, p. 5.

9 DAY, R. and DAY, J. (1977) 'A review of the current state of negotiated order theory', *Sociological Quarterly*, 18, p. 132.

10 STRAUSS, A. (1978) *Negotiations: Varieties, Contexts, Processes and Social Order*, San Francisco, CA, Jossey-Bass.

11 DAHRENDORF, B. (1959) *op cit*, p. 194.

12 *Ibid.*, p. 265.

13 This idea is well represented in the literature on industrial relations. See, for instance: BENDIX, R. (1956) *Work and Authority in Industry*, New York, Wiley.

14 STINNETT, T.M. (1966) *Professional Negotiation in Public Education*, New York, Macmillan, p. 11.

15 CORWIN, R.G. (1970) *Militant Professionalism: A Study of Organizational Conflict in High Schools*, New York, Appleton-Century-Crofts, p. 109.

16 *Ibid.*

17 BLAU, P. (1968) 'Social exchange' in SILLS, D.L. (Ed) *International Encyclopedia of the Social Sciences*, v. 7, New York, The Macmillan Co. and the Free Press, p. 457; also BENDIX, R. (1956) *op cit*.

18 SHORTER, E. and TILLEY, C. (1974) *Strikes in France: 1830–1968*, London, Cambridge University Press, p. 338.

19 SCHATTSCHNEIDER, E.E. (1960) *The Semi-Sovereign People: A Realist's View of Democracy in America*, New York: Holt Rinehart and Winston, p. 3.

20 COBB, R.W. and ELDER, C.D. (1972) *Participation in American Politics: The Dynamics of Agenda-Building*, Baltimore, MD, John Hopkins University Press, p. 83.

21 *Ibid.*, p. 115.

22 SCHATTSCHNEIDER, E.E. (1960) *op cit*, p. 65.

23 *Ibid.*

24 DAHRENDORF, R. (1959) *op cit*, p. 257.

25 MEAD, G.H. (1934) *Mind, Self, and Society*, Chicago, IL, University of Chicago Press.
26 On the growth of specialization, see MARCH, J. and OLSEN, J.P. (1976) *Ambiguity and Choice in Organizations*, Bergen, Norway, University of Norway Press.
27 LIEBERMAN, M. (1982) *Public Sector Bargaining: A Policy Reappraisal* Lexington, MA, Lexington Books, D.C. Heath and Co, p. 143.
28 STRAUSS, G. and FEUILLE, P. (1978) 'Industrial relations research: A critical analysis', *Industrial Relations.* **17**, 3, October, 259–77.
29 ERCK, W.M. (1983) 'An analysis of the relationship between teacher collective bargaining activities and altered managerial behavior in selected Illinois school districts', doctoral thesis, University of Illinois.

3
The Hand of History: Generations in Institutional Perspective

While this book concentrates on the organizational dynamics of teacher unionism, there is also an important institutional counterpart: national unions, administrator groups, school boards, and the attentive public also go through labor relations generations...or something very like them. The history of generational change, of heresy supplanting the old orthodoxy, extends back to the first national unions and forward to the most recent teacher union national conventions. Like our organizational versions of generations, each generation of unionism as an institution embodies a distinct organizing idea.

The Private Sector Roots

Since the mid-nineteenth century, which marks the beginning of a nationwide labor movement, unions have adopted three quite different ideologies about their fundamental purposes. Expanding product markets — made possible by advances in transportation and mechanization — threatened the security of skilled workers, who faced competition from women, immigrants, and less skilled workers. In the process, 'they were also converted from the dignified status of "producer" to the common one of "hired hand"'. Out of these circumstances the wage system itself came under attack, first from the short-lived National Labor Union formed in 1866 and then from the Noble Order of the Knights of Labor, the country's first large-scale labor organization.

Founded in 1868 on the ruins of a blacklisted Philadelphia garment workers union, the Knights of Labor, under the leadership of Terence

Powderly, became a strong voice for the elimination of the wage system:[1]

> Powderly's ultimate objective was producer cooperatives. He was not wage conscious, and constantly emphasized the fact that strikes could not solve issues like apprenticeship, administration of justice, child labor, or laws of supply and demand.[2]

Powderly urged workers to put their funds into cooperatives that would again make them their own masters. During the depression that followed the panic of 1873 the Knights flourished, their activities cloaked in secrecy and ritual. They departed from the history of narrow trade unionism, inviting anyone over 18, 'regardless of race, sex or skill', to join their ranks, excluding only such 'undesirables' as salesmen, bartenders, doctors, lawyers and bankers.[3]

By 1886 the Knights' membership had reached 700,000. But internal conflicts ensued with members seeking different goals than were sought by the leadership. To Powderly's embarrassment, the Knights began engaging in strikes for higher wages, including a successful walkout and boycott against railroad financier Jay Gould. The national attention that focused on this boycott attracted more members, and Powderly found himself heading,

> an organization whose expanded membership was now overwhelmingly composed of unionists who sought gains in the areas of wages and hours and who advocated the strike to achieve them, precisely the objectives and tactics abhorrent to the Knight's leadership.[4]

Not surprisingly, a new unionism took organizational form. The American Federation of Labor (AFL) was created in 1886 and prospered immediately. It was craft-oriented, pragmatic and non-revolutionary. Its aims were probably best expressed by Cigarmakers President Adolph Strasser in testimony before a Senate committee:

> We have no ultimate ends. We are going on from day to day. We fight only for immediate objects — objects that can be realized in a few years.[5]

The Knights, tarred with the brush of anarchism following the 1886 Haymarket bombings in Chicago, rapidly declined in popularity and, by the turn of the century, had virtually ceased to exist.

The movement of American labor from Powderly's Knights of Labor to Samuel Gompers' AFL represented more than just an organizational shift. It reflected a whole new generation of labor ideology. As Chamberlain, Cullen and Lewin put it:

> The passing of the Knights reflected the emerging acceptance by workers of the wage relationship and the recognition that small workshops were rapidly being replaced by aggregations of capital and professionally managed enterprises. The AFL survived and grew because it came to terms with the capitalist, private enterprise system, adapting to it rather than seeking to destroy it.[6]

This fundamental ideology was to remain strong through a half-century of bloody battles, the Sherman Anti-Trust Act, yellow dog contracts, the socialist challenges of the IWW, and the prosperity of the 1920s.

However, even as the labor movement was being formally legitimated by the Wagner Act of 1935, the AFL conception of craft unionism was being directly challenged. Major industrial complexes remained non-union, and attempts to organize them had been ineffective. Partly because the techniques of mass production were rapidly eliminating craft work in manufacturing, and partly because work activities in large industrial firms covered such a broad spectrum of tasks, it became virtually impossible to organize industrial firms along craft lines.

From Craft To Industrial Unionism

At this point John L. Lewis, whose mineworkers were dwindling in number, led and lost a fight to have the AFL shift from craft to industrial unionism. He argued, in essence, that unions should be organized by companies across entire industrial sectors and that floor sweepers, production workers, and skilled machine operators should all be included in the same bargaining unit.

Expelled from the AFL, the dissidents formed the Congress of Industrial Organization (CIO) and immediately launched major efforts to organize steel, textiles, rubber, and autos. By early 1937, United States Steel had recognized the steelworkers as an exclusive bargaining agent, and the rest of industry followed suit, albeit not without additional bloodshed. Autoworkers staged a sit-down strike at General Motors' Fisher Body plant before they were granted recognition. By the end of 1937, the CIO had a membership of 3.7 million, some 300,000 more than the AFL.[7] As time passed, even the AFL began to organize along industrial lines, particularly the machinists and the electrical workers. Today, despite continuing tension between the craft and industrial segments of the merged AFL-CIO, American unionism is fundamentally industrial in character. Over the past forty years the focus of union organizing activity and contractual demands has shifted dramatically toward a concern with the *firm* as the basic organizational structure for productive work. Unions have sought to control access to employment in the firm, health and safety protection, pensions, and effective mechanisms for adjudicating grievances.[8]

In advocating industrial unionism, the CIO was far more than a change in organizational form and leadership. Organization around the firm rather than the craft represents a fundamentally different idea about what unions are and what they should do. Industrial unions accept management's right to control work technology and to organize the means of production. Industrial unions seek to control the conditions of work, not the specific duties assigned various workers. By so doing, industrial unionism creates the conditions for unions to represent the unskilled laborer as well as the skilled craft worker. In retrospect, this change appears to have been inevitable. Though his words were controversial at the time, John L. Lewis was certainly right when he said in 1935, 'The craft union principle has become fundamentally ineffective in the face of modern conditions'.[9]

The 'New' Industrial Relations

In the last decade the supposedly stable system of industrial unionism has suffered a number of shocks, and once again questions are being raised about the underlying assumptions of unionism. Most apparent have been the shocks of retrenchment. Workers in a number of industries have had to make wage, benefit, and work practice concessions. In addition, there have been longer-run changes in industrial relations practices that form the basis for what some are calling a 'new' industrial relations.[10]

49

Union membership has declined from about one-third of the non-agricultural labor force to less than one-fifth, and the growth sectors of the American economy are largely non-union.[11] Management strategy has become more explicitly anti-union, with open assent being given to corporate policies on plant relocation away from union-intensive labor markets. Maintenance of a 'union-free environment' has become both an acceptable and an explicit policy in many corporations.[12] Meanwhile, policies of coexistence, if not active cooperation, have been encouraged at previously unionized plants.

Of even greater significance is the shift toward managerial initiative in introducing changes in work organization, shop-level employee participation, and even some forms of continuous employment guarantees. Many of these changes are taking place in non-union firms, and in the words of one observer, 'go beyond the simple goal of matching union gains [in other firms] to keep unions out'.[13]

In the face of these changes, the nation is witnessing a substantial rethinking of unionism. The AFL-CIO shows evidence of recognizing that work and workers have changed and consequently that 'unions must develop and put into effect multiple models for representing workers tailored to the needs and concerns of different groups'.[14] A recent report offered the possibility of abandoning the strike as labor's ultimate weapon, allowing individuals to seek wages above bargained minimums, and providing direct service to individuals outside collective bargaining units. In addition, the report recognized the need to embrace authentic quality of worklife programs and opportunities 'affording greater worker participation in the decision-making process at the workplace'.[15] As we will see, discontent with the current practice of unionization and a search for a new unionism is evident among teachers as well.

Generational Change Among National Teacher Unions

Whereas the histories of American industrial relations illustrate the general pattern of successive ideas around which unions were built, the histories of teacher unions reveal the same three specific ideas we have found in the school districts we studied. The central belief system of teacher unionism has dramatically changed from meet-and-confer within an administratively-dominated hierarchy to a tradition of independent teacher voice through collective bargaining. We believe that the central belief system is again in tension and that the shape and structures of the era of negotiated policy will emerge within national unions just as they do at the local level.

The First Generation of teacher unionism emerged from the progressive, civil service movement that sought to reform big city government, bring modern management to bear on education, and introduce the elements of a progressive curriculum. The trade unionism of the day, indeed, any essentially independent teacher organization, was an anathema in this setting. It is thus ironic that the seeds of widespread unionization were planted within this orthodoxy of supposedly beneficent bureaucracy. Yet, as we shall see, what we have come to know as meet-and-confer labor relations grew and flowered late in the development of the First Generation, when schools were forced to recognize that teachers were not well represented by the existing system.

Although the Progressive Era reforms are familiar territory to students of school organization and politics, their special relationship to labor helps illustrate the dynamics of labor relations generations. Much of the tension between teachers and school administrators can be understood in terms of the conflict between the three aspects of Progressive Reform: the municipal reform movement, the doctrine of business efficiency most commonly known as scientific management, and the pedagogical theories of progressive education. These three aspects of reform were hierarchically linked. Progressive educationists and scientific managers each depended on the freedom from political patronage brought about by municipal reform. Progressive education also required strong management in order to internally restructure schools and wrest control from traditionalist teachers schooled in the 3Rs and the parents who were suspicious of the new education.[16]

At the outset, the three reforms had very broad support among educators. Teacher groups, including the American Federation of Teachers, supported removing control of the teaching staff from the board of education and placing it 'in the hands of the professional expert, the Superintendent of Schools'.[17] The progressive educationists were also committed to administrative reform. John Dewey, the leading spokesman for progressive pedagogy, initially lauded key changes being made by the administrative progressives.

The tenet of a unitary community assumed that an overall 'public interest', addressing the needs of the entire community, could best be pursued by insulating political decisions from the biases and pressures of special interest groups and making decisions without regard for particularistic economic or ethnic needs or values.

In order to support the ideology of separation of schools from politics, it had to be argued that there is a special, politically neutral body of knowledge about how students learn and schools operate, and that people who run schools possess this knowledge. This is the cornerstone of the doctrine of neutral professional competence underlying the rise of school superintendents, city managers, and merit-based civil service systems in federal, state, and municipal governments. This doctrine, which is at the core of the scientific management movement, insists that administrators both can and should 'operate as professional experts...making value-free and apolitical decisions'.[18]

In turn, the belief that competent administrators were politically neutral allowed reform politicians to develop a strong alliance with school reformers seeking the incorporation of 'business efficiency' into the management of education and other public services. Demographics aided the transition — a growing industrial economy, immigration of large numbers of foreigners, and the migration of workers from farm, to town, to metropolis, all supported the consolidation of schools into large, complex, heavily administered organizations while it politically neutralized the new urban residents.

Business efficiency required that the outputs of education be known and quantified and that 'educational experts' could produce those outputs in various local school settings. It was simply a matter of social engineering: the application of the correct technology to the specific setting. Schools came to borrow heavily, and often badly, from Frederick Taylor's system of scientific management. They translated a concern for return on investment to an inquiry into unit costs. Thus, Frank Spaulding, one of the period's leaders, was to question 'Why is a pupil recitation in English costing 7.2 cents in vocational school while it costs only 5 cents in technical school? Is the "vocational" English 44 per cent superior to the "technical" English or 44 per cent more difficult to secure?'[19]

The Problem of Bureaucracy

The latent tensions within bureaucracies surfaced quickly and eventually led to teacher organization. Even while progressive reformers were proclaiming the importance of professionalization, they were formalizing and stratifying education so that teaching did not share in professional self-determination. Teachers, principals and superintendents were all technically 'educators' but divisions among the strata became so great that, 'in effect they [were] separate'.[20] As John Dewey wrote, administrative structures drove the development of a 'new curriculum'. Class size, the arrangement of classes and the assignment of teachers, their selection, grading, pay and promotion defined the 'reality of education'.[21] Ultimately, it was difficult to express the vision of cooperative, democratic schooling within the hierarchical bureaucracy which issued from administrative reform. Dewey himself recognized the need to balance bureaucratic control with teacher influence; he carried Card No. 1 of the American Federation of Teachers until his death.

Within the bureaucratic form created by progressive reformers, teachers became protected employees. They were given substantive and procedural rights by civil service statutes aimed at eliminating the all too prevalent risk of capricious dismissal by cost conscious or ideologically vindictive school boards. Pay systems and advancement became rationalized and the development of salary schedules that paid all teachers according to years of service and education became common. Teachers' desires for improved occupational status, according to the progressive vision, were to be realized through raising the overall status of the educational system. It was assumed that the status of teachers would rise in direct proportion to improvements in the training and expertise acquired by all members of the new profession. Standards of education for entering teachers, and indeed, the actual level of their education, rose steadily. Compensation for the teachers, it was assumed, would rise in response to public confidence and respect — not as a result of either market forces or teacher organization. In an argument heard with increasing frequency today, reformers insisted that the public would be grateful for improved teacher performance, and would see the wisdom of offering high salaries to attract able young people into the profession.

If teachers were poorly paid, it was asserted, the best way of improving salaries was improving performance. U.S. Commissioner of Education, William T. Harris, in 1905, noted:

> The teacher whose salary is low...will try to improve his skill in teaching... He will study to perfect himself in fine manners. He will pass under review his moral judgments... What teacher could not improve his position and find a more adequate salary for himself?... There is, in fact, a great lack in number and quality for the highest positions and best salaries that are offered in the United States. [22]

On the whole, the progressive vision was grounded on woefully inadequate premises. School finance did not respond to public support because schools were tied to property tax revenues. Tax revenues did not keep pace with either inflation or the demand for schooling. Even during the 1930s, when prices did not go up and birth rates were low, demands on the schools increased because the percentage of teenagers going to high school rose steadily. Rather than taking the interests of teachers as their own, scientific school managers often focused on cost reduction and expansion of their own power. And school boards, rather than compensating teachers for their dedication and professionalism, tended to accept the premise that low salaries confirm the assertion that teaching is an easy job held by relatively fuzzy minded and unambitious workers.

The Early Rejection of Unionism

Among progressive reformers, embrace of the reform bureaucracy was combined with an explicit rejection of unionism. Independent unions were seen as incompatible with the new administrative orthodoxy on several counts. First, overt self-interest clashed with the selfless service ideology underlying the reformers' idea of professionalism. Second, teacher expressions of self-interest were taken as a failure of reform governments to discharge their responsibility to care for and control their employees. Teacher organizations were an embarrassment. Third, unionization threatened the ideal of politically neutral 'Blue Ribbon' elite governance of the schools.

The elite opposed the vision of unionism almost from its origins in

1897, when Margaret Haley and her elementary teacher colleagues formed the Chicago Federation of Teachers. In 'fighting for the rights to which they were entitled',[23] Haley and her associates sought to raise teacher salaries from the $825 maximum which had been in effect for two decades, end tax abuse through which major corporations such as McCormick Harvesting, the Pullman Company and the *Chicago Tribune* escaped property levies, and reduce class size, which sometimes reached seventy children per room.[24]

In addition to her bread-and-butter trade unionism, Haley had a vision of how teachers should put together a nationwide organization — turning the National Education Association into an organization controlled by and 'administered in the interest of the thousands of teachers who were to contribute to its income'.[25] Haley was first noticed within the NEA when she rose to challenge Commissioner Harris at the 1901 Detroit convention. After Harris had cited statistics to show that public education was flourishing, one member of the audience suggested that wealthy philanthropists should give money to public schools. In response, Haley attacked the idea of big business support, saying that it would stifle the autonomy of teachers. Harris responded:

> Pay no attention to what that teacher down there has said for I take it she is a grade teacher just out of her school room at the end of the school year, worn out, tired, hysterical.

Harris assured his audience that the new industrialists were the great benefactors of the schools. Haley, fresh from her Chicago tax crusades, disagreed.[26].

In 1909, Haley's close personal friend and strong union supporter, Ella Flagg Young, became superintendent of schools in Chicago. She was a recognized force in Illinois politics, particularly with the Irish.[27] Young was also a student of Dewey's and a subscriber of his view of school democracy as a social necessity. To her, character development was as important a concept as it had been to the nineteenth century missionaries who organized public schooling in the United States but 'character' involved social deliberation and action as well as individual virtue.[28] Her PhD thesis, which she wrote at the age of 50, summarized her views on 'how teachers might participate in decision-making' within a democratic school system.[29] Haley called it 'the Bible of the teachers of the United States on the question of academic freedom'.[30]

As superintendent, Young instituted teachers' councils to advise the district on curriculum and thought it a logical contradiction for a democracy to so lack confidence in teachers that they could not be active participants in its decisional process. Perhaps most important, in terms of the developing ideology of school organization, she defined loyalty as a proper relationship between teachers and the common welfare of children, rather than an attachment to hierarchy or a political machine.

At first ambivalent on the question of collective bargaining for salaries, she changed her position after watching the cynical disregard with which the all male school board greeted salary requests from delegations of its female teachers.[31]

With Haley's support, Young became President of the NEA in 1910, but the presidency was substantially honorific in character during those years. The real power was held by the 'natural aristocracy' of college deans, presidents and professors — a group which was predominately male and intensely conservative in its view. Although they had the real power, the old boys viewed the situation with alarm. Harvard's Charles Eliot considered the women morally obtuse. He wrote,

> It is an extraordinary and very discouraging fact that whenever a large number of women get excited in some cause which seems to them in general good and praiseworthy, some of them become indifferent to the moral quality of the particular efforts by which it seems possible to promote that cause.[32]

Nicolas Murray Butler regarded Haley as a 'fiend in petticoats'.[33]

Tension between teachers and the reform movement's 'natural aristocracy', was only one indicator of the rejection of independent teacher interest. The second powerful symbol of rejection was the widespread popular belief that this self-interest was an illegitimate attitude for teachers to hold. At its root this belief reveals a tension that has not been fully resolved to this day, not in teaching and not in the other 'helping' occupations. As moral vocations, these occupations reject protection of worker interests in favor of commitment to service. In 1898, for example, the *Chicago Times-Herald* commented editorially on the formation of the Chicago Federation of Teachers with the charge that it sprang from 'a spirit not creditable to the high standards of professional ethics'.[34] And in an interesting assertion of the noneconomic character of the work, concluded that 'A teacher was not worthy of her salary who did not earn more than she was paid...'[35]

That viewpoint has endured. Sixty years later, Theodore Martin, NEA Director of Membership in the years prior to collective bargaining, was to proclaim,

> Unionism lowers the ideals of teaching. By emphasizing the selfish, though necessary, economic needs of teachers — salary, hours, tenure, retirement — unionism misses altogether the finer ideals of teaching and the rich compensations that do not appear in the salary envelope.[36]

Indeed, a superintendent from our study voiced similar comments in 1979:

> Teachers have lost their image as being public servants and are relegating themselves to being comparable to the dinner bucket, hard-hat union members. The community opinion is that the teacher really isn't interested in my youngster.

Teacher willingness to violate this ideal of selfless dedication and seek organized strength was explicit in the formation of the American Federation of Teachers. The AFT was founded in 1916, partly at the urging of Samuel Gompers, when representatives of three Chicago locals and one from Gary met in Charles Stillman's home in Wilmette, Illinois. Locals in New York City, Scranton and Washington, D.C., joined shortly.[37] By 1920 the total membership was 10,000.

The union movement, however, came under immediate fire. Coincidentally, the first organized attack on the unions took place in the same city and in the same year as the founding of the Cleveland Conference, one of school administration's most enduring elites. The year was 1915; the city, Cleveland, Ohio. The school board announced that it would not employ union members. Teachers had every reason to be fearful since private firms made widespread use of 'yellow dog' contracts whereby individual employees accepted their positions under the pledge that they would remain non-union.[38] The courts supported the teachers in Cleveland, however, and they were eventually successful in regaining their jobs, but the threat of dismissal had done its work. 'Teachers were then, as a few are today, timid folk. The idea of being fired, despite eventual remedies, was frightening'.[39] The tactic spread. In Chicago, the school board lost a legal challenge to a blanket firing order of union members, but the courts upheld the 1916 non-renewal of sixty-eight teachers, forty of whom were union members. Some twenty-eight of the dismissed unionists had been rated 'excellent' by the superintendent. In the days before tenure, the Illinois Supreme Court ruled that 'the board has the absolute right to decline to employ or to employ an applicant for any reason whatsoever or for no reason at all'.[40]

Teachers also learned the hazards of unionism from examples elsewhere. In September 1919, the Boston police union called a strike, and three-quarters of the uniformed officers followed their leaders. Widespread disorder and looting followed. Governor Calvin Coolidge fired all the strikers, hired replacements, and chilled public sector organizing for forty years with his remark to AFL President Gompers: 'There is no right to strike against the public safety by anybody, anywhere, anytime'.[41]

Union expansion halted abruptly. Chicago temporarily pulled out of the AFT in 1917 and, nationally, during the 1920s, the Federation was 'dead although it refused to lie down'.[42] It was not to experience growth again until the Depression.

Progressive Administrators Also Organized

In 1915, as noted above, school administrators organized the Cleveland Conference (whose annual gatherings are now held in Chicago) in a deliberate effort to strengthen their control over school progress and policies. The Cleveland Conference wasn't really a conference at all but rather, as historians Tyack and Hansot have aptly described it, a deliberately formed, by-invitation-only, elite network.[43]

The original members included Leonard P. Ayers, of the Russell Sage Foundation; Abraham Flexner, consultant to Andrew Carnegie whose 1910 report is credited with reforming medical schools in the United States; Frank Spaulding, a superintendent and scientific management advocate; Elwood Cubberly, author of the leading text on school administration and Dean of Education at Stanford University; and George Strayer and Edward Thorndike of Teachers College, Columbia.[44] Neither Ella Flagg Young or Margaret Haley attended — nor for that matter did any other woman until the 1960s.[45]

Administrative orthodoxy also spread through other means. Progressive reform professors of administration gained control over superintendent hiring as specialized training became more important in the developing bureaucracies of scientifically managed school districts. The school survey movement, which flourished in the years after 1910, emerged as a vehicle for bringing expert opinion to bear on the operation of school districts. Not incidentally, it was also a mechanism for bringing emergent male-dominated administrator groups together to discuss how best to give their special concerns greater weight.

Progressive administrators set out to turn educators into professionals. They recognized that although the norms of a profession require an ethic of public service and standards of high competence, powerful institutionalization is brought about through privatization and control. To become a profession educators had to seek the status of private government, the withdrawal of active public scrutiny and deference to 'the experts' in setting policy. School administrators took on the mantle of expertise, aggressively pursuing control over who has entry, what training and licenses are required, and what standards of conduct define the work.

Among the primary instruments for defining teaching from the 1920s to the 1950s was the National Education Association. The progressives created a truly national structure that regularized the relationships between local, state and national organizations. The Representative Assembly, which continues today as NEA's policy body, was the creation of George Strayer in 1918. The most important characteristics of the NEA were its comprehensive membership and its administratively-dominated structure. The NEA became the one organization that could speak for education. It included everybody in public education: teachers, superintendents, and the university educationists. The teachers, of course, represented the vast majority of the members. And women, some of them classroom teachers, often served as presidents. But control over the organization, and thus over the profession, was placed in the hands of male superintendents. As an organization, the NEA took on the same hierarchical characteristics as did the school districts.

The NEA grew rapidly in the years after World War I. Membership expanded from about 8,500 in 1917 to more than 141,000 in 1927 and 200,000 by 1940.[46] Concurrently, there were structural changes as the organization discarded its clubbish characteristics and added the departments and commissions appropriate to a national service organization — research, health, thrift, racial well-being, science instruction, practical arts and even foreign relations. During the '20s, the Association acquired a permanent headquarters in Washington, and a staff of fifty. One view of reform is that the NEA became a truly national organization, rational in its selection and representation procedures, 'from a small group led by college professors and school superintendents into a large and truly national group with the potential for representing classroom teachers'.[47]

Control of NEA policy and control of the occupation, however, remained firmly in the hands of the superintendents. This control was facilitated by the fact that administration had become a career while teaching was still a job. Superintendents changed jobs, on the average of once every five years, but they stayed in the occupation for most of a lifetime.[48] By contrast, teachers left their jobs to start families or to move into other occupations. Administrators also had the opportunity to reform the informal networks of association. The structure of their jobs permitted them more freedom of movement and control over their schedules. Teachers were confined to their classrooms, largely isolated from other adults. Superintendents formulated NEA programs and policies — frequently attending meetings of the NEA and its Department of Superintendence with travel funds supplied by their districts.[49] Teachers seldom attended, and when they did they often had to pay their own transportation cost and provide for substitutes out of their own pockets.

In the main, though, the establishment of a uniform and hierarchically-dominated system of public education was a work of deliberate statecraft. Journalist, muckraker, and social activist Upton Sinclair described the annual superintendents' meetings in a sinister light, saying that they were a

> great clearing-house, where the bosses exchange experiences and perfect the technique of holding down the salaries of the teachers, breaking up their organizations, eliminating the rebels from the system, and making fast the hold of the gang.[50]

While William Donely's sympathetic portrait of the NEA during that period was titled 'Teachers to the Fore', Sinclair's rendition of the same years was headed 'Teachers to the Rear'.[51]

The Invention of Meet-and-Confer

As the dissatisfaction of teachers became more obvious, the established school hierarchy needed a mechanism to address their real and pressing problems and to relieve internal tensions. Early Progressives recognized that teachers had a special interest in their own wages and salaries. Given substantial variations across school districts, a few small steps were taken to accommodate that interest. As early as 1919, for example, there were reports at the NEA's national convention of teachers' councils formed in different cities to deal with such problems as curriculum, textbooks, the merit system, the length of the day and salary.[52] By 1938, the NEA Educational Policies Commission was to go on record as favoring increased participation with a statement that concluded, 'It is sound procedure to provide for the active participation of teachers in the development of *administrative* policy'.[53]

Nevertheless, the post-war years were punctuated with increased teacher restiveness.[54] Salaries that looked good during the Depression were less appealing. School district enrollments grew rapidly, and there was a chronic shortage of teachers. Teacher organizations became more active, and isolated strike activity began to be seen. In 1946 there was a walkout in Buffalo and, a year later, work stoppages in New Haven and Minneapolis. In New York City, increased militancy of high school teachers was attributed to the new single salary schedule that deprived secondary teachers of their marginal wage advantage over their elementary school colleagues and, in their view, their elite status. By 1960, a negotiation proposal was presented to the NEA Representative Assembly meeting in Los Angeles.[55] It was extremely mild in tone stating only that the NEA 'recognized that representative negotiations by teachers with their governing boards concerning conditions of employment is compatible with the ethics and dignity of the teaching profession'.[56] The resolution failed, and the NEA was to wait two more years until its Denver Convention to adopt the rudiments of what it called 'professional negotiation'.[57]

There were concurrent changes in other public sector occupations. In 1962, John F. Kennedy signed Executive Order 10988 giving federal workers the right to organize and bargain, although it explicitly forbade strikes, and forbade negotiation over the 'mission of the agency'. State and municipal legislation enabling bargaining by public school teachers began to be seen. Wisconsin passed a statute in 1959. New York City and Philadelphia enacted 'little Wagner Acts' modeled on the 1935 federal statute governing most employees in the private sector. Other jurisdictions followed.

Meanwhile, in New York City, the United Federation of Teachers took more direct action. They struck for recognition and the right to bargain. The one-day strike involved in 1960 only about 4600 of the city's 39,000 teachers, but it proved sufficient to activate the support of organized labor and the city's politicians, who, while publicly decrying a strike, still viewed the right to bargain as sacrosanct. A representation election was held the following June. In the spring of 1962, the much more visible strike described at the beginning of this book signaled that the era had indeed changed.

The Institutionalization of Meet-And-Confer

On its face, the meet-and-confer period was an exercise in pure pragmatics; crafting rhetoric to meet the expectations of American teachers who were not yet ready to embrace unionization, and crafting a political vehicle for the NEA, which needed an organizational response to the AFT successes in the big cities. It was certainly both a political and a pragmatic vehicle. But it was also an ideal that stood as a way of accommodating differences within the existing institutional framework. It represented the last attempt to purchase the cooperation of all the elements within an omnibus profession.

The aggressiveness of the NEA and the AFT during the 1960s can be traced partly to organizational concerns. The AFT was being encouraged, even pressured, by the AFL-CIO to expand. Private sector unionism had started to decline, and public sector employees were one of the few vital areas available for organization. The NEA feared an aggressive AFT, having lost the 1961 recognition battle in New York City.[58] That and the AFT's organizing successes in the early 1960s clearly spurred the group of young organizers within the NEA to action. The NEA 'urban project' was launched in 1962 specifically to stem the tide of AFT activity.[59] The answer, in part, was 'meet-and-confer' activity operating under the name 'professional negotiations'. NEA organizer, Donald Baer recalls an early 1960s meeting in the Drake Hotel in Chicago:

We were going to lose the Chicago school district and we were having semantic problems. We couldn't be for bargaining, but we could be for something else. We wanted something to sell to a pretty staid, old membership.[60]

By 1962, a few Associations had been recognized to represent teachers in conferring with management; Long Beach, California, and Denver, Colorado among them.[61] That same year, Executive Order 10988 allowed unionization of federal employees and the NEA published 'Guidelines for Professional Negotiation'. By mid-1963, twenty 'professional negotiating agreements' had been secured in seven states.[62]

The AFT — indeed all of collective bargaining — was at first viewed as an 'urban problem' by the NEA. But the reaction to the AFT's successes spread meet-and-confer to places that would not have touched traditional unionism. The AFT was, in many respects, the bogeyman that scared school officials into adopting and even pressing for meet-and-confer arrangements. The AFT's union label became a target in organization, as was its image as urban and ethnic: Jews and Roman Catholics threatening the Protestant heartland.[63]

By 1965, the Kansas school boards and teacher associations had drafted joint guidelines for 'strengthening teacher-administrator-board relationships'. The 'need' section begins with the words, 'When the 1962 strike of the New York City teachers hit the front pages...' The Kansas guidelines, like others around the country, staked out the territory for meet-and-confer:

Involvement of teachers. The legal responsibility for the adoption of school policies belongs to the board exclusively. However, before arriving at a decision with respect to important policies which affect the work of teachers, the board should make sure that teachers have participated cooperatively in the preparation of the recommendations which it will have under consideration. In the event the board feels the recommendations to be unwise, it will engage in good faith discussions with representatives of the teachers before taking action on the recommendations.[64]

Resolutions such as these, and a series of books and pamphlets, established the framework and the ideal of meet-and-confer.

The central belief of meet-and-confer is that teachers have the right to organize and represent themselves. However, it is important to note that meet-and-confer exists within the context of the administrative bureaucracy, and it leaves existing formal authority undisturbed while at the same time promising increased teacher influence. Teachers would become influential because their personal interests would be perceived as coincident with and support of school district goals. The relationship was perceived as essentially cooperative, and the superintendent was thought of as a person to 'assist each group' and not the 'agent of the board'.[65]

These activities had an effect. The belief began to spread that teachers were supposed to participate in decision making; they were supposed to be heard. As enlightened districts began to meet with teacher organizations, their willingness to change was noted by teacher leaders. Former California Teachers Association staff member Lionel De Silvia, reports, for example, that 'these districts, their boards and their superintendents were our friends'.[66] Nevertheless, the meet-and-confer era needed a mechanism for resolving the persistent disagreements that had become the common experience of many districts. It was found in the idea of 'professional sanctions'.

Politically, sanctions were important because they were *not* strikes. Backed by the distinctive ideology of a shared interest in public service, sanctions gave teachers leverage without forcing them to blame administrators for their problems. Whereas strikes emphasized bringing economic and political pressure to bear on boards and administrators, sanctions were seen as a 'moral force'.[67] Where strikes emphasized the direct pursuit of the welfare needs of teachers, sanctions were much broader than simply power plays to support 'professional negotiations'.[68] Sanctions were used to punish school systems, not to pursue particular agreement of goals. In the two most widely known cases, sanctions were brought against whole states — Utah and Oklahoma. After persistent failure to provide adequate funding for education, these states were 'blacklisted' and teachers discouraged from working there.[69] The NEA executive committee 'enjoined' members from outside the state from taking jobs in Utah or Oklahoma, and in the latter case set up relocation centers for teachers seeking to leave the state.[70] Advocates of the sanction strategy hoped, above all, to avoid dividing the house of education. The enemy was outside; and the power of sanctions lay in the 'good will of the people' who can be expected to 'demand high quality educational services for their children (and) not accept substandard services for them'.[71]

Legalization of the Meet-And-Confer Process

By 1965, some eleven states had adopted legislation giving teachers the right to organize. Nowhere was the ethic of Meet-And-Confer more clearly expressed than it was in California's Winton Act. For the ten years (from 1965 to 1975) California experimented with a statutory form of meet-and-confer that mandated wide-ranging discussion with teachers but forbade formation of collective contracts or the election of exclusive representation for teachers. What surprised even the drafters of the statute was that it was taken seriously by both teachers and school boards throughout the state.

Drafted in the Los Angeles office of the California Teachers Association, the statute was intended partly as a political instrument for undercutting the influence of the AFT in California. The statute called for proportional representation by all employee organizations on district-wide employee councils. The AFT, the drafters knew, 'didn't have the members' to control these councils. The bill was intended as a substitute for collective bargaining, not as a precursor to it. Its sponsors expected it to be used in only 10–20 per cent of the districts in the state.[72]

Quite the opposite happened: almost everyone began to set up negotiations councils. Gordon Winton, who carried the bill in the legislature, recalled that no sooner was the ink dry than the school boards association,

> ...sent a letter to all school boards in the state telling districts to go through the motions of meeting and conferring, and then to do whatever you want. The CTA, on the other hand, sent out a letter to all its chapters telling them to get busy and form negotiations councils.[73]

Well over 90 per cent of the school districts in the state engaged in the process.

Teachers quickly began to see its limitations. They recognized that the process was both structurally flawed and ideologically offensive to many board members. Many teachers felt it lacked the power to seriously influence the views of resistant board members and cynically called the process 'meet and defer'.[74] Some schools were 'resistant to really getting people involved in the decision-making process—what we now call participatory management'.[75] Soon, all were forced to recognize that the law failed to either limit the negotiating agenda or force settlements. Districts were dismayed to discover that the Winton Act opened almost everything to discussion. Districts and teachers were equally disappointed to find that when they sat down to talk, they could not easily come to agreement. *Their differences in interest were real and persistent.* And the California law, indeed the ideology of meet-and-confer had no solution to real conflicts of interest other than to fall back on the sovereign authority of school boards.

By the early 1970s it became apparent that neither labor nor management was very happy with the act. Teachers came to see their interests as separate from those of the administration, and the CTA leadership insisted that 'the adversary relationship is now crystal clear to the majority of teacher organizations'.[76] Superintendents and boards, appalled that the courts would so readily broaden the scope of compulsory negotiations, began to think that *real* collective bargaining might actually be an improvement.[77] Eventually, all parties came to support compromise language in a 'little NLRA'-type bargaining statute that narrowed the scope of bargaining and included neither an explicit prohibition nor protection for strikes. Circumstances had coerced management support for the law. They knew that a bargaining bill was going to pass regardless of their support. One bill had already passed the California legislature in 1972. It was vetoed by Governor Ronald Reagan, but his successor, Edmund G. Brown, Jr. was pledged to support bargaining legislation.[78]

Thus, the state adopted full-fledged collective bargaining, less out of idealism than through disappointment and frustration with its meet-and-confer predecessor. The man whose name was to be attached to the bargaining bill, State Senator Albert Rodda, knew well of the frustrations of meet-and-confer labor relations. He had once been president of Local 31 of the California Federation of Teachers and one night was called to appear before the board of the junior college where he taught.

...they were challenging my right as a representative of teachers to appear before the board. After half an hour of such interrogation I said, 'I came here at your invitation; I did not come here to be badgered. You have not addressed the issues which I wanted to present to you and I'm not going to continue my presence here'. And I left. I can still remember going home on the old street car.[79]

Experiences like this rupture the fabric of common interest and make a mockery of professional service motives among teachers. Without support for these high motives, teachers quickly embrace the adversarial stance implicit in the 'good faith bargaining' requirements of second generation labor relations.

Notes

1 RAYBACK, J.G. (1951) *A History of American Labor*, New York, Macmillan, p. 146.
2 *Ibid.*, pp. 146–7.
3 *Ibid.*, p. 145.
4 DULLES, F.R. (1966) *Labor in America*, 3rd edn, New York, Crowell, p. 141.
5 CHAMBERLAIN, N.W. CULLEN, D.E. and LEWIN, D. (1980) *The Labor Sector*, 3rd edn, New York, McGraw-Hill, p. 100.
6 *Ibid.*, p. 101.
7 FOSSUM, J.A. (1979) *Labor Relations: Development, Structure, Process*, Dallas, Business Publications, Irwin-Dorcsey, p. 35–38.
8 BARBASH, J. (1969) 'Rationalization in the American union', in SOMERS, G.G. (Ed.) *Essays in Industrial Relations Theory*, Ames, IA, Iowa State University Press, p. 154.
9 LEWIS, J.L. (1937) 'Towards industrial democracy', *Industrial Versus Craft Unionism*, New York, H.W. Wilson Co, p. 151.
10 KOCHAN, T.A. and PIORE, M.J. (1984) 'Will the new industrial relations last?: Implications for the American labor movement', *AAPSS Annals*, 473, May, pp. 177–89.
11 JURIS, H. and ROOMKIN, M. (Eds) (1980) *The Shrinking Perimeter: Unionism and Labor Relations in the Manufacturing Sector*, Lexington, MA, Lexington Books.
12 GARBARINO, J.W. (1984) 'Unionism without unions: The new industrial relations', *Industrial Relations* 35, 1, Winter, pp. 40–51.
13 KOCHAN, T.A., MCKERSIE, R.B. and CAPELLI, P. (1984) 'Strategic choice and industrial relations theory', *Industrial Relations*, 23, 1, Winter, pp. 16–39.
14 AFL-CIO COMMITTEE ON THE EVOLUTION OF WORK, (1985) *The Changing Situation of Workers and Their Unions*, Washington, DC, AFL-CIO, p. 18.
15 *Ibid.*, p. 18.
16 MITCHELL, T.K. 'A brief examination of the progressive education movement in Chicago and San Francisco' unpublished manuscript.

17 EATON, W.E. (1975) *The American Federation of Teachers, 1916–1961: A History of the Movement*, Carbondale, IL, Southern Illinois University Press, p. 34.

18 IANNACCONE, L. (1977) 'Three views of change in educational politics' in SCRIBNER, J. (Ed.) *The Politics of Education: NSSE Yearbook, 1977*, Chicago, IL, University of Chicago Press, p. 281.

19 CALLAHAN, R. (1962) *Education and the Cult of Efficiency*, Chicago, IL, University of Chicago Press, p. 72.

20 FREIDSON, E. (1984) 'The changing nature of professional control' in TURNER, R.H. (Ed.) *Annual Review of Sociology*, 10, p. 17.

21 DEWEY, J. (1969) *The Educational Situation*, New York, Arno Press and the New York Times, originally published by the University of Chicago Press, 1904, pps. 23, 24, 25, 27 and 29.

22 DONLEY, M.O. JR., (1976) *Power to the Teacher: How America's Educators Became Militant*, Bloomington, IN, Indiana University Press, p. 18–19.

23 BRAUN, R.J. (1972) *Teachers and Power: The Story of The American Federation of Teachers*, New York, Simon and Schuster, pp. 22–3.

24 *Ibid.*, p. 24. Also HERRICK, M.J. (1971) *The Chicago Schools: A Social and Political History*, Beverly Hills, CA, Sage Publications, p. 101.

25 TYACK, D. and HANSOT, E. (1982) *Managers of Virtue: Public School Leadership in America, 1820–1980*, New York, Basic Books, p. 186.

26 *Ibid.*

27 BRAUN, R.J. (1972) *op cit*, p. 26.

28 TYACK, D. and HANSOT, E. (1982) *op cit*, p. 194.

29 *Ibid.*, p. 198.

30 *Ibid.*, p. 194. From SMITH, J. (1977) 'The influence of Ella Flagg Young on John Dewey's educational thought', *Review Journal of Philosophy and Social Science*, 2, pp. 148 and 143–54. See also, YOUNG, E.F. (1906) *Isolation in the School*, Chicago, IL, University of Chicago Press.

31 *Ibid.*, p. 200.

32 *Ibid.*, p. 186.

33 *Ibid.*, p. 186.

34 HERRICK, M.J. (1971) *op cit*, p. 95.

35 *Ibid.*, p. 95.

36 MARTIN, T.O. (1957) *Building a Teaching Profession*, Middletown, N.Y, Whitlock Press, p. 161 quoted in COLE, S. (1969) *The Unionization of Teachers: A Case Study of the UFT*, New York, Praeger Publishers, p. 4.

37 BRAUN, R.J. (1972) *op cit*, p. 30.

38 They would continue to be widely used until 1932 when the Norris-LaGuardia Act forbade them.

39 BRAUN, R.J. (1972) *op cit*, p. 30.

40 *Ibid.*, p. 33.

41 *The Encyclopedia of American Facts and Dates* (1970) New York, Thomas Crowell, p. 453.

42 BRAUN, R.J. (1972) *op cit*, p. 34.

43   TYACK, D. and HANSOT, E. (1982) *op cit*, p. 130.
44   *Ibid.*, p. 131.
45   *Ibid.*, p. 133.
46   DONLEY, JR, M.O. (1976) *op cit*, p. 30.
47   *Ibid.*, pp. 29–30.
48   MARCH, J.G. and MARCH, J.C. (1979) 'Almost random careers: The Wisconsin School superintendency, 1940–1972', *Administrative Science Quarterly*, 22, 3, March, pp. 377–409.
49   SINCLAIR, U. (1924) *The Goslings: A Study of American Schools*, Pasadena, CA, Upton Sinclair.
50   *Ibid.*, p. 227.
51   DONLEY, JR, M.O. (1976) *op cit*, p. 28; SINCLAIR, U. (1924) *op cit*, p. 263.
52   DONLEY, JR, M.O. (1976) *op cit*, p. 22.
53   STINNETT, T.M., KLEINMANN, J.H. and WARE, M.L. (1966) *Professional Negotiation in Public Education*, New York, Macmillan Co, p. 7.
54   The first bargaining contract with a public school district had been signed in 1944 in Cicero, Illinois.
55   STINNETT, T.M., KLEINMANN, J.H. and WARE, M.L. (1966) *op cit*, p. 8.
56   *Ibid.*, p. 9; from *Addresses and Proceedings* (98th Annual Meeting of the National Education Association (Los Angeles), Washington: NEA, vol. 98, 1960, pp. 153f).
57   *Ibid.*, p. 11.
58   DONLEY, JR, M.O. (1976) *op cit*, p. 53.
59   CRESSWELL, A.M., MURPHY, M.J. with KERCHNER, C.T. (1980) *Teachers, Unions and Collective Bargaining in Public Education*, Berkeley, CA, McCutchan Publishing Co., p. 94.
60   BUSHMAN, P. (1982) 'Collective bargaining in California public education: Historical perspective', unpublished Ph.D. dissertation, Claremont Graduate School, pp. 83–4, from personal interview.
61   DONLEY, JR, M.O. (1976) *op cit*, pp. 70–1.
62   *Ibid.*, p. 76.
63   BUSHMAN, P. (1982) *op cit*, p. 36.
64   STINNETT, J.M., KLEINMANN, J.H. and WARE, M.L. (1966) *op cit*, p. 94, from 'Guidelines, Topeka: Kansas Association of School Boards and Kansas State Teacher Association' May 1965, p. 10.
65   CAMPBELL, R.F., CUNNINGHAM, L.L. and MCPHEE, R.F. (1965) *The Organization and Control of American Schools*, Columbus, OH, Merrill, p. 210, quoted in STINNETT, T.M., KLEINMANN, J.H. and WARE, M.L. (1966) *op cit*, p. 116.
66   BUSHMAN, P. (1982) *op cit*, p. 58.
67   STINNETT, T.M., KLEINMANN, J.H. and WARE, M.L. (1966) *op cit*, p. 122.
68   *Ibid.*, p. 121.
69   *Ibid.*, p. 136f.
70   *Ibid.*, p. 144.
71   *Ibid.*, p. 122.

72 Former CTA Executive Director Arthur Cory in BUSHMAN, P. (1982) *op cit*, p. 68.
73 *Ibid.*
74 *Ibid.*
75 William Cunningham, former Executive Director of the Association of California School Administrators in *ibid.*, p. 97.
76 John Donaldson in *ibid.*, p. 72.
77 Two cases in particular expanded the mandatory scope of discussions: Yuba City and San Juan, 1973–74.
78 The vetoed measure was Senate Bill 400 sponsored by George Moscone.
79 BUSHMAN, P. (1982) *op cit*, p. 70.

4
Changing Perceptions Across the Generations

Field Data and the Generational Concept

Introduction

While no single research finding can prove conclusively that public school labor relations follow a generational pattern, several streams of evidence flowing in the same direction would appear to provide strong support. Excerpts from our case studies and interviews will be presented as a means of describing each generation and grounding our conclusions about the generational phenomenon in field data. In this chapter, interview and questionnaire data are analyzed to illustrate the close relationship found between labor relations generations and perceptions of administrators, teacher organizations and school board members.

Questionnaire analysis was carried out during the second phase of a two-year study of seventy-three California and Illinois school districts supported by the National Institute of Education. The key concepts of labor relations generations had emerged during the first phase of the study when we undertook detailed ethnographic studies of complete bargaining cycles in eight school districts. These districts — four in each state — ranged in enrollment from fewer than 1000 to more than 100,000 students and the period of investigation ranged from five months to more than eighteen months.

In the second phase of the study, we visited a carefully selected sample of sixty-five school districts in the two states. We talked with approximately 250 persons, each for about eighty minutes, and analyzed 1038 returned questionnaires.

The sixty-five districts chosen for the interview and survey study were selected so as to be representative of all California and Illinois school districts in both type (elementary, secondary and unified) and size (very small, small, middle sized and large). Six clusters of districts were identified in each state, so as to ensure that all geographic regions were represented and that rural, suburban and urban districts were included. Seventy-two districts were included in the sampling plan, but data from seven of these districts was incomplete and they were eliminated from consideration when statistical data analysis techniques were brought to bear on the final data.

Interview and Survey Data on District Labor Relations

Interview and survey data were collected in each district. Tape recorded interviews were conducted with the superintendent (in a few cases the assistant or associate superintendent for personnel), with the President or chief negotiator for the teacher organization, and with a school board member (most often the President). Additional interviews were undertaken in districts with particularly active or unusual labor relations. In addition, questionnaires were distributed to representatives of six key groups in each school district:

1   school site administrators;
2   district office administrators;
3   teachers;
4   elected union officers;
5   all school board members; and
6   active citizens.

Questionnaire distribution was handled by the district superintendent and the teacher organization leader.

The Interviews

Interviews with administrators, union leaders and school board members used a combination of exploratory and structured questioning techniques.[1] Each respondent was asked to characterize the current status of labor relations in the school district, to describe the events and processes that led up to the present situation, and to evaluate the impact of teacher unionization on school operations and programs. Interviews generally lasted more than 60 minutes; a few took as much as two hours.

Interviewees generally discussed issues openly and worked hard to ensure that specific events in their local district were adequately interpreted. In addition to confirming that the evolution of labor relations practices follows the overall pattern identified in earlier case study districts, the interview data details a broad array of unique and richly textured processes of change.

The Survey

In addition to information on personal background and organizational work roles, the survey questionnaire used in this study asked respondents to describe critical actions and characteristics of the teacher organizations, management groups, and school boards within their respective districts. The intent was to capture the range of feelings on issues found to be controversial in our eight case study districts. For example, respondents were asked to indicate the extent of their agreement with statements such as:

The teacher's organization is strong and well organized,
or
The teachers' organization acts responsibly.

Similar statements were crafted to measure opinion about the school administration and the school board:

The administration of this school district is successful in running the schools,
or
The school board in this district is well organized and efficient

In each area, respondents were presented with a series of statements and asked to indicate the extent of their agreement (or disagreement) with each statement. A seven point scale was used, ranging from 'strongly disagree' through 'no opinion' to 'strongly agree'. (The complete questionnaire is reproduced as appendix A.)

The questionnaire data demonstrate that large differences in belief about district administrations, teacher unions and local school boards can be traced to two factors: (i) actual labor relations experiences in each school district; and (ii) the organizational roles of individual respondents. The linkage between belief systems and the characteristics of specific labor relations experiences is particularly important because it helps confirm the generational pattern of labor relations development. The exact nature of this linkage is examined in detail in the remainder of this chapter. The relationship between organizational roles and beliefs about labor relations is of particular importance to the impact of labor relations on school governance, and these data are presented in chapter 8.

The first problem in analyzing the impact of district labor relations experience on individual beliefs is to find a reliable way of categorizing the labor relations situation in each district. Analysis of belief systems can proceed once we find a way, within the data provided by the respondents, to assess which of the hypothesized labor relations generational phases each district is currently passing through. Once the districts have been appropriately classified, it is relatively easy to examine changes in individual beliefs across the generations.

Conflict and Legitimacy: Classifying Districts by Generation

Identification of the generational phase through which a district is passing involves measuring two key variables: the level of labor relations *conflict* and the degree to which unions are seen as providing legitimate representation of teacher interests. These two variables were measured in each district surveyed and the resulting measurements were used to place each district into one of the five generational phases (i.e., First Generation, First Intergenerational Conflict, Early Second Generation, Late Second Generation, or Second Intergenerational Conflict).

Conflict level measurements were taken from the tape recorded interviews of administrators, teacher leaders and school board presidents. Each leader was asked to characterize the overall tone of labor relations in the district on a five point scale ranging from 'high conflict' through 'uneasy truce', 'some trust' and 'working relationship' to 'cooperation'. Answers were assigned numbers on an ordinal scale, and then averaged to produce an overall conflict level score for each district.

Districts were divided into 'high conflict' and 'low conflict' districts on the basis of whether the averaged conflict score was above or below the 3.9 average score for all sixty-five districts.

As described in chapter 2, conflict plays a major role in the movement of school districts from one generational period to the next. Conflict is expected:

1   to be low during the First Generation — teachers during this period believe that their interests are adequately recognized by administrators and the board without organized representation,
2   to rise sharply during the First Intergenerational Conflict period — feeling neglected or exploited, the teachers organize to press for recognition of their basic interests,
3   to remain moderately high during the Early Second Generation — though formal recognition is granted, teacher unions are still not fully accepted,
4   to fall substantially as the district moves into the mature Late Second Generation period — though acceptance may not be universal, fear and anxiety subside and the labor relations process becomes relatively routine.
5   Finally, conflict is expected, to rise again as the Second Intergenerational Conflict period begins — dissatisfaction with the established pattern rises sharply as problems are articulated and new approaches are offered.

Within this conflict pattern the two mature generational periods are sharply distinguished from the highly visible intergenerational conflicts and the Late Second Generation phase. By itself, however, a measurement of the conflict level does not allow us to distinguish the two mature generational periods from each other (both are relatively low in conflict) or to delineate the boundaries of the other three phases (they all involve high conflict).

To fully distinguish among the five different generational phases, we need to examine the extent to which teacher organizations are viewed as *legitimate*. Conflicting beliefs about the legitimacy of teacher unions and the processes of collective bargaining are vividly expressed and overtly challenged during the First Intergenerational Conflict period. If the generational process works as hypothesized, teacher organizations involved in this intergenerational conflict phase would be seen as having little legitimacy in the eyes of the school board. Districts still in the First Generation period would also be expected to report low school board acceptance of teacher organization legitimacy. Since the question remains largely abstract and untested, we might expect First Generation legitimacy levels in some districts to be somewhat above those reported during the First Intergenerational Conflict period.

Once the First Intergenerational Conflict period has passed, however, teacher organization legitimacy would rise to a moderate level. It remains only moderate, however, until the collective bargaining process has been in place for some time and the Late Second Generation phase begins. Of special concern to the generational concept scheme is the assumption that legitimacy, once established, will tend to persist — even into a Second Intergenerational Conflict where the primary issue is teacher organization influence rather than the bargaining process itself.

If the generational concept adequately captures the flow of events in the schools, the following would be true about the legitimacy scores:

1 legitimacy would be low to moderate during the First Generation;
2 it would sink to its lowest level during the First Intergenerational Conflict period;
3 it would rise somewhat during the Early Second Generation; but
4 would become quite high during the mature Late Second Generation period, and
5 would remain high during the Second Intergenerational Conflict period.

Teacher organization legitimacy was measured using a questionnaire item which asked individuals to indicate on a seven point scale agreement or disagreement with the following statement:

> *The school board in this district accepts as legitimate the rights of teachers to bargain collectively.*

Responses to this question were scored as follows: first, mean scores were calculated for each of six sub-groups within the total sample (teachers, teacher leaders, principals, superintendents, school board members, and active citizens). Each district was then assigned a legitimacy score by averaging these six subgroup mean scores. Three legitimacy levels were established — low, medium, and high.

Table 1: Classification of Sample Districts by Generational Phase

Generational Phase	Teacher Organization Legitimacy	Conflict Level	Number of Districts	Rater	
				Hits	*Misses*
First Generation	Low-Med	Low	19	11	8
First Intergenerational Conflict	Low	High	9	7	2
Early Second Generation	Med	High	20	15	5
Late Second Generation	High	Low	12	10	2
Second Intergenerational Conflict	High	High	5	4	1
		Total:	65	47	18

Goodness of fit $X^2 = 5.60$ (df = 4; $p > .20$)

Analysis of the rater 'misses':	
First generation (eight misses):	6 classified Late 2nd, 1 as Early 2nd, 1 as 1st Intergenerational Conflict.
First Intergenerational Conflict (three misses):	2 classified Early 2nd, 1 as First Generation
Early Second Generation (five misses):	3 classified as Late 2nd, 2 as 1st Intergenerational Conflict.
Late Second Generation (two misses):	1 classified as Early 2nd, 1 as First Generation.
Second Intergeneral Conflict (one miss):	Classified as Early 2nd.

The results of cross classifying the sixty-five sample districts by teacher organization legitimacy and labor relations conflict level are shown in table 1. As indicated in the last two columns of this table, two knowledgeable members of the research team were asked to review the qualitative data from each district and place them within the generational development framework. In forty-seven of the sixty-five cases there was perfect agreement between the qualitative rating and the statistical classification. A goodness of fit Chi-squared statistic was used to test the reliability of the classification agreement between raters and the computer generated numerical data. As indicated on the table, the calculated Chi-squared value is 5.60, indicating that the relationship between these two methods of classification should be viewed as reliable.

For the most part, disagreement between the researchers' subjective judgments and the statistically data-based classification of the districts represents the natural errors of borderline cases. Half of the eighteen 'misses' involved disagreement over whether districts belong in one developmental step or the next one:

— five involving decisions about the beginning or ending of the First Intergenerational Conflict period, and

— four involving movement into or out of the Late Second Generation period.

Six of the remaining nine 'misses' involve disagreement about whether districts are still in the First Generation period or have gone through both the Intergenerational Conflict and Early Second Generation phases and are now experiencing the Late Second Generation period. These six 'misses' are particularly interesting. They are districts where formal bargaining has been going on for some time (which is why the field researchers confidently placed them in the Late Second Generation). At the same time, however, most respondents in these six districts reported only moderate agreement with the proposition that the local school board recognizes as legitimate the right of teachers to organize. Thus, while these districts have well developed teacher bargaining systems, ideological change has been slower to develop.

The reasons for this mismatch between organizational reform and belief system change differed from district to district. In some cases, management had encouraged teacher unionization. This made it unnecessary for the teachers to win public support for their cause and may have undercut the normal process of ideological change. In other cases, the teachers organized and won contested union recognition elections, but beliefs were not changed because school board members, citizens and even some teachers quietly continued to question their legitimacy. This may have happened because local community cultures were generally supportive of teacher unionization or because the board and administration did not believe they should engage in overt conflict.

Exactly where these districts should be placed in our developmental scheme is open to some question. In some cases mature Second Generation labor relations systems may not require full acceptance of teacher organization legitimacy. More likely, however, these six districts are best thought of as being First Generation districts whose belief patterns will gradually change. We suspect that there will be substantial public controversy and conflict before movement into the Second Generation becomes complete. In any event, the number of questionable cases is relatively small and should not unduly disturb statistical analysis of the data.

Having developed a statistical tool for classifying district development, we were able to confirm its validity through analysis of information about the nature and extent of teacher union power and influence contained in the interview tapes. Tapes for each district were reviewed to identify specific high conflict events and to determine the extent to which teacher unions had become active in school board elections and/or superintendent contract renewal. In some cases, the tapes contained direct evidence of limited teacher union influence. This evidence was also systematically recorded.

Since the administrators, union leaders and school board members interviewed were asked to tell the story of labor relations in their own way, it was not always possible to identify the timing of overt conflict episodes. It was possible, however, to identify the highest conflict events to have occurred during the evolution of the labor relations system in each district. The incidence of these highest conflict events is shown in the top part of table 2. A review of the entries in this part of the table largely supports the classification of the districts. Only two of the nineteen First Generation districts reported any high conflict event (the one with a reported strike obviously involves an error in classification). Of the nine First Intergenerational Conflict districts, only one did not report active conflict. This is either a classification error or an oversight in the interview responses. Of the thirty-seven districts that had moved into or beyond the Early Second Generation phase, all but seven reported overt teacher conflict.

A second measure of teacher union strength and activity concerned involvement in school district governance. Three specific indicators of

Table 2:   *Labor relations activities by computer assigned phases*

	First generation	First intergenerational conflict	Early second generation	Late second generation	Second intergenerational conflict
Total number of districts:	19	9	20	12	5
Highest Conflict Events					
Strikes	1	2	6	1	0
Other job actions	0	0	3	1	0
Impasses	0	0	2	2	2
Public debates	1	0	3	3	2
Inter-union conflicts	0	2	0	2	1
Denied recognition	0	1	0	0	0
Active teacher unrest	0	3	2	0	0
Union involved conflicts	2	8	16	9	5
No conflict reported	17	1	4	3	0
Governmental Involvement by Unions					
Superintendent turnover	0	0	3	2	1
Board election action	0	9	11	7	3
Incumbent defeat	0	0	4	0	1
Union involved	0	9	5	2	1
Union not involved	19	0	15	9	4
Other Indicators of Limited Union Influence					
No contract with union	16	2	0	0	0
Reported weak union	5	1	2	0	0

union influence in governance were identified. In six cases superintendents were forced out of office as a result of labor unrest. In thirty districts teacher organizations were reported to be visibly active in recruitment of candidates and election of school board members. In five cases this involvement was reported to have led directly to the defeat of an incumbent board member. Teacher unions were directly implicated in governance decisions in seventeen of the sixty-five districts in the sample. The distribution of the seventeen cases is compatible with their generational classification. None of the nineteen First Generation unions was reported to be involved in district governance, while all nine of the First Intergenerational Conflict unions were reported to be taking an active part in the governance process. Districts assigned to later generational stages, as expected, report mixed levels of union involvement in governance.

As shown at the bottom of table 2, the interview tapes provided two other indicators of union development. Sixteen of the nineteen First Generation districts were operating without a teacher contract. In two of the First Intergenerational Conflict districts contract agreements had not yet been reached. In all other cases signed contracts were in effect. In eight of the sixty-five districts we were told that the union was weak or very weak. Six of these districts had not yet passed out of the First Intergenerational Conflict phase, the other two had just exited this phase.

The distribution of the sixty-five districts according to the reported conflict level and teacher organization legitimacy is summarized graphically in figure 3. The nineteen districts falling into the First Generation period, characterized by low to moderate legitimacy and low conflict, tended to be smaller and more rural and to have labor relations systems dominated by administrators or strong school board members who operated in a 'meet and confer' mode. Conflict was generally low because teachers either were satisfied with this arrangement or were not sufficiently organized to challenge the prevailing labor relations system.

The nine First Intergenerational Conflict districts reported high conflict involving unions not perceived to be legitimate. This conflict, without accompanying recognition of the teacher organization's legitimacy, is generally a signal that teachers are pressing for more explicit and formalized bargaining arrangements against the active resistance of school board members and their administrative representatives.

The twenty Early Second Generation showed signs of continued

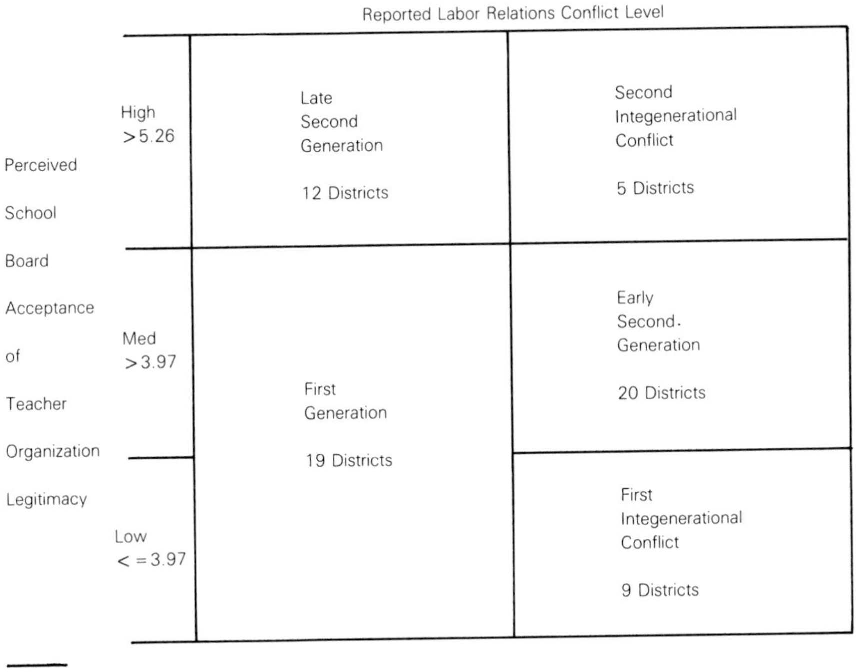

Reported Labor Relations Conflict Level

Perceived	High > 5.26	Late Second Generation 12 Districts	Second Integenerational Conflict 5 Districts
School Board Acceptance of Teacher	Med > 3.97	First Generation 19 Districts	Early Second· Generation 20 Districts
Organization Legitimacy	Low < = 3.97		First Integenerational Conflict 9 Districts

Figure 3: Generational placement of research districts

conflict, but had begun to moderate resistance to the legitimacy of formalized collective bargaining. The twelve districts classified as Late Second Generation were experiencing a much lower level of conflict with a simultaneous increase in the board's willingness to accept teacher organization legitimacy. Finally, the five districts with broad acceptance of formal bargaining arrangements and renewed conflict were seen as entering into the Second Intergenerational Conflict period.

Differentiating Among Districts in the Different Generations

Recognition of the close correspondence between the statistical classification of district generational phases and the research team's identification of labor relations incidents encouraged a more detailed analysis of how beliefs about teacher organizations, school administrators and school boards change as districts pass through the generations. After clustering respondents into groups based on the generational develop-ment of labor relations within their school district, we were able to use multiple discriminant analysis to test the extent and statistical reliability of changing beliefs. Multiple discriminant analysis is a technique for identifying the underlying factors that most effectively distinguish response patterns among sub-groups in a large sample. The technical aspects of multiple discriminant analysis are explained in more detail in appendix B.

Three separate discriminant analyses were performed. The first examined respondent views of the character and actions of the *teacher organization*. The second looked at how ten questions regarding *district management* actions change through the generational evolution. The third looked at ten items probing feelings about *school boards*. In each case the discriminant analysis identified a sub-set of the questionnaire items that powerfully and reliably distinguish among the five genera-tional groups.

How Views of the Teacher Organization Evolve

The first discriminant analysis of the questionnaire data revealed two basic changes in beliefs about the nature and role of teacher unions as labor relations evolve through the generations. In statistical terms, the changes in questionnaire response patterns were both large and reliable. In more than 42 per cent of all differences the generational classification of the sixty-five school districts was linked to respondent perceptions of the teacher organizations.

The most dramatic change in belief about the teacher organizations concerns their willingness to act responsibly and the degree to which they are successful in dealing with school management. The second shift in perception concerns the competence of teacher leaders and their inclination to act politically in pursuing union interests.

Success versus responsibility

As school districts pass through the various phases of generational evolution, perceptions regarding two key aspects of teacher organiza-tion behavior tend to move in opposite directions. Respondents who agree with the assertion that the teacher organization in their district 'acts responsibly' tend to disagree with the statement that they are 'successful in dealing with school management'. It may seem paradoxical that teacher unions are viewed as most responsible when they are being least successful in pursuing their basic interests — and ironic that increasing success in pressing their demands leads to the belief that they are not acting responsibly. This paradox is consistent with the general American discomfort with unionization, however. Americans broadly support the abstract rights of workers to organize for protection and mutual benefit, but they rarely believe that decisions forced on management by worker organizations actually improve the operations of a company or increase the quality of service to clients and customers.

As indicated in figure 4, the generational concepts developed in chapter 2 are strongly supported by sharp differences in belief separating generational subgroups among the sample districts. The nineteen First Generation districts are characterized by a slightly positive discriminant function centroid, indicating that respondents in these districts tended to see teacher organizations as responsible but not very successful. As labor conflict rose sharply in the nine First Intergenerational Conflict districts, this view changed dramatically — intergen-

Figure 4: Plot of Discriminant Function Centroids For Opinions of Teachers Unions by Labor Relations Generations

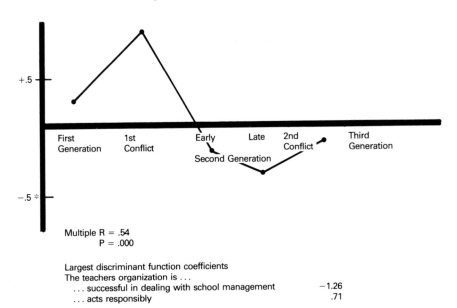

| Multiple R = .54 |
| P = .000 |

Largest discriminant function coefficients	
The teachers organization is ...	
... successful in dealing with school management	−1.26
... acts responsibly	.71

erational conflict erased the belief that teachers are successful but enhanced confidence in their willingness to act responsibly.

The fact that teacher organizations are seen as most responsible (and least successful) during the period of Intergenerational Conflict is politically very important. Without the broad-based political support that comes from public confidence in the willingness of teachers to act responsibly, union leaders would find it impossible to gain popular support for the idea of a strong independent teacher organization or to make a convincing case that collective negotiation of enforceable labor contracts is a legitimate way of resolving conflict in the schools.

As we will describe more fully in chapter 5, in each of our eight case study districts, teacher organizations were unable to move through the First Intergenerational Conflict period, or to establish the good faith bargaining relationship characteristic of Second Generation labor relations, until they had mustered enough public support to defeat incumbent school board members or force the early departure of a school superintendent. This was just as true in California, where a collective bargaining statute supported the right of teachers to organize, as in Illinois where no law requiring school boards to recognize teacher unions had yet been enacted. In short, responsible action by teacher organizations (or at least the widespread perception that their actions are reasonable) is a political prerequisite for successful movement into and through the First Intergenerational Conflict.

As indicated in figure 4, once the Intergenerational Conflict phase is concluded and districts enter the Second Generation period of good faith bargaining, there is an even more dramatic shift in belief about the teacher organizations. As data from the twenty Early Second Generation districts indicate, once they win the Intergenerational Conflict and become established as fully fledged unions, teacher organizations tend to be viewed as successful but irresponsible in their actions. As the tension and conflict associated with the Early Second Generation gives way to a climate of accommodation and compromise during the Late Second Generation period, this view becomes more exaggerated. At this point, the belief that teacher organizations are responsible partners in school policy and program development reaches its lowest point, while the belief that they are successful in pursuing their own interests in relation to management reaches its zenith.

While the number of districts identified as entering into a Second Intergenerational Conflict period is small (only five districts are so identified), the up-turn in the responsibility line shown in figure 4 suggests that a renewal of overt conflict between teachers and management groups is once again accompanied by changed perceptions of union success and willingness to act responsibly. Detailed case studies confirm what these data suggest: renewal of labor conflict after a mature Late Second Generation relationship has developed is the result of aggressive board and management actions and indicates reduced success for the teacher organization.

Competence versus influence

The second dimension on which beliefs about the teacher organization change as districts pass through the generational phases of the labor relations process concerns the issues of competence and political influence. Questionnaire respondents were asked to indicate the extent to which they believed that teacher organizations within their respective districts:

1   have competent leadership;
2   support political candidates; or
3   actively try to influence school board policies.

As indicated in figure 5 responses to these questions provided very reliable discrimination among the generational groups. The first two items (competent leadership and support for political candidates) were positively correlated, indicating a general belief that political activity is expected from competent teacher leaders. The third item (trying to influence the board) was negatively associated with perceived competence and support for candidates.

Interview data collected from district leaders helps to clarify the significance of this discrimination pattern. Evaluation of teacher organization leaders is, we discovered, as much a moral as a technical matter. In the views of most district leaders, it is a mark of fairness and competence for teachers to participate in electoral politics by recruiting and supporting candidates favorably disposed to their interests. Seeking to influence board policymaking is morally reprehensible, however, and is seen as an indication of incompetent leadership.

As the graph in figure 5 indicates, teacher organizations in the nineteen First Generation districts were given a near zero score on this discriminant function. The question of political fair play and leadership

Figure 5: Plot of Discriminant Function Centroids For Opinions of Teachers Unions by Labor Relations Generations

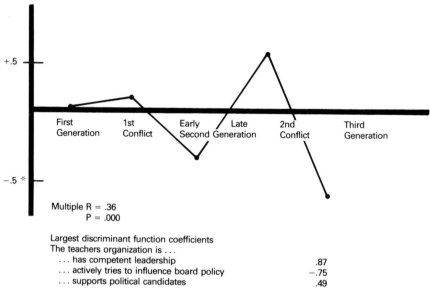

competence is of no special significance in these districts. The issue becomes increasingly important as districts move through the generational process.

During the First Intergenerational Conflict period, when teachers are seen as most responsible in their actions and unsuccessful in their dealings with school management, the issue of their political fairness remains relatively unimportant. Once organizational legitimacy is established, however, leadership judgments come to the fore. During the Early Second Generation phase respect for organizational leadership drops off, while the perception that teachers are improperly pursuing political influence rises.

In the twelve districts characterized by the low conflict and high sense of legitimacy associated with mature Late Second Generation development, respect for teacher leaders reaches its highest point. Teacher groups appear to be more circumspect in their dealings with the board and to be pursuing political influence through candidate sponsorship. During this phase, districts can usually avoid rancorous public conflict. District policymakers learn to live with, if not always to love, their teacher organizations.

As evolution in labor relations continues, however, belief that teacher organizations are competently led and politically circumspect declines sharply. Among the five districts identified as moving into the Second Intergenerational Conflict period, criticism of the political behavior of teacher unions was most noticeable. Interview data confirmed the tendency of observers in these districts to believe that teacher groups have gained 'undue influence' over school board decisions and are using that influence to take unfair advantage of administrators and the public. In these more mature districts, conflict is typically sparked by board members or lay groups demanding changes in the basic relationships between teacher unions and the district management.

How Views of the School Board Change

Beliefs about the character and role of school boards also change rather dramatically as districts move from one generational period to another. Two powerful and statistically significant discriminant functions resulted when responses to eleven questions about school boards were analyzed. Once again, more than 42 per cent of the variance in school district placement in the various generational phases was related to respondent views about school boards.

Satisfaction versus preoccupation

The most powerful discriminant function, accounting for nearly 30 per cent of the variance in district placement, might be called a school board 'satisfaction index'. Two questions provided most of the explanatory power of this function. The first asked respondents whether they agreed or disagreed with the proposition that 'The school board in this district is satisfied with the current relationship it has with teachers'. The second key question probed agreement with the statement, 'The school board in this district is preoccupied with collective bargaining issues or problems'.

As indicated by the discriminant function scores for these two questions shown in figure 6, survey respondents who believe that the board is satisfied with its working relationship with the teacher organization tend to see the board as not unduly concerned with collective bargaining problems. While the negative correlation between

Figure 6: Plot of Discriminant Function Centroids For Opinions of School Boards by Labor Relations Generations

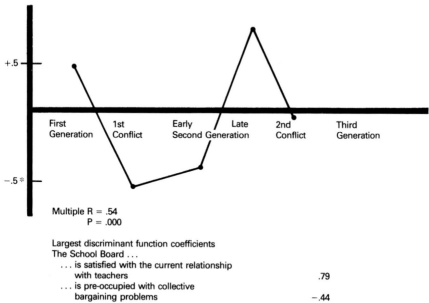

Multiple R = .54
P = .000

Largest discriminant function coefficients
The School Board . . .
  . . . is satisfied with the current relationship
    with teachers   .79
  . . . is pre-occupied with collective
    bargaining problems   −.44

responses to these two questions is far from perfect, it is, nevertheless, true that a declining belief in board satisfaction is generally associated with the perception that preoccupation with collective bargaining is on the increase.

Changes in school board satisfaction/preoccupation scores as districts move through the generational process are displayed graphically in figure 6. Just as would be predicted by the generational theory, board satisfaction is relatively high in First Generation districts. It drops dramatically as districts enter the First Intergenerational Conflict period, and rises only slightly after the conflict ends during the Early Second Generation shift to formal collective bargaining. In the twelve districts that had moved into the period of more placid and routinized Late Second Generation labor relations, however, satisfaction levels were fully restored. Indeed, these districts reported the highest levels of satisfaction.

Overall satisfaction dropped and pre-occupation with bargaining problems climbed once again as districts entered the Second Intergenerational Conflict period. Just as the theoretical framework predicts, these perceptual shifts are most emphatically *not* a matter of gradual and uni-directional movement from conflict to accommodation. There is a movement from conflict to accommodation *within* the Second Generation, of course, but it begins only after the First Intergenerational Conflict period ends and ends abruptly as districts pass out of the Late Second Generation period into the Second Intergenerational Conflict phase. Most observers would recognize that boards are relatively satisfied during the period before teacher groups initiate overt demands for recognition as a formal bargaining unit. It is not generally recognized, however, that the most fully developed districts experience a resurgence of board dissatisfaction and preoccupation with labor relations problems.

Efficient organization, openness and conflict

A second discriminant function based on the eleven questionnaire items regarding school boards is presented in figure 7. The extent of respondent agreement with four key statements account for most of the explanatory power in this discriminant function. These four items were:

The school board in this district...

1 is well organized and efficient;
2 makes all important decisions openly and with adequate input from all interested parties;
3 is preoccupied with collective bargaining issues or problems; and
4 is characterized by high conflict, loud debates, and split votes on important issues.

In this function, all four questions are positively correlated and displayed positive discriminant function coefficients. This means that, while their views differ from one generational phase to the next, respondents in all five generational periods tended to share a common level of agreement (or disagreement) with these four items.

The substantive meaning of these perceptions of school boards becomes clear once we realize that the lowest level of agreement for all items is found in the nine districts undergoing the First Intergenerational Conflict process. As shown in the plotted line in figure 7 the nineteen First Generation districts had negative scores on this discriminant function. They were, however, well above the First Intergenera-

Figure 7: Plot of Discriminant Function Centroids For Opinions of School Boards by Labor Relations Generations

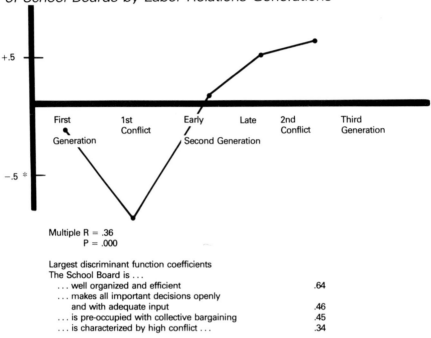

Multiple R = .36
P = .000

Largest discriminant function coefficients
The School Board is . . .
. . . well organized and efficient	.64
. . . makes all important decisions openly and with adequate input	.46
. . . is pre-occupied with collective bargaining	.45
. . . is characterized by high conflict . . .	.34

tional Conflict cluster. Moreover, agreement rises sharply once the conflict is over, and continues to rise as districts move into the Late Second Generation and Second Intergenerational Conflict periods. What respondents are reporting is that school boards faced with demands for teacher union recognition are typically seen as poorly organized and closed to input from legitimately interested groups. Moreover, districts undergoing this transitional process often fail to focus directly on the emergent labor relations problems and are given to rancorous debates and split votes.

This picture is compatible with both the generational concept we have been presenting and the more typical 'conflict to accommodation' picture found by other researchers. It suggests that school boards typically resist teacher organization by simultaneously denying the legitimacy of their demands and attempting to close the governance system to what is perceived to be the illegitimate demands of special interest groups. As the conflict over teacher recognition deepens, boards tend to deny that labor relations problems are the real issue, insisting that they should be indifferent to what they believe to be

90

inappropriate and self-serving claims by teacher organizers. The conflict is real, of course, and takes its toll by leading many in the district to view the school board as poorly organized and creating a climate of rancorous conflict within the board.

Such a perception naturally contributes to the willingness of teachers, parents and even school administrators to look upon collective bargaining as an effective vehicle for recognition of teachers' legitimate grievances and for redressing the board's inadequacies. As interview and intensive case study data confirm, unionization becomes broadly accepted once school boards have been successfully characterized as insensitive to the legitimate interests of teachers. This insensitivity is often characterized by teacher organizers as a matter of bad faith and callous disregard, but it comes to be seen by citizens and administrators more as a matter of unproductive conflict, breakdown in board organization, or a failure of the board to focus on real issues.

How Views of the School Administrators Change

Beliefs about the administration within school districts also change significantly as labor relations evolve through the generational phases. Although respondents were asked to report on a number of different aspects of district management, a single question accounted for most of the differences among respondents when they were clustered according to the generational development of their school districts.

Dealing responsibly with the teachers

As indicated in figure 8, one very powerful discriminant function separates the generational clusters. That function accounts for about 26 per cent of the differences in generational phase placement (Multiple $R = .51$, $p = .000$). The question accounting for most of this variance is the one which read:

> The school administration in my district...
> ...acts responsibly in dealing with teachers.

Since the discriminant function coefficient for this item is negative (-1.16), the high score for districts in the First Intergenerational Conflict reflects a belief that managers in districts passing through this

Figure 8: Plot of Discriminant Function Centroids For Opinions of Administrators by Labor Relations Generations

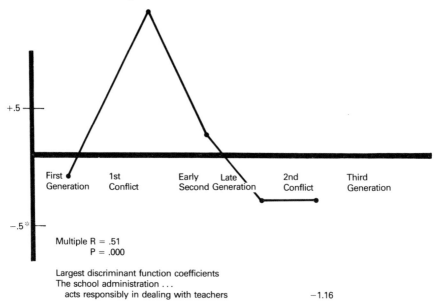

Multiple R = .51
P = .000

Largest discriminant function coefficients
The school administration . . .
acts responsibly in dealing with teachers   −1.16

phase were definitely *not* being responsible in their dealings with teachers. Before the onset of this conflict period, managers are seen as much more responsible. And again, after the peak conflict period is over, belief that administrators act irresponsibly fades away. By the time the mature Late Second Generation phase develops, confidence in administrators returns to the generally positive level reported before union organizing efforts began. Even when the Second Intergenerational Conflict period begins, administrators continue to be viewed in a generally positive way.

Once again, there is an important political message in this plot line. Teachers cannot get the support needed to organize and demand union recognition until they are able to convincingly claim that school administrators are irresponsible and insensitive. The statistics of the questionnaire responses are amply supported by poignant stories from teacher organizers who told us repeatedly that violations of ordinary decency and common sense by school board leaders and school administrators were responsible for their willingness to take on the emotional and physical burdens of organizing teacher unions. We found many of these stories believable. More to the point, so did rank and file teachers and ordinary citizens whose support was crucial to the organization of teacher unions.

Summary: Conflict and Legitimacy Across the Generations

The data reviewed in this chapter provide strong support for the generational development framework for interpreting the evolution of teacher unionism in the public schools. Beliefs about teacher organizations, school boards and school administration behavior change dramatically and systematically as the generational phases unfold. At the critical moment of transition between the First Generation, meet-and-confer, period and the good faith bargaining procedures used in Second Generation districts, teacher organizations are perceived to be acting responsibly in their dealing with districts, but they are also seen as being relatively unsuccessful in representing the basic interests of their members. School boards, by contrast, are believed to be dissatisfied in their dealings with teachers. They are also seen as relatively inefficient and closed governance systems that do not give adequate attention to important labor relations issues. Rounding out the picture of movement through the First Intergenerational Conflict, is the perception that district administrators are not being responsible in their dealings with teachers. In short, this period of high conflict and rapid change is characterized by broad support for emergent teacher organizations and a commensurate lack of confidence in school boards and administrators. Given this overall pattern of belief, it is little wonder that teacher organizations are able to muster the emotional commitment and political support needed to force districts to recognize them as exclusive representatives for teachers.

In the small group of districts undergoing the Second Intergenerational Conflict phase, political conflict is just as intense, but its character is quite different. Teacher organizations are seen as rather more successful and less responsible, confidence in teacher organization leadership drops, and the organization is seen as trying to directly influence school board policy decisions. At the same time, school board members (who were being castigated for inefficiency and remoteness in the earlier conflict phase) regain the confidence of most observers and are perceived to be taking a leadership role in reshaping the labor relations process. Administrators, criticized for acting irresponsibly during the first conflict episode are now seen as being basically responsible in their dealings with teachers. In short, the second intergenerational transition period is driven by school board and management legitimacy, and is aimed at 'reforming the reform' produced by the first transitional conflict period.

It would be helpful to know whether the changed views expressed in the questionnaire responses are only perceptual and ideological changes or whether they are linked to substantial changes in the *behavior* of key actors within local school districts. Taken alone, the questionnaire data cannot resolve this important question. Changes in belief can just as easily be responses to changes in interest and desire as to new circumstances within the districts. Several researchers have begun to explore other types of data, however. Dorothy Jessup explored changed behavior patterns in four local school districts and concluded that ideological changes are closely linked to significant behavioral shifts.[2] In another case study, Pamela Mayhall documented important behavioral changes in a district passing through the various generational phases.[3] Confirming data from our eight case study districts can be found in Wayne Erck's doctoral dissertation.[4]

John Cooper engaged in secondary content analysis of our interview tapes establishing an independent measure of labor conflicts[5] and high instability levels associated with the use of negotiators who were not school district employees. His findings are consistent with our own more general conclusion that outsiders tend to be associated with increases in labor conflict. David Morton used our data to create a labor strife index and relate strife to variables in the organization's environment.[6]

The next three chapters will elaborate on the ways in which the belief system changes mapped by the questionnaire data are linked to school district organization, governance and work behavior changes. The evidence will show that both teacher organizers and their critics muster the political support needed to change the *status quo* only if they are able to point to real events and stimulate significant behavioral changes within the school system. The strong ideological beliefs documented in the questionnaire findings are like the seed crystals dropped into a super-cooled liquid. They capitalize on existing conditions to stimulate dramatic changes in behavior — reorganizing the entire social field within the school system. Unless the field is ready for change, however, these ideological crystals will merely dissolve into the fluid social system and disappear — branded crazy or irresponsible by leaders throughout the system. Data from the history of labor relations in the private sector, together with the detailed study of the evolution of teacher unionization in eight case study districts clearly point to the gradual accumulation of dissatisfaction which leads to rapid, sometimes convulsive, changes in basic labor relations in school districts, particular private sector firms, or throughout whole industries.

Notes

1 KERCHNER, C.T. and MITCHELL, D.E. (1981) *The Dynamics of Public School Collective Bargaining and its Impacts on Governance, Administration and Teaching*, Report G-79-0036 to the National Institute of Education. Washington, D.C., NIE. (ERIC Document Reproduction Service No. ED 211 925).
2 JESSUP, D. (1985) *Teachers, Unions and Change*. New York, Praeger.
3 MAYHALL, P. (1987) 'Development of labor relations in a large Southwestern school district based on a generational framework', unpublished doctoral dissertation, University of Arizona.
4 ERCK, W.M. (1983) 'An analysis of the relationship between teacher collective bargaining activities and altered managerial behavior in selected Illinois school districts', unpublished doctoral dissertation, University of Illinois.
5 COOPER, J.L. III, (1985) 'Organizational predictions of hostility in labor-management relations in public education', unpublished doctoral dissertation, Claremont Graduate School, Claremont, CA.
6 MORTON, D.C. (1982) 'Contextual predictions of labor strife in selected California school districts', unpublished doctoral dissertation, Claremont Graduate School, Claremont, CA.

5
From Meet-and-Confer to 'Meet you at the Barricades'

The meet-and-confer era of First Generation labor relations continues to live on in some school districts. Almost 30 per cent of our survey sites were classified as First Generation districts. While these districts tended to be small and rural — eight of them had fewer than 400 students — this was not universally the case. One of the districts had more than 13,000 students and was in a growing suburban area.

The First Generation districts we studied shared a common sense that the authority of the administration and the school board to represent *teacher* interests was healthy and legitimate, and it was, therefore, largely unchallenged. One small rural district in Illinois reported no organization at all among the teachers, no elected offices, no salary committees. One teacher in this district, who had spent most of his career in a neighboring district, enthusiastically reported a 'feeling of mutual respect, and less interference with my daily classroom activities' in his new job. 'A lot of day-to-day decisions are made by teachers themselves', he reported, such as 'decisions on how to divide up playground duties'. Teachers reported a willingness to work for lower salaries because they were freed from the hassles and constraints they felt were present in larger districts (and also from the discipline and drug problems that they perceived as drawbacks elsewhere). To be sure, their salaries were low. Several years ago, when the state passed legislation setting the minimum teacher salary at $10,500, the staff in this district got a hefty raise. The superintendent characterized the district as very conservative fiscally and indicated that salaries were a matter of 'doing the best we can without putting an extra tax burden on the community'.

Another superintendent characterized his school as being run by 'coffee-cup administration'—informal flows of communication between teachers, administrators and community leaders. These flows included a conduit to the board in the person of one teacher who 'just attends' even though 'he's not elected or anything'. The superintendent described the teacher's role: 'On occasion he is asked for an opinion...but he doesn't inject unless he's asked'.

These places also share a belief that unions are improper, partly because they challenge legitimate authority. As the superintendent put it: 'Teachers are trying to gain control over their destiny, but under the (Illinois) Revised Statutes Chapter 122 the authority for operating and running the school belongs to the board of education'.

It is the 'damage' to the public service image of teachers, however, that drew the most passionate comment. There is an expectation of self-sacrifice attached to teaching, and first generation administrator's concept of professionalism is tied much more to self-sacrifice, than it is to self-determination. 'If you don't do anything more than you get paid for you become a laborer and leave the ranks of the professions', noted one superintendent. A teacher in the district suggested that 'unions were started for the right reasons in the nineteenth century, but they've gotten out of hand. Teachers are professionals; they don't belong in unions'.

Solving problems on an individual level serves as a substitute for, and a preventative of, group action. The same teacher reported that, 'Mr. [Superintendent's] door is always open. Whenever there is a problem, the question isn't whether we have a contract but whether we get to talk to Mr. [Superintendent]'.

The irony of this situation is its instability. Bonds of trust, communication and grants of mutual confidence by the faculty and administration appear to be mutually reinforcing and protective. One might expect them to be highly stable. Instead, we found that the relationships were highly fragile, particularistic, and easily damaged. Because conflict was not expected and was improper, no institutional mechanisms existed to manage staff conflicts when they did develop.

Those who strayed beyond the norms of the organization quickly became branded as radicals or outsiders by the administration. One superintendent described a teacher, the wife of a 'miner who works in a union', as a person who, attends every [union] meeting there is, plasters the bulletin board full of notices, has the [union] rep down here weekly. Anytime she can make an issue out of something, she does. She has about alienated the other teachers though. But if somebody has a problem with something, like we cut our art teachers' time back, then that teacher runs to her right away.

This trouble-making 'outsider' had taught in the district for nineteen years.

The seeds of change seemed present. Even a member of the school board, a board which is on record with a threat to fire teachers if they ever strike, perceived the emergence of a legitimate teacher interest in unionization saying, 'If I were a teacher, I'd probably fight for one'.

While most school districts depart from the First Generation before they know they've gone, we found one which had pointedly elected to retain its First Generation beliefs. The administration of this district, let's call it Millerstown, looked at collective bargaining, but decided it liked its meet-and-confer relationship with the teachers better. It ran a successful no-agent campaign and defeated the teachers' bid for unionization. The equipment of meet-and-confer is in place: a faculty senate, open representation before the school board, and a highly organized administrative structure.

Prototypical of the First Generation, Millerstown exhibits an apparently genuine belief in the legitimate authority of the school administration, and support for administrative efforts to secure employee cooperation. The uncooperative, however, are not welcome here, and teachers speak of coercion and of driving teachers out. Most teachers, though, told us they trusted the administration.

The district bristles with purpose. 'We're in a war on illiteracy, and we're literally going to stamp it out', the Superintendent insists. He came to town a decade ago with the announced plan of raising reading scores, which were below the state average, to the 90th percentile. They are close.

The Superintendent, a man of substantial will and strong beliefs stated, 'We believe in competition. We believe in high standards. We believe in dress codes — we still have dress codes. We don't believe in collective bargaining. We believe in local control. We believe in the educational team being able to respond to the needs of the community and of the individual parents quickly...so we have two high schools and their feeder systems broken up into an Assistant Superintendent of the red attack unit and the Assistant Superintendent of the blue attack unit'.

Military metaphor is part of the local dialect in the Millerstown schools. The Assistant Superintendent is the attack leader; the associate in charge of personnel, the fighter cover; the Director in charge of psychologists and special education, the hospital medical corps. The Superintendent himself is known as 'the general', although we didn't hear anyone call him that to his face.

Within this no-nonsense and somewhat authoritarian structure, teachers maintain a measure of self-determination through an active faculty senate, the President of which noted: 'The administrators are very willing to work with us; listen to our complaints'. There is a budget committee within the Senate, and the board has been inclined in recent years to follow its recommendations about how to divide the budget. An administrator noted, 'If they want to spend it on class size instead of personnel salaries, then we don't fight it'. There also appears to be a good bit of autonomy within school buildings in the curriculum as well as dividing of supply and equipment money. There is no mandated curriculum, but scores in reading and math are closely monitored. Noted the Assistant Superintendent:

> You don't superimpose programs on a teacher because then he has a perfect cop-out. He can say, 'Hey, that was *your* program, that's not my program'. But by letting the teacher develop his own program, he's now going to fight to the death to defend that program...

Also characteristic of a First Generation district, there is an air of informality in decision making. The President of the Faculty Senate, for instance, could not recall ever seeing a copy of its by-laws, and administrative decision making is characterized as 'very flexible'. The Faculty Senate President does, however, understand leverage: 'They are very good at cooperating...the threat being that if we are unhappy we might eventually want to go union'.

At the end of our study bonds of trust and common mission still held the district together, although it was already apparent that this social glue would not last indefinitely. In the face of a board chairman who was 'hanging tough' on teacher dismissals, teachers started to consider how to protect themselves. The President of the Faculty Senate reported that teachers were asking for help, but that he could only reply that the senate had no power. Some of the dissidents were considering talking to a lawyer; others were talking union.

From the First Generation to Intergenerational Conflict: The Homestead Story

The First Generation of labor relations dissolves when teachers begin to articulate a new idea: that the interests of teachers and school managers are often different and that teachers *should be* represented by an autonomous organization and binding contracts rather than informal agreements with school administrators. Typically, intergenerational conflict periods are strife-ridden, dynamic and highly visible. They are characterized by vigorous articulation of controversial new ideas and by growing awareness of self-interest on the part of both workers and managers. Open conflict often leads to the replacement of leaders who believe in the 'old idea' with those who believe in the new one. To the participants (and even to the observer) these are tumultuous, exciting and sometimes frightening times when actions are given moralistic, almost religious, interpretations and when the simplest act is easily turned into a test of one's loyalty to the new or old order.

The critical elements of an intergenerational conflict are best seen in the concrete events of a particular school district. California's Homestead Unified School District illustrates the process well. A number of circumstances combined to exaggerate the intergenerational conflict process in Homestead, with the result that good-faith bargaining had a difficult birth and a traumatic infancy. Nearly all of the teachers, administrators and school board members who lived through this period could remember the details vividly and were quick to tell us their story.

Background

Homestead is a northern California school system with approximately

38,000 students. Our story starts with the era of steady growth in school enrollments and budgets that followed World War II. Made up of a cluster of suburban communities seeking to realize the postwar dream of tranquility and prosperity, Homestead boasted a stable organization whose major problems revolved around the need to accommodate and educate the rapid influx of baby-boom children. Board members tended to have been involved in various school-related citizen support groups or in the civic affairs of one of the surrounding communities. By tradition, one board member was an employee of the district's largest industrial landowner and thus the guardian of the local property tax rate. At election time, school policy issues were muted or non-existent, and candidates were distinguished in terms of their backgrounds and experience, not their ideologies or policy positions.

During this period, labor relations were peaceful. Nonetheless, by the early 1970s, the teachers were feeling some need to insure that their interests were represented within the school policy system as became evident when the Homestead Teachers Association (HEA) hired a full-time executive director. With passage of California's Public Employment Relations Act (the Rodda Act) in 1975, it was an easy and natural step for the teachers to select their Director to represent them in their dealings with the district.

District management was also remarkably stable in Homestead: the district had only three superintendents between 1950 and 1980. The third of these superintendents, John Burroughs, served for four years (1976–80). He was a central character in the intergenerational struggle that followed passage of the Rodda Act. Like most other suburban school districts during this period, Homestead was not tax rich but showed few outward signs of financial stress until enrollment began to decline sharply during the mid-1970s. Although local support for budget increases was not strong (the last bond issue, proposed in 1970, was defeated by a 9 : 1 ratio), enrollment growth kept pushing budgets up, assuring that managers would have flexibility and discretion in dealing with the manifold needs of a growing organization.

The Intergenerational Struggle

The extended period of First Generation labor peace began to unravel in 1975 when declining enrollments precipitated a budgetary crisis. The district enrollment had decreased by about 25 per cent over a five-year period. The only way to cope with this decrease, without firing teachers, was to allow both class size and real teacher salaries to drop substantially. By 1975 teacher salaries in Homestead were among the lowest in the twenty-seven districts in the immediate area. Purportedly because he could not deal with the ensuing budgetary problems, the man who had been superintendent for a decade abruptly retired in the middle of the 1975–76 school year. John Burroughs — widely recognized as an advocate of an open, participative management style — was warmly welcomed by both teachers and community. As the school's financial situation deteriorated, however, his position became more equivocal. 'The board had been less than candid with me', he reported. 'Within months of my arrival, I found we were a million and a half "in the sock"'. Burroughs saw no alternative but to propose school closures as a way to balance the 1976–77 budget.

At an earlier time, or in another school district, Burroughs might have been able to undertake this fiscal and organizational surgery without serious resistance. But in Homestead his actions set off a heated debate and organizational activity. A dynamic young teacher, Dan Riley, emerged from the ranks of discontented high school teachers to challenge the HEA leadership (whose attitude toward Burroughs was generally cooperative) and to demand both a greater union role for the HEA and higher salaries for teachers. Riley galvanized teachers' resentment over being the victims of budgetary problems they had not been told about and did not participate in creating. He appealed to the teachers' feeling that they were being robbed of their dignity and self-worth in a system that gave them no power.

Riley captured the presidency of the HEA in May of 1977. The Executive Director promptly resigned, and the district prepared for what nearly everyone expected would be a teacher strike. Riley's forcefulness and ability to rally support can only be described as charismatic. 'I don't know what there was about him', commented a later union leader, 'but when he spoke the room was electric with excitement'. Certainly the district administration had never had to deal with anyone quite like him. And they found him all the more shocking because he was 'one of ours; not a goon from the union'. To the outside observer, it is not Riley's charisma but his function in catalyzing the first intergenerational conflict that is important. He was drawn from the ranks of mid-career high school teachers, and he was male. These characteristics enabled him to identify with, and symbolically represent, those who felt they had suffered most from the indecision of Burroughs' predecessor. Moreover, Riley's election as Union President was hotly contested, and his victory was seen as an obvious mandate for militant unionism.

Burroughs and the school board responded to Riley's election by hiring Stan Adams to represent them in negotiations with the HEA. Adams was an experienced labor attorney with a reputation for resistance to union contract demands. They also withdrew a tentative salary offer in excess of 10 per cent and instead opened formal negotiations with the proposal that the teachers get no raise at all.

The Strike

Athletic coaches fought the first round in August when they refused to ready teams for play in the fall. Then on 11 September 1977, 70 per cent of the Homestead teachers walked out of class. On 16 September a temporary restraining order was issued. The union ignored it. The strike continued until 24 September when a fact-finding panel was appointed. the panel, comprised a state senator representing the board, a state assemblyman representing the teachers, and a chairman. The visibility and prestige of the panel reflected the fact that the conflict had become a broad public issue.

Events culminated in a tumultuous public meeting on 13 October when the fact-finding panel presented its report to the school board. One member of the panel claimed that he had found $600,000 which could be used to fund teacher salary increases. Board members counterclaimed that this money was restricted and could not be used for salaries. Two ministers, who had attempted to mediate the dispute, put forward what they proposed as a 'memorandum of understanding' between the parties, but they were summarily told by a board member to 'sit down and shut up'.

At this meeting the board made it clear that they would not agree to a 10 per cent salary increase for teachers (even though their initial willingness to make an even larger offer had been widely publicized). Indeed, the final settlement included only an 8 per cent salary increase.

Needless to say, the teachers were angry. And they were not alone. A substantial group of outraged citizens launched a recall effort against the board in hopes of breaking the stalemate. Thus, before any contract was settled, the struggle between the board and the teachers had moved into the electoral arena.

Nearly a year passed before enough signatures were collected to force the recall issue onto the ballot. At the general election on 7 November 1978, the recall election was held, and three of the five school board members were forced out of office. Because two of their replacements were strongly backed by the HEA, most observers expected rapid settlement of a contract favorable to the teachers and an early return to a stable, low-conflict school board.

The anticipated quick change in labor relations did not materialize. To the union's dismay, the new board members adopted the view that fiscal responsibility, not labor peace, was mandated in their election. While they accepted as legitimate the HEA's claim to represent teacher interests, they established this as the *starting point* for serious bargaining, not as a requirement that they accept teacher demands uncritically.

In the aftermath of the election, the HEA broke into pro- and anti-Riley factions. The anti-Riley faction succeeded in electing the new HEA President, who was immediately faced with the problem of a bitter and apathetic constituency. Swamped with grievances, Fran Erickson, the new Executive Director, came to believe that the district administration was being disingenuous and did not really want to solve labor problems.

Feelings about the two new board members were also bitter. In the view of most rank-and-file teachers, one of the candidates they had supported was totally coopted by the Superintendent, while the second — though independent of both teacher and administrative influence — was ineffective, frequently finding himself on the short end of a 4–1 vote. Union members didn't quite know how to interpret what had happened. The sense of betrayal ran deep. One union leader remarked bitterly that, 'You could elect Jesus Christ himself to this board and he would go sour on you'.

Even though he embraced participatory management concepts, Superintendent Burroughs was never able to establish a level of trust with the teachers. In 1977 he devoted most of his energy to developing an innovative school site management system aimed at creating school site councils (made up of parents, teachers and principals) responsible for the assessment, implementation, and evaluation of all programs. He seemed not to notice that the board's stubborn resistance to all contractual demands — especially as the resistance was symbolized in the hard-nosed lawyer Stan Adams — completely undercut his proclaimed intention to have teachers share in the decisionmaking process. So completely was the teachers' animosity to the old school board transferred to Burroughs that by 1979 it became axiomatic that anything the superintendent wanted, the HEA opposed. As one teacher put it, 'Anything to do with his [Burroughs'] greater glory was anathema to teachers'. At the district high schools, the curriculum councils (elected committees of teachers who formally advised principals on most matters) voted not to participate in Burroughs' management plan.

Burroughs' relationship with the board was also shaky. The board that hired him had been recalled, and his relationship to the new board remained somewhat distant. In 1979 he told us, 'Look, I have no illusions about my ability to survive here'. In part, the weakness of his position can be attributed to his endorsement of the proposal that labor relations matters be turned over to Adams at a time when labor issues were the most important ones facing the district. Burroughs' innovative management plan, however effective it might have been in other circumstances, simply did not address the district's most crucial problems.

In addition, labor conflict and the recall election stirred up community dissatisfaction over educational matters. Expressing dismay over the 'minimal learning and lack of discipline' in the schools, a group of parents asked to have a 'fundamental' school established in the district. They were ultimately successful, but they suffered through two years of frustration as (according to their reports) administrators delayed, blocked, or altered their plans.

Ending the Conflict: The 1979 Negotiations

It was against this background of political upheaval and organizational discord that the 1979 contract negotiations began. Both sides said they wanted labor peace, but neither side could offer an olive branch with much fruit on it. The union was still under threat of decertification, and its leadership was afraid that any sign of conciliation would bring a 'soft on management' charge from the challenging pro-Riley faction. Management was saddled with two figures who had become devils in the

105

eyes of the union: the Superintendent and the Attorney-negotiator. So personalized was the animosity, that no action taken by the board would have been seen as a genuine move toward reconciliation. For her part, Erickson (the HEA Executive Director) was never fully trusted by management, who doubted her ability to control the union and thus to deliver on any agreement that might be reached. This distrust was intensified by a feeling that she could not be trusted with confidential communications.

The Superintendent maintained very little contact with the union during the 1978–79 year. As negotiations continued, he withdrew even further; indeed, he was out of the country during some of the most tense bargaining moments. Although Burroughs and the board were genuine in their desire for labor peace, the image cultivated by Stan Adams was definitely not that of a conciliator. His reputation as a tough and unreasonable bargainer had been confirmed in both bargaining and grievance resolution sessions. Adams believed that having precise and sharply-limited language in labor contracts — or no language at all — was the district's best defense against grievances. Many teacher proposals were routinely dismissed as improper for incorporation into a labor contract because they were 'out of scope', 'too vague', or 'unreasonable'. Hence, negotiation sessions took on a powerful symbolic meaning for both parties. The teachers saw them as an expression of the district's commitment to ignoring teacher interests and rights. Management, more by default than by conscious choice, saw them as a way to divide the teacher organization and to reaffirm its conviction that Burroughs' participatory management plan (not collective bargaining) was the best way of bringing teachers into the decision-making process.

As bargaining continued, *persons* rather than issues became the focus of conflict. More and more, Adams became an emblematic figure to the teachers. His presence at the table was read by teachers as confirmation that they were not being taken seriously. And Burroughs' refusal to deal with this problem came to be interpreted as a sign that the district was not being well managed. Similarly, Erickson became an emblematic figure to management, a sign that the union was irresponsible and dangerously out of control. It is not accidental that, within nine months of the 1979 contract settlement, all three of these symbolic figures left the district.

As negotiations drew to a close in the late fall, Adams' position became a public issue. Labor relations were an important issue in the board election held in November. Dan Stevens, one candidate in a field of nine, campaigned on a platform of ending labor strife in the district. He made a specific pledge that if elected he would see that Adams was fired. Stevens was elected, Adams resigned within a week, and the contract was settled shortly thereafter.

The financial problems that had plagued the district during all of Burroughs' tenure were brought to a head by the inclusion of a large salary settlement in the 1979 contract. The district had, for several years, blunted the effects of declining enrollment by allowing class size to decline and keeping sparsely enrolled programs in operation. This required letting teachers' real income slip as well. It was obvious the 1979 wage settlement would require a major reorganization of the school system. Burroughs opted for one major dislocation rather than trying to struggle through another five years of chronic financial weakness: he ordered ten of the district's schools be closed in a single year. That Burroughs was already packing his bags may explain his willingness to make this courageous proposal. The board had periodically made his tenure a public issue, and by the spring of 1980 he had taken another job.

The school closing plan moved forward. It was a substantial jolt to the district organization, creating massive problems of layoff and transfer of staff. From a labor relations perspective, it was important for another reason. For the first time in the history of the district, problems were seen as a matter of joint concern for both management and the teacher union. Following the contract settlement, Fran Erickson (or the union's Elected President) appeared alongside the Assistant Superintendent for Personnel at each of the schools proposed for closure to explain the contractual and legal procedures to be used in dismissing or transferring staff and to outline teachers' rights of appeal. There were still battles to be fought — hearings before the Public Employment Relations Board and other confrontations — but the union's position not only as an important advocate for teacher interests but also as an accepted partner in management decision-making was now clear.

The HEA position was also strengthened by the inclusion of an agency shop provision in the 1979 contract. The district insisted on separating the teacher vote on agency shop from the ratification of the rest of the contract, but both carried. With approval of agency shop came both financial and organizational security for the union. The clause also helped to reinterpret the mission of the teacher organization as the representative of all teachers in the district. One die-hard supporter of ousted union President, Dan Riley, symbolically confirmed the importance of this change when he showed up at union headquarters with his agency shop fee — in pennies. As the staff went about the onerous task of counting and rolling the coins for bank deposit they were heard to reflect aloud on the questionable parentage of the reluctant member. Fran Erickson captured the core meaning of the event when she cautioned the staff to remember that, 'he paid...he's *ours*'.

Her symbolic role played out, and exhausted from the struggle, Fran Erickson left the district at the end of that academic year.

Key Elements in the Intergenerational Conflict: A Post Mortem

Events in Homestead illustrate all of the key events that separate meet–and–confer First Generation labor relations from the Second Generation of good–faith bargaining. The processes of *Discontent*, *Crisis*, and *Institutionalization* are all present in the Homestead case, and, as we shall illustrate, in other districts.

Discontent: Finding Flaws in the Old System

Dan Riley brought Homestead into the Second Generation by organizing around latent, diffuse discontent and by providing a *vision* of a better work life, which teachers could achieve through their collective bargaining contract. In order to be successful, Riley had to convince the teachers that the old system would no longer work and that overt expression of self-interest was consistent with teachers' social status and work roles. This argument of necessity and consistency with self-concept is common to all organizing. Ten years before the Homestead Education Association strike, Lieberman and Moskow said much the same thing as they painted the ideological argument for collective bargaining on the basis that teachers had broad range interests that could solve real school problems:

The physician has an interest in professional autonomy, in his medical supplies and equipment, in the quality of nursing and other supporting activities, and in his overall conditions of professional practice. It is erroneous to think that non-professionals are uninterested in such matters, but there is widespread acceptance of the professional's legitimate involvement in them.[1]

This picture of collective bargaining could be seen as wholly consistent with what the public wants from the public schools. Some authors even argued that the institutionalized conflict generated by annual contract negotiations serves to socialize teachers — adding to their esprit de corps.[2] Whereas early First Generation theorists believed that the unitary organization of schools under the executive leadership of a superintendent would ultimately result in the 'professionalization' of teachers, these new leaders argued that the administrative dominance inherent in bureaucracies was the enemy of professionalism:

Centralized authority and system-wide uniformity are difficult to reconcile with decentralized decision-making, which is the central component of professionalism. If classroom teachers are to professionalize, therefore, they must gain more control, perhaps the primary control over key matters.[3]

In addition, Riley immediately picked up another theme sounded in the earlier literature: the importance of a sharp separation between teachers and administrator. Lieberman and Moskow, for example, pictured administrators not as independent, neutrally competent professionals, but as persons subject to powerful pressures from multiple interests, intent on pursuing their own career goals and self-interests. Citing recent research on role theory, they noted that

many superintendents frankly stated that their job was to persuade teachers to accept the board's position, and that they could not hold their jobs unless they did so.[4]

Collective bargaining was a tool, they said. Whether it would be used to make education more effective was still an open question. But the undergirding assumption was that collective bargaining could be made to work in the public schools:

Thus, the approach here is not so much to praise a tool which

109

has conclusively demonstrated its value in public education, as it is to show what must be done in order to use this tool effectively.[5]

But Dan Riley knew that before good faith bargaining could produce results, it had to be legitimated as strong and independent. He sided with those who argued that demonstrations, strikes, and other concerted activities were appropriate means for teachers to use in maintaining control over their own work. He shared the view that — far from disqualifying the teacher from wearing the professional label—such activities expressed a professional commitment to high-quality schooling.

Attaching anger to symbols

Through using the language of self-determination and attaching it to the symbols of professionalism, Riley was able to articulate the frustration and anger of a large group of teachers who felt 'neglected' and abandoned by the system. In Homestead, these tended to be male high school teachers with eight–twelve years experience. They thought of themselves as the traditional breadwinners for their families, and over a number of years had seen their real family incomes decline. Objectively, they were not the most vulnerable teachers in the district — younger teachers lost their jobs as enrollment declined — but the Riley faction was able to convert its discontent into anger and action.

Such conversion to action is virtually universal in the conflict change process. Teachers are recruited to the cause through the telling and retelling of 'horror stories' of abuse, neglect, or insensitivity suffered at the hands of school boards or administrators. Teacher leaders have typically lived through one or more of these horror stories and can tell the story as firsthand participants. Every teacher we talked to, in both California and Illinois, had a story to tell about the particular moment when he or she was converted from being 'just a classroom teacher' to accepting responsibility for leadership in the teacher organization. The nature of these 'moments' varies, but they all seem to produce an effect similar to a religious conversion. Willard McGuire, former president of the National Education Association tells his story:

It was in the spring, I hadn't been teaching for very long, and the school board made its decisions about salaries for the next year. Two friends of mine who were in their third year of teaching were not given tenure, and there wasn't any pretense that they were not needed next year. It was just that the school board didn't want any more tenured teachers. One of the teachers who was a friend of a board member got the largest raise. The rest of us got a middle amount, and the old-age teacher who was about 55 at the time got a tiny raise because the school board knew he was too old to move on to a new job.

Though the specifics are different, the mood is the same in Raoul Teilhet's story. Teilhet, former President of the California Federation of Teachers, recalls:

> This whole thing started over textbooks. Max Rafferty was the state school superintendent, and we had this awful high school social studies text — unbelievably naive. Our activity started when a bunch of us gathered together to try to use another one.

Radical leadership

By organizing teachers in opposition to both the existing union leadership and the current school administration, Dan Riley was immediately branded a 'radical', a description so universally attached to him that it became akin to a title: Radical Dan Riley. The same is true of all teachers-turned-organizers, and they *are* radical in the classic sense of insisting that the problems they experience are symptomatic of *fundamental* problems confronting the school system. But they are not necessarily radical in the popular sense of being brash, irresponsible, or unwilling to cooperate with others. Nor do they all embrace the same set of political beliefs or actions. Some advocate striking, others recoil from the very idea. Some, like Riley, are charismatic political organizers; some are conceptualizers and writers; others, like Riley's successor in the HEA, are pragmatic organizers with a keen sense of when to compromise and when to hold out for more. The classical radicalism of these teacher leaders — their belief that unionization is the answer to deep-seated problems in the educational system — is the driving force behind the conflict that separates the meet-and-confer generation from the era of good-faith bargaining.

Crisis: Bringing Conflict into the Open

Ideas, even radical ones, typically remain abstract until some critical event provides the occasion to put them into practice. The event provides a specific decision to organize around and affords the radical leader the opportunity to expand the conflict by searching for converts among previously non-involved persons.

Critical turning events

In Homestead, the enrollment-driven fiscal crisis served as the critical turning event to galvanize teachers into action. But the event does not have to be of the same type of magnitude as that found in Homestead. In our observations of California and Illinois school districts, we found three different types of precipitating events that marked the transition from personal dissatisfaction with the First Generation to overt agitation: issues, personnel changes, and changes in labor law. Policy or administrative behavior issues frequently trigger crises. In one school district, a poorly handled requirement for teachers to produce written lesson plans became the *cause célèbre* of the union organizers; in another, it was the creation of English classes with forty-two students. In many districts, the critical issue is fiscal: salaries that have slipped to 25 per cent below the state average, the lack of any raise, or the offering of a 2 per cent raise in a year of substantial inflation. Fiscal issues are frequently shrouded in distrust and skepticism. As one board member remarked about his superintendent:

> The Superintendent got them into...trouble by making the budget so difficult that nobody could understand where we were at, or what was going on in the district financially. The teachers were screaming that there was money, and he would insist that there was no money. [California:District 23:Board member][6]

Other frequently cited issues included teacher transfer or layoff policies, adoption of new programs without teacher consultation, or new teacher duty assignments.

Often less visible, but generally more corrosive to the smooth functioning of a school district, are issues that involve the actions of particular school officials. School executives, particularly superintendents, are the most frequent targets of union organizers. For instance, an Illinois board member reported that the new Superintendent was brought in

> to ramrod through a desegregation program. He made it clear that *he* was in charge and running the shop. If I'd been a teacher and heard his introductory remarks to teachers as they were reported to me, I would have left the room and tried to organize the teachers. [I:3:B]

The target is not always the Superintendent. In one district, we were told about a Principal who made the teachers feel that

> they are always suspect, always wondering whether they'd get rehired or not, or whether he's going to step into their classrooms at any moment and jump on them about something or other.

Personnel changes serve as triggering events in many school districts. We are not referring here to the personnel changes that accompany or are created by the first Intergenerational Conflict process. Dan Riley's rise to power in the HEA and his subsequent replacement, as well as the arrival and departure of Stan Adams as the district's chief management negotiator, were critical elements in the unfolding intergenerational conflict process in Homestead; they did not precipitate it. The departure of John Burroughs' predecessor as Superintendent did, however, play a significant role in triggering the intergenerational conflict cycle. In other districts, conflict was triggered when key personnel changes occurred on the school board or within the teaching staff. In one small, rural California district, an older teacher, affectionately called 'Mother Johnson' by the rest of the faculty, determined that a teacher contract was not necessary, and the other teachers went along with her judgment. Not until she retired was the first contract negotiated. Similarly, in a small Illinois district, the triggering event was the hiring of fourteen new teachers who persuaded the older ones to push for more recognition and less paternalism. The union President in another Illinois district cited the combined effect of adding new teachers and changing the District Superintendent. As he put it,

> That was at the time we started changing superintendents. So

we more or less went on the defensive to try and protect what we had. The previous Superintendent had nothing written down, and that was fine. We did not know who was coming in, so we said, 'OK, we have this now, we do not want to lose it'. [I:13:T]

Legal changes represent a third type of precipitating event that creates the occasion for an intergenerational conflict to 'go public'. In many school districts, the statutes drafted by a state legislature, or a key court decision permitting districts to recognize teacher unions, galvanized local leaders into action. Some districts accepted the new legal status of bargaining with little or no overt conflict, perceiving either that the law 'required' bargaining or that opposing the change would invite unmanageable and corrosive conflict.

The following is a typical comment heard in districts where the transition was relatively peaceful.

We felt we should comply and conform to the whole wave of bargaining throughout the state, to be in line with it. We didn't feel we had much choice about it. [C:29:B]

Many districts thought that recognition of the teacher union would bring little change. Perhaps school boards had already met informally with teachers to talk about salaries, and neither party expected formal bargaining procedures to change their working relationships. And in some cases they were right, at least temporarily. One rural California district appeared virtually unchanged four years after passage of the Rodda Act. When we asked to see a copy of the current contract, the superintendent had his secretary retrieve a document from the files. On inspection, we realized we had been given the *original* typewritten and signed contract. On the last page were a series of initials indicating that the original contract had been reinstated each year without changes. No one had ever found a reason to make copies of the contract for distribution.

In contrast, less than five miles away, another small rural district, responding to the same statutory changes, suffered such serious labor difficulties that negotiations with its six teachers involved the full gamut of high conflict tactics: picketing, television cameras, newsletters known as 'hit sheets', and active teacher campaigning against incumbent school board members. It is difficult to say what a 'typical' response to the adoption of new law involves, but we did find that the changes were frequently much deeper and more conflict laden than either teachers or administrators had expected.

Open Conflict

Once teachers are motivated to action by a specific event, open conflict begins, and the Homestead case illustrates several typical events. The open conflict, which began with the 1977 strike, created a 'crisis of legitimacy' for the HEA. Agitation was so unusual for these teachers that they were seen as acting in bad faith and 'not the way a teacher ought to behave'. Both sides engaged in recrimination and name calling. In Homestead, as elsewhere, school board members and administrators maintained that the radicals in the teacher organization did not represent the interests of the 'really dedicated' teachers.

In turn, the pro-Riley faction came to question not just the specific actions of managers but also their fitness to hold office. Indeed, Homestead teachers (as well as many others during this period) frequently said that 'this school would run better if there were no principal — (s)he just gets in the way of our work'.

School boards differ substantially in their initial reactions to teacher demands for collective bargaining. Particularly in blue-collar towns, boards tend to be receptive to formal bargaining as a way of 'spelling things out', of rationalizing work rules, or of recognizing the rights of workers. In white-collar communities there is usually strong resistance to formalization of the bargaining process but a greater appreciation for expanding teacher job definitions. Frequent use of the word 'professional' in these communities connotes sympathy for the plight of teachers as underpaid workers who bear a heavy responsibility for the future of children. Generally, however, unionization is taken as a signal that teachers have forfeited any real claims to professional status. School board members are often given to moralizing about the downfall of teaching at the hands of the union. In one rural California community where teacher organization had followed efforts to organize farmworkers, a board member stopped the interview in mid-stream, slammed his fist on the table, and declared, 'They're all bandits; anyone who would ask a public school for more money is a bandit!'.

While substantial power resources are brought to bear during this period of open conflict, the struggle is won or lost at a symbolic level.

Meetings, demonstrations, newsletters, even job actions, threats of dismissal, and outright violence are of little value unless they are accompanied by, and used to support, a set of easily understood and broadly-appealing political symbols. For the teachers, the two key symbols are 'dignity' and 'protection'. Teacher dignity finds concrete expression in many different ways. It is frequently connected with salary decisions, though the concern is not so much with absolute salary level as with the way in which the decisions are made and the relative distribution of raises and fringe benefits between teachers and administrators. In one district, teachers became militant

> ...about two years ago when the board gave administrators 2 per cent more than the teachers... Right then, the teachers started getting mad. [C:T]

In many cases, however, the dignity symbol attaches to policies and practices that have nothing to do with finances. In one of our case-study districts, the union President's access to the school board agenda became a major issue. The board's denial of access was widely interpreted to mean that the administration had no respect for teachers. Leave policies, access to curricular decision-making, lavatory facilities, even the use of bulletin boards and mailboxes are frequently seen as revealing the extent to which school officials appreciate teacher dignity. The protection symbol is generally associated with both economic and psychological security for teachers. While protection against layoff or involuntary transfer is the 'big ticket' item in this domain, teachers frequently become much more emotional over problems related to the supervision and evaluation of their work. Most union locals develop elaborate strategies to shield teachers from what is widely perceived to be arbitrary and capricious evaluation by administrators.

As the conflict continues, management's verbal assurances that it intends to protect its teaching staff are greeted with increasing skepticism. As one union leader put it,

> I always try to consider the ulterior motive that the administration has for doing something. [C:T]

Another said,

> There's a lot of information in this district that has been unethical. Outright lies have been told and written — this has happened for the last ten years. [C:T]

On the management side, the dominant symbol is 'discretion'. In labor relations parlance, this discretion is called 'management rights' and is frequently negotiated directly into a contractual agreement. In general, however, managers choose not to specify the boundaries of their discretionary authority, preferring to believe that teachers are obligated to comply with *any* management directive that does not explicitly violate a specific contractual agreement or legal right.

Typically, the intergenerational conflict grows more intense and more public until a crisis is reached and a clear symbolic victory is won by one side or the other. Sometimes the turning point is a strike or demonstration, sometimes it is the settlement of a hard-fought contract or the acceptance of a contested item into a previously non-controversial labor contract. In each of the case-study districts, the moment of crisis and the ultimate resolution of the conflict depended upon a change in key personnel. In fact, the forcing of one or more people from office is the most common way of confirming the success of one side. When management wins, union leaders lose their jobs. When unions succeed in forcing recognition, one or more management career may be derailed.

Although the period of crisis *varies widely in scope, duration and intensity from one district to another*, we found that virtually everyone is able to recognize when a symbolic victory has been decisively won by one side or the other, and nearly everyone can identify the specific events signaling that victory. In Homestead, the turning point was not the 1977 strike but the recall election in which three school board members were defeated. While this signal event did not lead to teacher domination of school board decision-making, as many had expected it would, it dramatically altered management's approach to bargaining and started a process that ended in Stan Adams' resignation as chief management negotiator.

As the conflict broadens, the reasonableness of the administration becomes a major issue. Finally, the conflict itself becomes the issue. Continued conflict begins to make the administration look arbitrary or, at best, unskilled. As one teacher in a tiny district put it:

> The people around here have little truck with unions, but they're starting to ask why the superintendent can't keep six teachers in line. [C:25:T]

Indeed, many of the teachers' complaints struck a responsive chord in parents and often in board members. What the teachers want begins to 'sound nice and reasonable'.

If conflict continues, public pressure builds to solve or end it. Politically, this gives the teacher organization the upper hand. Contractual gains during this period are usually not very substantial, however. Even the most conspicuous of teacher organizations, those in the big cities, have been unable to protect their members against the effects of economic cutbacks and population movements that have cost thousands of teachers their jobs.

Accommodating and Reorganizing

More important than the period of crisis and symbolic victory for one side or the other is the abiding pressure within school districts for labor peace. The prescription of 'good management' in America's schools depends at least as much on maintaining a modicum of order and civility within the organization as controlling organizational productivity. This means that managers must move quickly to establish a modus vivendi with the teacher organizations once it has won symbolic legitimacy for the new unionism ideology. One superintendent describes this pressure for settlement:

> Last year we go to the point where the teachers went public in a sense. They advertised my salary in the newspaper, they carried on open communications with the community — you get the half-truths in the bulletins from the teachers. And we as a district, quite frankly, retaliated...I think in many ways it tore the community up. It was more of disease kind of thing...I had a number of coffee klatches, to involve the community, and I think they did the same kind of thing...I don't think that either side garnered any large support. We didn't get a lot of support. The Chamber of Commerce and Rotary and so on, would be somewhat supportive of the administration, but I think that a distaste for the conflict was what was going on. [C:19:S]

Turnover of Individuals

Frequently the first intergenerational conflict is brought to a close with another round of personnel changes among the individuals responsible for labor relations. Negotiators for both labor and management frequently leave or are discharged, most often because they have become symbols of the old order, the order which refused to recognize teacher organizations as legitimate bargaining agents. Homestead's Superintendent Burroughs said of Stan Adams, the lawyer who had staunchly defended management interests in early negotiations with the teachers: 'He's competent, but the air is so poisoned that he has to go. Better him than me'.

Sometimes the departure of key people is encouraged because they cannot adapt their behavior to the requirements of the new situation. Having staked their reputations on preserving the old order, they find themselves caught between embarrassment and obstructionism. In one California district, both the militant President of the teacher organization and the crusty management negotiator had to quit in the middle of a strike — sacrificial lambs on the altar of labor peace. Such personnel changes symbolize the transition to a new era of labor relations and give everyone a chance to shift from ideological posturing to pragmatic compromise.

At times, we found the teacher organization holds an election in which successful militant leaders are removed from office to make way for a new leadership group ready to establish less vitriolic working relationships with management. Teachers require militant leadership in order to get organized and to get their basic interests articulated. But they must abandon that leadership in order to restore order and settle long-term contracts.

Thus, conflict fades at the end of the first intergenerational period. The symbolism attached to contract negotiations, the day-to-day interactions of teachers and school administrators, or the handling of key issues shifts from moral purity to pragmatic decision-making and second generation bargaining begins.

Epilogue: People Out of Season

While the movement of school district labor relations through an intergenerational conflict period is fairly easy to trace, it must be remembered that individual actors do not necessarily see themselves in the light of this dynamic process. Indeed, most of the people we interviewed held a normative view of 'how things are supposed to be' that took no notice at all of the shifts in the basic form and meaning of labor relations from one generation to another. This lack of understanding on the part of key actors accounts for much of the conflict associated with the transition between generations. It also makes the transitions possible by blinding the participants to the possibility of failure.

In Homestead, each of the three main characters (Superintendent Burroughs, HEA executive director Erickson, and chief negotiator Adams) was decidedly 'out ahead of' or 'lagging behind' the intergenerational conflict process. Adams, like most labor professionals, was a committed Second Generation negotiator. He felt that collective bargaining was an efficient way to handle basic conflicts and that if each party would just 'take its best hold' at the bargaining table, decisions could properly balance the interests of all parties. He emphasized keeping order and writing contracts that made keeping order possible. His mannerisms and 'hardnosed' approach to bargaining would have been viewed as appropriate and fair in a situation where teachers felt that their legitimacy was not in question. But, alas, teachers were more concerned with proving that they had dignity than with settling specific differences during the intergenerational conflict period. And they viewed Adams not as a tough bargainer but as a representative of those who rejected their claim to legitimacy. Adams had to leave the district before the Second Generation labor relations system — which he understood and tried to utilize in dealing with teachers — could be fully accepted.

Burroughs' management style was also out of step with the needs of the First Intergenerational Conflict process. He held views that are usually successful during the quiescent periods that come late in either the First or Second Generation. He believed that teachers would prefer collaborative participation to explicit negotiation of decisions. He also believed that managers must take ultimate responsibility for the shape of school district programs and policies. Burroughs saw his 'open management' plan as an alternative to the formalization of conflict and development of explicit bargaining relationships with teachers. He failed to recognize that teachers had a greater need to establish their independent worth and identity than to win particular policy decisions made regarding their working conditions. What for Burroughs was cooperative decision-making the teachers came to see as a denial of their dignity.

Erickson wanted to move directly into a mature Late Second Generation relationship with the school board. Ironically, she became the symbol of the continuing conflict that she sought to avoid.

She was forced to posture as the leader of a teacher union bent on establishing its power and flexing its new-found muscle, rather than on moving into pragmatic decision-making and long-range planning. However, she could not let go of the symbols of righteous indignation and hostility toward the district's central office in order to establish this mature relationship. Since she, like Dan Riley, came to power out of teacher frustration, she could not avoid becoming a representative of teacher outrage. And she genuinely believed in the healing powers of conflict: beating Adams and winning concessions from the district were fun, they tested her mettle, and they gave her an opportunity to display symbolic 'dignity' for her fellow teachers. But the wounds would have to be healed by someone else.

Notes

1 LIEBERMAN, M. and MOSKOW, M.H. (1966) *Collective Negotiations for Teachers: An Approach to School Administration*, Chicago, IL, Rand McNally, p. 8.
2 CARLTON, P.W. (1969) 'Educator attitudes and value differences in collective negotiations' in CARLTON, P.W. and GOODWIN, H.I. (Eds) *The Collective Dilemma: Negotiations in Education*, Worthington, OH, Jones Publishing Co., p. 33.
3 CORWIN, R.G. (1969) 'The anatomy of militant professionalism' in CARLTON, P.W. and GOODWIN, H.I. (Eds) *The Collective Dilemma: Negotiations in Education*, Worthington, OH, Jones Publishing Co., p. 241.
4 LIEBERMAN, M. and MOSKOW, M.H. (1966) *op cit*, p. 373, citing GROSS, N., MASON, W.S. and McEACHERN, A.W. (1958) *Explorations in Role Analysis: Studies of the School Superintendency Role*, New York, Wiley.
5 *Ibid.*, p. 17.
6 Notations to our field interviews are given as follows: The state, either Illinois or California; the school district identified by number, and the source — a school board member, superintendent, teacher, parent, or union leader.

6
The Second Generation: The Era of Good-Faith Bargaining

The Second Generation stands as evidence that the trustee relationship paramount in the First Generation meet-and-confer labor relations comes to be seen as failing to represent teachers' interests in the governance of schools, their operation, and in shaping teaching work. Thus, the onset of the Second Generation legitimates teacher self-interest and initiates the dynamic tension between the ideal of collective bargaining and its organizational reality. Collective bargaining is the lynchpin of the Second Generation, and with collective bargaining come the structures and processes of negotiation, contract administration, and continuous interaction between employer and the union. All these address the practical problem of managing conflict.

During the First Intergenerational Conflict, the need to control labor strife has an immediate, almost palpable, meaning. It is uncontrolled conflict (or the fear of it) that brings states and school districts to the Second Generation: thus, the institutionalization of Second Generation labor relations statutes and administrative machinery is a promise that labor conflict can be managed, and that school districts can be managed too.

When intergenerational conflict passes the crisis stage, the first task is restoring order. To do so requires relinquishing First Generation assumptions about the role of conflict in governing and operating schools. In the First Generation, it is generally assumed in both theory and practice that conflict in schools is an individual matter based on personality or social role. Permanent group conflict within the school organization is a new concept, and it requires managing conflict rather than suppressing it.[1]

Managing conflict involves establishing new collective bargaining ideas and playing out the tension between the new ideas and organizational reality. As suggested in chapter 2, the generation comprises two phases, the Early phase concerned with establishing the idea and institutionalizing the structures, and the Late phase concerned with pragmatic compromise and accommodation to reduce tension and achieve real results.

In the Early phase, labor-management conflict drops from the peaks of the First Intergenerational Period, but tension often remains high because establishing a union requires simultaneously learning to negotiate aggressively and to settle pragmatically. In the Second Generation's Late phase, public conflict virtually disappears as bargaining becomes more routinized and more exclusively the province of labor professionals. At the same time, diffuse, trusting, and even cooperative relationships develop between teacher union leaders and school administrators. The substance of labor relations becomes less a matter of contract and more a matter of what the parties informally agree to and how they socialize one another.

The structures of collective bargaining — the union organization, the contract, negotiation, impasse resolution, and contract administration — remain the same in both the Early and Late phases of the Second Generation, but the organizational meaning of these structures changes. As the interactionist mode of social change suggests, the socially constructed meaning of events is altered over successive rounds of contract negotiations.[2]

Snapshots of Schools in the Second Generation

This dynamic is most vividly seen in two school districts which have created Second Generation relationships. The case of Thresher Unified School District, which entered the Second Generation almost against its will, shows that the structures and procedures of collective bargaining can operate even when a district is undergoing political upheaval and administrative fragmentation. The case of Riverview City School System demonstrates the ability of Late Second Generation labor relations to address and solve thorny internal and external problems by integrating the activities of the union and administration at the bargaining table, in electoral politics, and through personal interaction between leaders.

Thresher Unified: Procedural Stability Amid Political Strife in the Early Second Generation

Labor relations in the Thresher Unified School District demonstrate the robustness of Second Generation structures and beliefs in the face of continuing ideological antipathy toward teacher unionism. Even though board members talk of repealing the bargaining statutes and make inflammatory public statements about unions, the district and union are learning to operate in the Second Generation. The union has taken on the characteristics of a permanent organization. It has an office and an executive organization, and it shares the services of a full-time labor professional. Its own teacher officers have gained experience and expertise in bargaining. The district's administrators, particularly the second- and third-echelon administrators, are mastering Early Second Generation behavior — bargaining tactics, grievance processing — and learning that the purpose of bargaining is to reach agreement, not to slay the enemy.

Surprisingly, it was the superintendent's actions several years ago that sent the signal of legitimacy to the union. Just as the district was being formed as an amalgamation of smaller school districts, the board asked Deputy Superintendent Harold Quinn to negotiate with the teachers under the state's meet-and-confer statute. Quinn established himself as a teacher supporter by negotiating a written agreement called the *White Paper* with the teachers at a time when written agreements were not common. Quinn called the agreement 'generous'. Teacher association president Ken Wilson characterized it as 'paradise'. Fringe benefits improved dramatically, and teachers gained liberal job control rights: the ability to leave campus at any time, no restrictions on work hours, few mandatory after-school duties. Quinn says he was trying to build a coalition of educators and to ensure an era of good feeling for the district by giving teachers a significant voice, but one modulated by himself. To the teaches, however, Quinn's embrace signaled the legitimacy of collectively bargained agreements over educational policy.

The following year, the old Superintendent was ousted, and Quinn, with teacher union support, was named Superintendent.

When California's collective bargaining law became effective in 1976, the union set to incorporate the *White Paper* into contractual language. Quinn, the board, and a new labor attorney wanted to 'start from ground zero'. The meet-and-confer agreement was not a contract, they said, and its contents were inappropriate for a contract. 'No backward movement', said Wilson and the union. In a series of statements to the press and parent groups, Quinn and three board members attacked the legitimacy of collective bargaining and the union. The teachers counter attacked, charging the administration with incompetence and callousness. The bargaining impasse continued for two years.

There was still no agreement by the time of the 1977 school board campaign, and teacher unionism became an election issue. One candidate was elected on a platform of: 'No Unions; No Taxes'. The platform, of course, was pure bluster: The state's labor statute required the district to recognize a properly chosen bargaining agent, and school tax issues were decided largely in the state capitol. But the election was a symptom of political feeling in the community. Another candidate, Anne Beeman, spent an unprecedented $17,500 to attract 3500 votes and in her victory statement remarked that the 'voters have defeated a strong bid by the teachers' union for control of a major school district governing board'. Teacher-supported candidates lost.

In May 1977 the teachers mounted a three-day strike. While the strike brought the teachers closer together and won them support of some community members, it did not bring them the contract terms they wanted. But the real loser may have been Quinn, who during the next two years lost control over the collective bargaining process and nearly lost his job.

The board began to criticize Quinn publicly, and in a bizarre series of events: (i) Quinn announced that he was looking for a new job; (ii) the board told Quinn it was going to buy out his contract and ordered him to go on vacation; (iii) Quinn sued the board; (iv) the community launched an unsuccessful but spirited recall campaign against board members; (v) Anne Beeman reversed her previous stance and voted to extend Quinn's contract; (vi) Quinn dropped his suit; and (vii) Beeman was elected school board President.

The ongoing public battle between the Superintendent and the board, as well as other intramural fights within the district administration, distracted attention from negotiations. But bargaining did take place. During the eighteen months we observed Thresher, the teachers clearly exhibited Second Generation norms. Not all the teachers could be considered unionists. Indeed, many of them thought that the union's job actions were clumsy at best. But every teacher we talked to expected the union to get an agreement with the administration. And they all wanted an enforceable agreement, a contract. For the teachers, the *White Paper* agreement reached some five years earlier symbolized an important status passage. They considered their organization the legitimate body to negotiate with the administration, and they acted accordingly.

For second-level Thresher administrators, the transition to a collective bargaining technocracy was relatively easy (it was the relationship between themselves and the Superintendent that was difficult). They had schooled themselves in the law and in collective bargaining techniques. They had observed the different techniques of the three attorneys hired and fired by the district during its first four years in collective bargaining. They behaved as if their job was to reach agreement with the union, not to act upon the campaign rhetoric of the school board members. Indeed, while Beeman and other board members had vowed to 'get' the union leadership and throw out the union, these threats were never taken seriously by administrators.

Ultimately, for Quinn — and even for Beeman — the structures of collective bargaining proved to have a powerful hold. The natural logic of bargaining ends in agreement. When there are no agreements, the organization is perceived as 'not doing its job', and it must act to erase this impression. As her personal fight with Quinn drew to a close and she assumed board presidency, Beeman became personally involved in pressing for a settlement with the teachers.

Riverview: Compatibility and Challenge in the Late Second Generation

Riverview is an old industrial and commercial city whose physical character suggests that 'some things never change', but the handsome old houses and brick factories only partly reflect reality. School enrollment has grown over 30 per cent in the last decade, but enrollment from the central part of the city has declined. As population has shifted to the suburban housing tracts, political influence has shifted too — from old, elite families to newly-established interest groups. These changes have placed the schools under substantial economic stress and have realigned the political forces into a new coalition. Teachers are an organized and powerful element in this new establishment, but their hold is tenuous.

Riverview teachers enjoy a Late Second Generation relationship with their district. The union is strong, and it accommodates to, and cooperates with, the school administration. This relationship has not always existed. In the recent past, Riverview was one of most conflict-torn school districts in the state: four strikes; angry public meetings; vicious political campaigns. Even now, the Late Second Generation is under attack by those who believe that the union has grown too powerful and the district's performance has become shoddy.

The first substantial labor contract with the teachers was negotiated in the late 1960s. At one time a rather honorific task rotated among volunteer teachers, negotiations are now conducted by the local union's full-time trained personnel. The union enjoys widespread support among the district's 1000 teachers and is viewed as one of the best run in the state.

Joseph Henry, the current Superintendent, was the district's negotiator for those early contracts, but he relinquished this position shortly after assuming the superintendency in 1971. A period of substantial labor unrest followed including a two-day strike in 1971 and a one-day walkout the following year. Relationships did not improve in 1973–74 when the teachers appointed a new negotiator, a man described as 'exceptionally abrasive' by even the most generous observers. There was another strike in 1975, and the district was not successful in keeping the schools open.

During 1976–77 the teachers changed their chief negotiator once again and management followed suit. The level of confrontational rhetoric declined, and a new relationship developed around 'a mutual goal of achieving labor peace'. Still another, largely economic, strike took place in 1978. At this point it became clear that the ebb and flood of labor relations threatened the district's financial capacity, so labor and management decided to do something about it.

In one sense, the economic stress is easy to explain: Riverview was running out of tax money. No additional tax levy for the general education fund has been approved since 1964, and the last successful construction bond referendum — chiefly to build schools in the district's new suburban areas — was held in 1974. Tax levy referenda failed twice in 1979, despite the best efforts of the school board, the active support from the Citizens Advisory Council, and the overwhelming participation of the teacher union. Aging voters in the more established neighborhoods voted no. As one put it: 'Look, I've already sent my children through this school system, and besides the teachers get all the money anyway, not the kids.' The board, the union, and the administration agreed that labor conflict would have to be aggressively managed if a referendum was to be passed.

Both labor and management considered a successful tax referendum an absolute necessity. The union understood the district's financial position. The schools were not in financial crisis, but only because programs in physical education and music had been cut and because teachers had agreed to salary terms that did not keep pace with the cost-of-living. Without a tax increase the till would be empty. With a tax increase the school board could restore program cuts and pay teachers a 'decent' raise.

Both sides also understood that strikes poison the well of public support. The results of the 1979 referendum made it clear that the majority of voters (those who did not have children in public schools) regarded a teacher's strike not simply as the natural extension of a wage dispute but as a sign that the schools were not tightly controlled financially. According to the board President: 'The people I represent believe that we haven't yet made significant cuts and eliminated the fat from the budget. They won't approve a referendum till we first get our house in order.'

That the public perception differed from the organizational reality made the situation even more difficult. Widely acknowledged by his peers to be a shrewd and careful fiscal manager, the Superintendent guided the board in adopting a long-term financial strategy which included gradual program adjustments rather than abrupt, massive reductions in either programs or personnel. The percentage of the budget spent for teacher salaries had not increased for a decade. But because of his careful shepherding of funds and incremental adjustments in programs, the very real financial problems of the district were not apparent to the public. And because of the repeated strikes, the union appeared more avaricious than the data suggest it was. The district's financial plight had to be made clear, but without attributing blame either to a greedy union or to an overly compliant board. A successful referendum required a modest wage settlement and labor peace.

The onset of negotiations and the decision about whether to hold another tax referendum came at the same time. Orchestration of these events required skillful and trusting relations between the Superintendent and the union President. There could be no strike. Just after the failure of the 1979 referendum, the Superintendent and the union President privately agreed to try another tax referendum the following year. The union President also agreed that the teachers would not strike. Later, after making revenue projections, the two agreed to a 7 per cent salary increase. This agreement took place before the negotiating teams met for the first time.

In the spring, when the bargaining teams actually began to meet, a serious and potentially disruptive event took place. A school board member advocated extensive changes in the 'policy' aspects of the contract, and there was a growing mood on the board to get tough with the teachers. Thus, the Superintendent's real bargaining task was to convince the board that it should not alter the contract but that it should discuss wages only. The board finally agreed, with the understanding that a wage agreement be reached by 30 June.

At this point, of course, neither the board members nor the teachers' bargaining team were aware of the proposed '7 per cent solution'. The Superintendent and the union President had to guide their respective sides toward this end. They were successful, and in June the parties agreed upon a contract that was substantially what the union President and the Superintendent had sketched out in January. The way was paved for a tax campaign involving the active participation of both the board and the union.

Reflections on the Elements of Labor Relations

These two cases illustrate the key elements of the Second Generation and set the stage for explaining its dynamics. The first element is *the union* itself. During the First Generation the union is a domesticated organization, dependent on the school district. In the Second Generation, the union becomes organizationally independent and presents school organizations with a major discontinuity. The shock of the new union bothered Thresher Superintendent Harold Quinn, whose self image as an educational leader was battered by the realization that 'my teachers' wanted to negotiate chin-to-chin. The problem for Riverview Superintendent Joseph Henry, whose board was chafing to attack the teachers' contract, was to legitimate the union's role in organizational problem solving.

The second element of the collective bargaining relationship is *the contract*. Quinn intuitively recognized that the new relationship was powerfully shaped by the contractual nature of the agreement. His wariness about expanding the contract was coloured by his distaste for the union as an organization. Still, he well understood the binding nature of contracts, and he feared them. In contrast, our snapshot of Riverview reveals a district *managed largely around its contract*. Henry's style, mirrored by the union leadership, was to find ways of solving practical problems — including those created by the contract itself.

Third, Second Generation labor relations involves establishing *bargaining structures and procedures*. In Thresher, second echelon administrators and union leaders spent a great deal of time trying to structure bargaining. Frustrated by their inability to reach timely agreements, the parties redoubled their efforts, experimenting with different negotiating styles, persons, and agendas in a search for something that worked. As we have seen, by the Late Second Generation, bargaining structures in Riverview were well-established but were not particularly important to the eventual outcomes. What counted was the interaction of elites: in this case a single representative of the teachers and Superintendent Henry.

The fourth element of good faith bargaining is *impasse resolution*. Although our snapshots do not focus on the strike experiences of Thresher and Riverview, both districts quickly learned that strikes are something other than a new toy. Both sought alternatives through mediation, fact-finding, and restructuring negotiations.

Fifth, Second Generation districts engage in *contract administration*. Thresher's attention was directed primarily at getting contracts, not administering them. But the emerging issue in the district was the Superintendent's relationships with his principals: how they were to be controlled, and whether they would agree to interpret district rules, and the contract itself in the same manner. In Riverview, contract administration was characterized by continuous bargaining at school sites, by little deals between principals and teachers that were kept quiet from 'the folks downtown'.

Union As Organization

It is not the requirement for interaction with teachers, but *which* teachers the school interacts with, that makes the Second Generation different from the First. In meet-and-confer arrangements and other types of administratively dominated labor relations, managers interact with the teachers who are most like themselves. But the First Intergenerational conflict causes unions to be led by leaders who are most unlike, and unliked by, administrators. As Neil Chamberlain put it in describing private sector unions, the difference is that these people 'do not share the same goal base'.[3] To the school district, it is like being asked to take on a permanent harassing agent.

Thus, the beginning of the Second Generation is often characterized by frustrating interpersonal experiences. In one of our study districts, the younger teachers had organized in opposition to the older ones, who had held department chairs and the principal's ear for years. In telling the story, the Superintendent drew back his chair and said with disgust, 'and *these* are the people who spend hours and hours talking around the superintendent's conference table', clearly indicating that he didn't enjoy the process. Even if the individuals once had close working relationships with school administrators, as was the case in Thresher, the change in values and perceptions makes the labor-management meeting at the beginning of the Second Generation a meeting of strangers.

The amazing transformation of the Second Generation lies in the acceptance, and even support and protection, of the union as an organization and of its leaders as individuals. As the Riverview case illustrates, the union President and the Superintendent, recognizing the mutual advantages in unionization, became locked in a close working relationship, taking on reciprocal obligations and making informal agreements.

School superintendents often come to value teacher unions because they not only stabilize but also formalize administration. As one said, 'Well, it makes everything a lot clearer. If I don't have a map, I don't know where we're going. But I can't imagine any school system that has been able to operate without written guidelines' [C:26:A]. The contract, he said, simply gave the rules additional validity. Or as a union President put it: 'It's clearer where the lines of authority are' [C:23:T].

Personality conflicts are diminished, and the rule of contract is recognized [C:30:T].

As the Riverview case illustrates, union leaders also lend their influence and personal support to school district goals. Even in Thresher Unified, the union President and Superintendent Quinn were able to bury the hatchet long enough to fly to the state capitol together and lobby for school finance legislation. Another union reported working on a bond issue campaign 'when the Superintendent needed some Indians' [I:21:T].

At the extreme, union-management collaboration involves a high level of interpersonal trust and a highly confidential relationship that would often be impossible if school board or rank-and-file teachers were fully aware of it. Such relationships are also extremely private. As one Superintendent said, 'I don't work with teachers, I work with the President of the Association' [C:25:S]. In one district, the union helped management through a period of severely declining enrollment and revenues by 'cooling out' about forty veteran teachers who were considered 'deadwood'. The district's enrollment had declined by at least one-third, forcing the closure of several elementary schools and a high school. Increased benefits for early retirement — benefits substantially greater than those of the state retirement system — were negotiated into the labor contract. Then, forty senior teachers were encouraged to take advantage of those provisions. Some were in programs that had been cut back, while others had been threatened with the possibility of dismissal for cause, so the union suggested that they accept the early retirement package rather than subject themselves to the rigors of dismissal procedures.

School superintendents and union leaders also begin to feel a sense of obligation toward one another, a desire to be mutually protective, both organizationally and personally. One superintendent who has just seen a group of moderate teachers take over control from the 'radicals' in his district said 'Between you and me, I tend to want to make this group successful' [C:19:S]. In another case, when an old firebrand emerged from inactivity and announced that he would run for the union presidency, the Superintendent quietly approached the union executive and asked if there was anything he could do to help influence the election.

Over time, credibility increases. The two leaders come to believe more strongly in the validity of the information that passes between them. Just as important, each believes in the ability of the other to honor commitments made. That is, if the Superintendent says that he can deliver a vote from the school board, the union leader believes that the vote will, indeed, be forthcoming. Similarly, if the teacher leader says that he can prevent a disturbance or sell the membership on an idea, the Superintendent believes that the promised result will follow.

Union Politics

Unions gain political importance during the First Intergenerational Conflict Period, so much so that the literature on public sector labor relations is perhaps preoccupied with a fear that unions will come to 'distort the normal political processes'.[4] Teachers, our respondents said, gain 'two bites of the apple', electioneering and collective bargaining, an unbeatable advantage over management. But the reality of union political behavior is different, and the meaning of political activity changes during the Second Generation.

During the First Intergenerational Conflict and the Early Second Generation, teacher organizations are very active in school board elections. Because electing public officials is one way in which they can flaunt their power and influence, unions organize electorally and are often successful at the polls. But they are often disappointed with the results. School board members elected with union support seldom back the union party line as vigorously as the teachers expect. Fran Erickson of the Homestead Education Association put it succinctly: 'School board members have a disgusting tendency to act like school board members.' Of the new school board majority elected in Homestead's union-supported recall election, only one remained a union loyalist, and he was so ineffectual that after regularly finding himself on the short end of 4–1 votes he decided not to seek a second term. In another of the study districts, other board members and the administration took great pains to isolate a pro-union board member. During preparations for collective bargaining, for instance, the substance of management's position was shown on overhead projections in a darkened room so that the maverick board member could not transmit copies to the union.

Teacher organizations frequently misunderstand the meaning of the political support they received during the First Intergenerational Conflict Period. The political support unions received was for *legitimiz-*

ing collective bargaining; it did not convey a promise of future support of union-supported policies or even teacher salaries. During the Second Generation, union leaders come to understand the distinction and to say, as one official did, 'we don't seek puppets anymore; just people who won't try to kill us with an axe'.

Political exposure also proves hazardous to teacher unions. In many communities, union involvement in local politics is considered illegitimate and thus self-defeating. As one teacher organization President in a large California city said, 'when the newspaper came out with the headline saying, "Teachers Major Force in Local Politics", I knew that we no longer were'. The emergence of teachers as a discrete political force fuels a backlash, which frequently signals the end to the Second Generation and the beginning of the Second Intergenerational Conflict Period.

Sensing the hazards of continued exposure, some unions adopt decidedly low-key approaches to school board politics in the Late Second Generation. Sometimes they drop political involvement altogether, figuring that the candidates they endorse don't help them very much if they win and that those they oppose become enemies of the union if they win. But the more frequent pattern is a less shrill endorsement of candidates who will support the union generally and a deliberate downplaying of the 'teacher power' theme. Private influence is substituted for public power.

The Bargaining Unit

To engage in collective bargaining one must have a bargaining unit: a group of employees whose job titles are legally recognized by the appropriate labor agency as the proper grouping of workers for the purposes of collective bargaining.[5] In the American industrial union tradition, the firm or organization, rather than the narrow craft or occupational specialty, has been the focus of bargaining unit determination. Smaller aggregations of workers are considered unfeasible. As industrial unionism has been incorporated into public education, unit determination has come to mean that virtually all teachers who work in the same school district became members of the same bargaining unit. Except for the very largest school districts, educational support personnel, such as psychologists and counselors, are generally included in the same bargaining unit.

The symbolic meaning of this omnibus grouping of employees changes over time. During the Early Second Generation, the bargaining unit represents teacher solidarity — solidarity necessary for union victory in the intergenerational conflict — and the means of clearly distinguishing 'them from us'. This distinction is dramatized in the frequent struggle over department chairs. Historically, the department chair has occupied a somewhat anomalous position, combining teaching duties with curriculum, scheduling and sometimes evaluation responsibilities. Particularly in senior high schools, department chairs clearly were more than first among equals. Collective bargaining has little tolerance for such differences in status. Unions we observed fought vigorously to define anyone who 'did bargaining unit work' as a teacher and thus rightfully a member of the unit. Labor boards usually agreed. Management, for its part, often reinforced the cleavage between teachers and managers by doing away with the position altogether replacing the chair with a full-time administrator. In those cases where the position was not abolished, the occupants often ceased to carry out coordinating or oversight functions, on the grounds that these functions constituted 'managerial, not teaching work'.

In the Late Second Generation, the emphasis shifts from the clear distinction between teachers and managers to the lack of distinction among teachers. The bargaining unit comes to stand for the homogenization of teachers in terms of what the school district expects from them and what they can expect in the way of job definition and contractual rewards. The concept of 'common rule', long a union defense against favoritism and particularism, comes to mean identical behavioral standards for all employees.[6] Part of the explanation for sameness rests with the internal political calculus of teacher unions. The majority of the bargaining unit members are 'regular classroom teachers', and the distinct minority are specialists in either a subject matter or an educational service, such as special education. Somewhat to our surprise, we found that the specialists in our study districts were unsuccessful in gleaning contractual concessions built around their particular job requirements. They often made proposals, but seldom were these proposals adopted. [On this point, our findings differ from those of some other authors. For instance, Goldschmidt *et al.*, found that special education teachers were successful in gaining clauses

135

dealing with special education policy in 44 per cent of the contracts they examined and with teacher compensation, training and other matters in 60 per cent of the contracts. What is not known from this finding, however, is whether the special education clauses reflect the political influences of a powerful subgroup within the union or whether the special education contract clauses simply mirror state requirements.[7]]

Gaining Union Security

Organizational security is the catchall term describing agreements which foster the permanence and stability of the union. Some access forms, which were highly controversial in the First Intergenerational Conflict period become routine in the Second Generation, provisions such as the union's right to post notices on bulletin boards and to place its communications in teachers' mail boxes at school. But union security also extends to items such as time off from work for union officers, payroll deduction of union dues, and — most controversial — the requirement that all members of the bargaining unit pay dues or fees to support the union. This *agency shop* issue is often the subject of an intense struggle between union and management at the beginning of the Second Generation.[8] Unions desperately want an agency shop to insure their position as exclusive representative and bolster the union treasury. (Agency shop proves a potent way of drying up support for an alternative and potentially opposing bargaining agent. After agency shop, the opposition must convince potential members to pay voluntary dues in addition to the mandatory fees they pay to the bargaining agent.) Management sees no reason to strengthen the union's position, and many school boards are ideologically opposed to the coercion involved in forcing teachers to pay union fees.

By the end of the Second Generation the union has achieved organizational security, and the term 'security' comes to mean the security of the regime: the durability of the current union and management leadership. Each leader has an interest in the longevity of his or her counterpart. The mutual support relationships described earlier become the tangible expressions of the security question. At this point, there are seldom any serious rivals from opposing unions, nor is there a remaining viable anti-union faction. The agency shop issue is usually muted, sometimes because school boards 'rise above principle', trading off agency shop for a bargaining concession from the union, and sometimes because the union has given up trying for that form of security, feeling that the fight is not worth the effort.

Contract as the Form of Agreement

Contracts are seen as *the* answer to labor relations problems, *the* means by which teachers can, in the words of one unionist, 'add fangs to the toothless tiger'. Without the right to contract and the machinery to enforce collective contracts, unions in the United States found they had nothing.[9] Because the contract is seen as the means to cement their gains, achieving contractual gains is of great importance during the Early Second Generation. Surprisingly, however, in the Late Second Generation only routine attention is paid to the status of the contract. Negotiations become what one labor scholar called 'the biannual tournament' over economic conditions. Both sides realize that the contract is, in Philip Selznick's words, 'an incomplete law of association'.[10] The union-management relationship spreads 'beyond contract' and is reflected in a broader organizational culture where the machinery of the union is used to address practical problems. The contract becomes but an artifact of that relationship. To understand the dynamics by which contracts move from centerpiece to artifact, one must first be aware of the differences between legally binding contracts and school board policies (the dominant form of agreement under the First Generation meet-and-confer model), and then, consider how continuing tension over the scope of bargaining and management rights influences what is actually negotiated during the Second Generation.

The most obvious distinction between contract and policy is that policy is the unilateral responsibility of the school board and contract is a bilateral agreement. While this distinction has high symbolic significance, its efficacy tends to be overrated. The supposedly unilateral policy authority lodged in the school board is subject to political influences and organizational as well as legal and fiscal structures. The responsiveness theories of school politics rest on the assumption that those who do not have formal authority have the ability to influence those who do. Thus, when we looked at meet-and-confer school districts, we often found teachers effecting policy. Such was certainly the case in Thresher Unified, where the teachers successfully influenced the school board to adopt the compendium of job-related policies called the *White Paper*. Policy is not necessarily as unilateral as it seems.

The more important differences between contract and policy are rooted in the content of the agreement and its legal meaning. Policy conveys organizational intent. Contracts convey individual or collective rights. Policy is an expression of where organizations intend to go and how, as a matter of standard operating procedure, they plan to handle contingencies. Policy is intended to guide individual behavior and create a general direction for the organization. Generally, departure from policy is reason for censure, or at least scrutiny, within the organization. Contracts specify what the organization is bound to do. They are intended to govern the actions of the organization and its agents in *all* cases. Violations can be adjusted in the courts or through administrative mechanisms.

Early in the Second Generation both labor and management recognize this important distinction, so it is not surprising that they develop strong and opposing beliefs about contracts. For labor, bilateral agreements are a response to the dignity symbol raised during the First Intergenerational Conflict, and contract enforceability addresses the protection symbol. Unions enter the Second Generation believing that everything of importance must be negotiated and included in the contract. Management disagrees, maintaining that *the shortest contract is the best one*. The battle over what is included in the contract is heavily fought during the Early Second Generation.

But as the Second Generation progresses, both labor and management come to believe that contracts seldom address themselves to fundamental organizational problems. Collective bargaining contracts are not purposive contracts which express an explicit economic exchange.[11] They do not obligate the union to specific performance outcome. They do not specify the services employees are to render, nor do they completely specify the limits on employee duties. In the Late Second Generation, the existence of a contract is looked upon more as a touchstone that provides legitimacy for 'a system of industrial self-government'.[12] In one sense, 'its function is to create a political community'.[13] A union executive we interviewed put the matter somewhat more bluntly: 'Having the contract doesn't get much done, but it ensures that they pay attention to me when I come to call'.

The Scope of Bargaining

The Second Generation tension over contracts focuses itself on the scope of bargaining. In the beginning, teachers expected collective bargaining to accommodate their broadly-based concerns about 'the standards of their practice and the quality of service provided to their "clientele"'.[14] But for management and most all state legislatures, limitations on the scope of bargaining became the substitute for the doctrine of sovereignty, a way of asserting that collective bargaining had not contaminated the policy-making process.[15] A legal line is drawn between contract and policy. Virtually every state statute declares that it distinguishes between those issues which are bargainable and those which relate to educational policy. Minnesota, for instance, expressly forbids bargaining over 'educational policies of the school district'. In an attempt to limit the language of the National Labor Relations Act, which imposes a duty to bargain over 'wages, hours and other items and conditions of employment' (Section 8d), California specifies which terms and conditions are negotiable: health and welfare benefits, leave and transfer policies, safety conditions, class size, employee evaluation procedures, union security and grievance process-ing methods.[16] Thus, a school board member could maintain that entering into collective bargaining did not alter the philosophy that the 'objectives of the school system, the goals achieved, shall be determined by the community itself and not by the professionals...'[17]

During Early Phase, the battle over scope of bargaining questions and over union involvement in decision-making is strong and contin-uous. But the unions stop pressing for an expanded role. In Thresher, the teachers participated on a budget cutback committee until they found themselves blamed for the reductions. In Homestead, teachers were so disaffected with the administration that they pointedly refused to volunteer for joint meetings. Robert Doherty maintains that indus-trial unions followed a similar path:

> A great many trade unions had also gone through the 'codeter-mination' stage and had learned in the process that the further their demands ranged from traditional trade union objectives, the more divisiveness was created among the membership. Teacher organizations are no less politicized than private-sector unions, the membership of teacher organizations are by no

means of one mind about what constitutes a good curriculum or a sound student discipline policy. Nor do teacher leaders, any more than trade unionists, want to face the political consequences of having helped frame a policy that turned out badly. [18]

The pressure for involvement in governance abates as both parties turn their attention to real problems as opposed to principles of participation.

Scope as 'Management Rights'

At the legislative level, concern over the scope of bargaining is expressed chiefly in terms of preserving the policy-making rights of elected public officials. In contrast, the school districts see the issue as preserving managerial flexibility and discretion. Because the locus of a decision and the outcome of that decision are closely linked, labor vies with management as each tries to move decisions into the arena where its potential influence is greatest. Management, for its part, attempts to hold on to the discretion associated with bureaucratic or administrative decision-making. Since these are precisely the areas of decision-making that impinge most deeply on the autonomy of the individual teacher, labor counters by seeking to broaden the scope of bargaining.

The scope of bargaining does expand, and bargaining effects policy. [19] However, where bargaining affects the curriculum or the technology of teaching it almost does so by indirection, and the policy impacts of contract come as spillovers, unforeseen consequences of fairly ordinary industrial union decisions about pay, hours, job classification, working conditions, and duties associated with each job. [20] Thus, what we have in the Second Generation is *accidental policy* which often goes unrecognized even as it is being made.

Bargaining as a Process

Just as contracts were seized upon as *the* answer to problems of teacher representation, negotiation was seized upon as *the* process. As a school district enters collective bargaining, it gives great attention to the basic structure of bargaining, which is treated as an implementation problem in much the same way as the district routinely treats other statutory dictates such as changes in categorical funding or new requirements for vocational education. School districts, like other bureaucracies, 'handle' problems by assigning responsibility for them; in the case of collective bargaining this responsibility often goes to some hapless Assistant Superintendent for personnel or business who has no previous experience with bargaining.

In the Late Second Generation, the explicit structures for bargaining — the bargaining team, scheduled meetings, and protocols for interaction — become less important than the ongoing interactions between elites. As one union leader put it, 'It's mostly just him and me. We could settle in thirty minutes, but it takes six months to bring the rest of the folks along'. Coming to agreement within the organization often proves more difficult than coming to agreement across the table, and union bargainers fear rejection of contracts by their teachers more than they doubt their ability to reach agreement with their counterparts in management. The bargaining relationship, in essence, becomes the rationale for a much broader set of interactions. The differences between the Early and the Late Second Generation, in terms of the bargaining process, can be viewed from three perspectives: the question of public access, the change in the symbolic meaning of bargaining, and the development of bargaining norms.

The Public Access Question

The public's right to interact in the bargaining process is a bigger issue in education than in almost any other theater of public-sector labor relations. Indeed, as was pointed out earlier, limitations on the scope of bargaining were envisioned as a means of protecting the public's interest. During the Early Second Generation, extensive efforts are made to structure negotiations so that the public has a continuing flow of information from, and ready access to, the process. For example, California's labor statute requires public disclosure of the topics for bargaining and public hearings on those topics. These public access provisions were written and backed by the state's League of Women Voters; and in two of our study districts, citizen organizations associated with the League had worked hard to develop procedures for citizen interaction in teacher bargaining.

Since our interest in this research was initially spurred by the public disclosure aspects of California's statute, we were surprised to discover, in the course of the study, how often the mechanisms for public participation go unused and how inconsequential public input tends to be. Indeed, the very people who press hardest to establish standards for public involvement seem to lose interest in the hearing process, once the ground rules are agreed upon.

According to the conventional wisdom that evolves during the Second Generation, the fewer the participants, the easier it will be to reach agreement. Thus, participation is actively discouraged: 'I have tried as hard as I can to keep it out of the community, and we were totally successful on that last year' [I:21:B]. Gradually, citizen activists are socialized to the norms of privatization. In one district, a prominent activist who had been trying to gain access to the bargaining process for a number of years was elected to the school board. Once on the board, however, she did not take a particularly active role in bargaining, nor did she advocate a strong role for the citizen. 'We kept things quiet last year', she said, 'and it was the easiest settlement we ever had. We're going to do the same thing this year'. In the final stage of this evolutionary process, even the propriety of allowing outsiders to influence the bargaining is questioned.

The Changing Meaning of 'Bargaining'

The move from public deliberation to private conversation is facilitated by a symbolic change in the meaning of the negotiations process. At the outset of the Second Generation, collective bargaining is viewed as the fulfillment of the revolution, the stuff for which the First Intergenerational Conflict was fought. Teachers vie for a chance to 'get to the table'. Soon, however, the newness wears off, and bargaining comes to be seen as a tedious chore best left to the experts.

The early days of bargaining constitute an intense period of training in which labor relations professionals, usually attorneys with little public school experience, disseminate the new standards for labor relations practice. More than a few modest law practices have benefited richly from this trend, leading one nonattorney member of California's Public Employment Relations Board to dub the state's bargaining law, a 'Lawyers Unemployment Protection Act'.[21]

Bargaining Norms

Genuine expertise grows rapidly, and with expertise comes strong belief about practice. The parties learn both from their environments and from their experiences; they copy other successful districts, and they respond to their own successes and failures. Early in the bargaining relationship, a bargainer's definition of a 'good' contract has its roots outside the school district in question. Both management and labor are substantially influenced by their training and personal beliefs, as well as by their knowledge of contract settlements in surrounding districts and practices in the private sector. Their bargaining priorities are determined primarily by these external influences rather than by any consideration of the problems facing their particular school district. This copycat behavior accounts for the high degree of similarity or 'institutional isomorphism' found among schools and for the ability of labor professionals to transmit these behaviors. [22]

As bargaining continues through a number of contracts, negotiators gain the skill to determine what contract modifications they really need: they also develop a sense of the emotional or symbolic content of particular offers or demands. Take the negotiation of binding arbitration of grievances, for example. There tends to be a movement from opposition on ideological grounds to acceptance on pragmatic ones. In the early period, superintendents typically say, 'If we ever give that away, they can have the whole store; I couldn't manage a school district that way.' But later on they change their view:

> Hey, before binding arbitration, we had a lot of grievances because it was a hassle [to the administration]...Now it has to be before an arbitrator and it was going to cost them [the teachers] $500 every time they go [C:19:S].

In our study, we found that misperceptions about the meaning and intent of the opposing team were widespread, but the risks of misunderstanding were not equally distributed. If teacher organizations appeared confused and incompetent, management tended to excuse them as either 'inexperienced' or 'not representative' of the teachers as a whole. In contrast, when management negotiators showed poor judgment or bad faith, teachers tended to interpret this behavior as a glimpse into the 'true character' of the district's managerial leaders. In short, ineptitude on the part of management has much graver consequences than does ineptitude on the part of teacher organizations, in terms of the risk of doing serious damage to working relationships in the district.

Impasse Resolution

No issue in public sector labor relations is more controversial than the right to strike. The academic conversation over public sector rights to strike has extended over the better part of the two decades; and, as with many academic conversations, events have had a tendency to overtake it. Yale University law professors Harry Wellington and Ralph Winter framed the legal argument for restricting the right to strike: If teachers are allowed to strike, 'they may possess a disproportionate share of effective power in the process of decision', and such power would 'skew the results of the "normal American political process"'.[23] Other interest groups, they argued, do not have the same level general interest or the sustained influence. On the contrary, opponents replied, the right to strike is preferable to union support for the political patronage system which results if unions are not allowed an economic weapon.[24] Those who would restrict the right to strike argued further that public employees provided essential services whose interruption endangered public health and safety. Nonsense, said their opponents, employees of private subcontractors performing the same functions — such as garbage collectors and bus drivers — are freely given the right to strike. As for schools, they take two-month vacations anyway.

State legislation generally prohibits strikes. Only ten states provide a limited right to strike, and in these states the right to strike is usually contingent on first exhausting conciliatory procedures.[25] However, there is a tendency for strikes to be legally tolerated even though they are not legally permitted. Strikes occur: an average of 145 a year nationwide for the years 1972–1980.[26] Strike prohibitions and the non-binding impasse resolution such as mediation, fact finding, or advisory arbitration have been generally ineffective.[27] However, the strike weapon has proven to be less than overpowering, and unions have grown cautious about its use. They have also become more accepting of binding interest arbitration, some form of which is allowed in nineteen states.[28] The National Education Association, for instance, supports both the right to strike and binding interest arbitration as means to break bargaining impasses.[29]

Regardless of national union views, each school district must come to terms with the strike question for itself. Early Second Generation unions have a tendency to strike — some would say because they don't know how to prevent strikes — and to put great emphasis on preparing for and winning strikes. Riverview's four strikes during the Early Second Generation were a source of pride to the union leadership. Although Thresher Unified experienced only one strike, it is still a source of conversation in the district with people trying to decide who won what.

In the Late Second Generation, school districts and unions come to eschew strikes, adopting the view that 'there are no winners'. This perspective is reinforced by professional norms which hold that a strike is a sign of mismanagement on the part of both the district and the union. Instead, they seek and utilize strike alternatives. Our study districts were characterized not so much by strikes as by the sometimes habitual use of fact-finding and mediation.[30] So great was the fear of overt job action that districts often failed to realize that a bargaining season which drags on months and sometimes becomes a year-round activity also has high costs.[31]

Contract Administration

Labor contracts require a means of authoritative implementation, and the American structure of enforcing contracts is the grievance. On the face of it, the right to grieve adds teeth to the contract: It provides a means of forcing that which has been agreed upon and defining that which is vague. But the grievance clause does far more. The right to grieve socializes teachers into using the teacher organization to resolve work-related problems. It establishes a new authority system at the school-site level and a communication system that often bypasses the building principal. Among the teachers we studied, the decision to use the grievance process rather than the decision to strike was the first expression of militancy and involvement in the union. Other teachers served an enabling function by supporting or urging the filing of grievances. As one grandmotherly type was overheard to say in a teachers' lounge, 'Honey, you don't have to put up with that horse poo anymore; you can file a grievance'.

Because of the grievance mechanism, the union building representative takes on importance as an alternative to the Principal for problem-solving and for communicating with the central office. And just as the evaluation mechanism has historically been a means by which the Principal disciplines and socializes teachers, so the grievance mechanism has become a means by which teachers socialize and discipline principals. Even the threat of a grievance can be powerful, as we found at one of our largest city school sites. Our initial impression was that relations there were remarkably pacific. In fact, only four written grievances had been filed that year. We soon discovered, however, that the district maintained a full-time employee whose sole function was to answer complaints and resolve disputes before they became grievances. Thus, even the threat of a grievance was enough to enlist the intervention of a central office staff member in modifying the behavior of the school Principal.

Grievances are also powerful agenda builders. In a world where managerial time and attention are scarce, the ability to file a grievance — which under the terms of contract, requires an answer — is a potent attention-getter. Grievances work their way into the agenda whether the administration wants them to or not. In addition, they are a medium of communication, signaling discontent and pointing to problem areas in the district. Particularly in smaller school districts, they quickly gain the attention of the Superintendent and the school board.

Finally, the grievance clause enables teachers to engage in what James Kuhn calls 'fractional bargaining'.[32] That is, small work groups can negotiate for themselves to win changes in work rules or working conditions. Most complaints can be couched in terms of health or safety violations or of unilateral changes in working conditions, both of which are generally grievable. Thus, teachers whose contracts include a strong grievance clause have substantial leverage when they approach principals to talk informally about changes they would like to see at the school. A grievance, if filed, is costly to the Principal's time and in some districts brings negative attention to the school site. (In one of the study sites, however, management applauded grievances seeing them as the hallmark of backbone and managerial aggressiveness.)

The Seeds of Change

At the beginning of his work on conflict, Ralf Dahrendorf puzzles over the observation that 'social structures as distinct from most other structures are capable of producing within themselves elements of their supercession and change'.[33]

We are faced with the same puzzle here. During the Second Generation, the familiar structures of collective bargaining are introduced, and school districts adapt to them, sometimes halting, sometimes painfully. Gradually, these mechanisms undergo a social reconstruction: they are turned to the use of school districts and to the support and stability of the current leadership. Words and actions take on new and shared meaning, conflict is effectively managed, and the parties involved are generally pleased with what they have created.

But Dahrendorf's seeds of change are planted. Their germination is illustrated by the case of Riverview, where the superintendent and the union leadership worked together to shape collective bargaining in such a way as to bring about a referendum for a much-needed tax increase.

As was pointed out earlier in this chapter, changing demographics changed school politics in Riverview. At one time, school board candidates were drawn primarily from the downtown business hierarchy, whose self-interest was generally compatible with the concept of quality education. This pattern began to change more than a decade before our study, as bedroom communities began to pop up around the central city and as many of the business proprietors and corporate executives moved to more socially prestigious communities outside the school district, commuting to work in the central city. The civic elite disintegrated and was replaced by an unstable coalition of four active groups: the *community elites* representing Riverview's old families and traditional economic interests, *the teacher union*; a collection of *watchdog groups* seeking lower taxes, better management, or some particular kind of education; a *citizens advisory council* representing professional and business interests.

The teacher union became an unusually potent force in school board electoral politics because it could mobilize a precinct-level political organization complete with poll lists, phone banks, precinct walkers, and rides to the voting booth. But its electoral activity has begun to produce a backlash. Prior to the time of our study, the board of education was always split over the issue of teacher contractual rights. The union was perceived as fighting only for its right to pursue just wages and working conditions through a contract. In 1978, however, a union-supported candidate upset an incumbent board member. The new board member carried the flag openly for 'teacher issues' and 'woke up the public and made them realize just how much power the teachers had gained'. During the same year, the union supported a successful candidate for the state senate and an unsuccessful candidate for city clerk. These activities were widely interpreted as being an attempt to extend the influence of the teacher organization into areas that were beyond its rightful purview.

Before 1978, all candidates who had teacher support were successful. Since 1978, all successful candidates have been elected without teacher support. The board still includes three members who were elected with the support of the teacher union, but it does not control their votes. Moreover, one of these board members will not run again, and another may eschew union support and endorsement in seeking re-election. Of more general concern to the union, however, is the critical turn that internal board politics has taken with respect to labor relations. Critics of the union were never able to marshall the votes necessary to break the union, but they have gained support around the theme of 'undue policy influence'. The contract is seen as too extensive. As the board President put it:

> I don't mind teachers making good money, but they should not have a contract which dictates policy to the board. If I had my way, I would reduce all their protections to one page. If we did this, the teachers would still be adequately protected, but the Board of Education could still determine policy.

It has become apparent in Riverview that the intergenerational struggle that legitimated collective bargaining did not legitimate teacher access to the policy dimensions of education. Even though relationships between the Superintendent and union President were accommodative and productive, an explicit role for the union in educational matters was the subject of political opposition.

Notes

1 PERRY, C.R. and WILDMAN, W.A. (1970) *The Impact of Negotiations in Public Education: Evidence From the Schools*, Worthington, OH, Charles A. Jones Publishing Co., p. 218.
2 BERGER, P.L. and LUCKMAN, T. (1967) *The Social Construction of Reality*, Garden City, NY, Anchor Press.

3 CHAMBERLAIN, N.W. (1948) *The Union Challenge to Management Control*, New York, Harper and Row, p. 72.
4 WELLINGTON, H.H. and WINTER, JR., R.K. (1971) *The Unions and The Cities*, Washington; DC, Brookings Institution, p. 137.
5 ROBERTS, H.S. (1971) *Roberts' Dictionary of Industrial Relations*, Washington, D.C., Bureau of National Affairs, p. 46.
6 DUNLOP, J.T. (1958) *Industrial Relations Systems*, New York, Holt.
7 GOLDSCHMIDT, S., BOWERS, B., RILEY, M. and STUART, L. (1984) *The Extent and Nature of Educational Policy Bargaining*, Eugene, OR, Center for Educational Policy and Management, University of Oregon.
8 The Agency Shop, a requirement to pay a fee for the union's services, has become the public sector equivalent of the Union Shop, a requirement that one actually becomes a member of the union as a condition of continued employment.
9 The history of labor relations before an enforceable right to union recognition or contract enforcement strongly support the idea that labor's strength lies in a legally protected right to negotiate. See for instance: CHAMBERLAIN, N.W., CULLEN, D.E. and LEWIN, D. (1980) *The Labor Sector*, (3rd edn) New York, McGraw-Hill, p. 109.
10 SELZNICK, P. (1980) *Law, Society, and Industrial Justice*, New Brunswick, N.J, Transaction Books, pp. 52–62.
11 *Ibid.*, p. 54.
12 *Steelworkers v. Warrior & Gulf*, 363 U.S. 574, 578–579.
13 SELZNICK, P. (1980) *op cit*, p. 152.
14 WOLLETT, D.H. and CHANIN, R.H. (1974) *The Law and Practice of Teacher Negotiations*, Washington, D.C, Bureau of National Affairs, p. VI-43.
15 For a review of the sovereignty doctrine see: HANSLOW, K. (1967) *The Emerging Law of Labor Relations*, Ithaca, NY, Institute of Labor Relations Press, p. 10f.
16 *California Government Code*, Section 3543.2
17 PERRY, C.R. and WILDMAN, W. (1970) *op cit*, p. 166.
18 DOHERTY, R.E. (1969) 'Labor relations negotiations on bargaining: Factories vs. the schools' in CARLTON, P.W. and GOODWIN, H.L. (Eds) (1969) *The Collective Dilemma: Negotiations in Education*, Worthington, OH, Jones, p. 221.
19 Bargaining expands through the judicial interpretation of statutes, through the interaction of labor and management, through the integration of new norms into the practice of teaching. For a review of the issue see: KERCHNER, C.T. (1978), 'From scopes to scope: The genetic mutation of the school control issue', *Education Administration Quarterly* 14, 1, Winter, pp. 64–79.
20 Among the major contract analysis studies: MCDONNELL, L. and PASCAL, A. (1979) *Organized Teachers in American Schools*, Santa Monica, CA, Rand; GOLDSCHMIDT, S. *et al*, (1984) *op cit*; SIMPKINS, E., MCCUTCHEON, A. and ALEC, R. (1960) 'Arbitration and policy issues in school contracts', *Education and Urban Society*, 11, 2, pp. 241–54; EBERTS,

R. and STONE, J. (1984) *The Effect of Collective Bargaining on American Education*, Lexington, MA, Lexington Books, D.C. Heath; JOHNSON, S.M., NELSON, N. and POTTER, S. (1985) *Teacher Unions, School Staffing, and Reform*, Cambridge, MA, Harvard Graduate School of Education.

21 GONZALEZ, R. (1978) 'New decision makers in education', *Sacramento Bee*, 15 January.

22 For a conceptual argument see: DIMAGGIO, P.J. and POWELL, W.W. (1983) 'The iron cage revisited: Institutional isomorphism and collective rationality in organization fields', *American Sociological Review*, 48, April, pp. 147–60.

23 WELLINGTON, H.H. and WINTER, JR. R.K. (1969), 'The limits of collective bargaining in public employment', *Yale Law Journal*, 78, 7, June, pp. 1107–27.

24 BURTON, JR. J.F. and KRIDER, C. (1970) 'The role and consequences of strikes by public employees', *The Yale Law Journal*, 79, 3, January, pp. 418–33.

25 FINCH, M. and NAGEL, T.W. (1984) 'Collective bargaining in the public schools: Reassessing labor policy in an era of reform', *Wisconsin Law Review*, 6, December pp. 1573–670, p. 1582. By supreme court decision in 1985, California teachers were determined to have no legal bar to striking. MORGAN, D. (1985) 'Public employees win strike right', *Los Angeles Times*, 14 May, p. 1.

26 *Ibid.*, p. 1583.

27 *Ibid.*,. p. 1585; MCDONNELL, L. and PASCAL, A. (1979) *op cit*, p. 63.

28 *Ibid.*, p. 1585.

29 NATIONAL EDUCATION ASSOCIATION, (1983) *NEA Handbook*, Washington, D.C, National Education Association, resolution E2.

30 FEUILLE, P. (1975). 'Final-offer arbitration and the chilling effect', *Industrial Relations*, 14, pp. 302–10.

31 KERCHNER, C.T. (1983) 'Bargaining costs in public schools: A preliminary assessment', *California Public Employment Relations*, 41 pp. 1–22; (1983) 'Correlates of collective bargaining process costs in California public education', *Collective Negotiations* 12, pp. 311–26.

32 KUHN, J. (1961) *Bargaining in Grievance Settlement*, New York, Columbia University Press.

33 DAHRENDORF, R. (1959) *Class and Class Conflict in Industrial Society*, Stanford, CA, Stanford University Press, p. viii.

7
Movement Toward the Third Generation: The Unexpected Crisis

According to conventional labor relations wisdom, and under theories of accommodation, the Second Intergenerational Conflict isn't supposed to happen. Social theories of accommodation posit long periods of stability, marginal adjustment and changes through negotiation within an established social order. But our generational theory, based on evidence from the schools, suggests that the Second Generation can have a relatively short lifespan — less than a decade — and that increased political conflict at the end of the Second Generation challenges the basic definition of labor relations in as fundamental a way as the conflict that introduced collective bargaining. Thus, the Second Intergenerational Conflict presents a special challenge to teacher unions, a challenge that resurrects the issue of the connection between policy and labor relations.

By way of introduction, we will first tell the story of a school district's passage through the Second Intergenerational Conflict period. Next, we will consider the question of generalizing one school district's experiences to others. And, finally, we will discuss the unique challenge that the Second Intergenerational Conflict poses to unions and management, but especially to unions.

Industrial City: Finding the Third Generation

With a total enrollment of just under 4000 students, Industrial City High School District includes two comprehensive schools and a vocational high school. The district boundaries cover two adjoining suburbs, one with a strong working-class heritage and another — somewhat newer, more middle-class town homes. Although the towns' populations vary economically, the two have a strong ethnic heritage and substantial family and community cohesion. A large proportion remain in the community after high school graduation or return to it after college. A majority of the board members and citizens we interviewed were born and raised in the same neighborhoods as their parents, and they view the schools as an extension of neighborhood and family culture. This attitude has two consequences. First, the quality of schooling is judged by the perceived fit between the schools and the community. As one interviewee put it, 'The schools here are pretty good. I went there and did okay, and I know that my child must be learning more than I did'. Second, influence and authority in the schools derive from personal association and tradition. As one respondent put it: 'Knowing who to see to get things done means a lot here'.

School board elections and partisan politics have been intertwined in Industrial City for many years. The connection partly reflects a politics of distribution among the district's two comprehensive high schools each of which is located in a different community, one Democrat and one Republican. Although school board candidates do not run under party labels, their associations with the party system are well known.

In the years prior to the mid-1960s the potential divisiveness of this political structure was held in check by an informal body called the community caucus, which virtually selected school board members. The caucus was overseen by a powerful local politician who maintained sufficient influence with both parties to be viewed as evenhanded in nominating members of each party to the school board. There was seldom a successful challenge to caucus candidates.

Industrial City also has a well-established teacher union. Formed fifteen years before our study, it has been a powerful force in the district ever since. In fact, no-one remembers for sure when bargaining started, but veterans in the school district recall informal agreements dating back to the 1940s. In the mid-1960s, when the school board announced that it would no longer meet with the teachers informally, the teachers formed a union. At about the same time an Illinois court handed down a decision that allowed school districts to recognize unions, and after a short strike the teacher union won recognition.

Just after the teacher's strike in 1966, the caucus system disintegrated to be replaced by a narrow 4–3 Democrat-controlled school board majority that would last for a decade. Partisan politics became overt, and it was generally represented to us that positions, from principal to janitor, were filled on the basis of a candidate's political loyalty and acceptability.

Within this framework a Late Second Generation relationship developed relatively quickly. It was built upon the allowance of political patronage in hiring and promotion and upon continuing factionalism in the school board itself. The school board was very receptive to teacher proposals. Contracts were generally easily negotiated and gave individual teachers substantial autonomy. For instance, contract clauses forbade evaluation of tenured teachers, prohibited management from altering the school day without teacher permission, and created a seniority system which eventually led to serious imbalances between available teaching specialties and student demand.

But more than the contract itself, the continuing factionalism of the school board resulted in close interpersonal relationships. Both union leaders and individual teachers had direct access to school board members. The board picked what were described as weak administrators and fired them frequently; thus, there were six superintendents in the space of a decade. As one union leader put it: 'Management in the past has been afraid to make decisions because they faced getting fired. The union had to be strong to make this place operate on all eight cylinders'. The union's growing access and influence particularly angered the school principals who perceived the relationship as collusion between the union and board.

After a decade of raucous controversy between the two school board factions, the public finally reacted. Rumors about school board irregularities had been circulating for some time: rumors about favoritism in administrative promotions and custodial employment, failure to use a bid-letting system for some district purchases, and advantageous placement on the salary schedule through overly 'generous' counting of post-baccalaureate education credits. By 1975 local newspapers were carrying almost-daily stories highlighting charges and counter-charges. Irregularities in bid-letting for a new building were alleged, and board members were accused of pressuring administrators to make purchases from particular suppliers.

In that same year, three independent candidates not aligned with either political party were elected to the school board. Within the next two years, three other board members resigned. As a result, the school board was dominated by new members, who clearly felt that they had a mandate to reform the schools. However, the new board was not made of new-broom-sweeps-clean members. They were steeped in Industrial City's labor tradition, and they were by no means anti-union. Nor were they out to reform the political party system. Their intent was simply to make the schools work.

While the theme of 'chaos in the school district' ran through all their campaigns, the new school board members did not represent a grand coalition; nor were they all backed by the same central community organization. Just as importantly, in their campaigns, the new board majority did not run against the teacher union. Only after the election did they come to see reform of labor relations as an important task. One board member commented:

> I don't think that the people who ran had any knowledge to any great extent of what they were getting into when they ran other than they wanted to rectify what they considered a fault in the district. They didn't know how to accomplish that when they first sat on the board. I didn't know what the [teachers'] contract looked like before I got on the board.

But after the election the diffuse feelings of dissatisfaction crystalized into a drive for strong, aggressive administration.

The old Superintendent, who was characterized as 'waiting to retire' was allowed to wait no longer, and the board set about employing an executive who had the skills to 'lead the district rather than observe its movement'. The superintendency search was exhaustive; after a series of interim appointments a new Superintendent was named in the spring of 1978.

The decision to hire the new Superintendent was given direction and impetus by the disgruntled school principals, who sensed that the new board majority would give them a sympathetic hearing. In a position paper, which attributed the district's difficulties to the union's influence, the principals complained about four specific areas of the contract:

> (i) The incorporation of 'school day' language in the contract — i.e., specification of the times when particular periods were to be dismissed as well as the starting and ending times for

the school day itself — had resulted in inflexibility of scheduling. Special events were difficult to schedule and required *ad hoc* negotiations between teacher building representatives and the principals.

(ii) The contract contained language that allowed teachers to grieve policies and practices of the school district as well as the contract itself. Such items as assignment of parking places, for instance, became the subject of grievances. As a result, principals grew timid, feeling that any show of authority on their part would be met with a grievance.

(iii) The contract effectively removed tenured teachers from performance evaluation.

(iv) The contract contained language that limited the principal's ability to assign teachers to extra duties. Prior to the 1966 contract, assignment to duties such as lunchroom supervision was left to the principal's discretion. Since that time, a rotation system had been in effect. According to the principals, this system prevented the assignment of the most effective teachers. According to teachers, the old system had allowed favoritism and an unfair distribution of unpopular duties.

In sum, the principals argued that the new Superintendent should be a person who understands labor relations and who could in their words, 'win back the keys to the store'. The board agreed.

The union leadership was frustrated by the new turn of events and the claim to undue union influence that lay behind them. The leadership had claimed for years that they were forced to be strong because the administration was so weak adding, 'We are just trying to make the system work better like we always have'.

But it was precisely the union's role in making things work better that disturbed both board members and other unionists. One state labor leader criticized the union for getting itself into the position of being accountable for the district's overall performance. He said: 'By being too strong, the teachers became associated with the district's leadership function and eventually were identified as part of the problem when things began to deteriorate... It's a terrible position to be in when labor begins to look like management — that's why we need managers: to take the heat'.

155

Thus, the new Superintendent came to office with what he called a 'mandate from heaven' to get control of the district's internal organization and its labor relations. It is generally agreed that he is tough. He believes in strong line authority, a classic public bureaucracy reinforced by rules, of which the labor contract itself is among the most important. Consequently, he drafted language which would make the contract an explicit instrument of the district's control mechanism.

The union, which had become strong during the decade of managerial drift, was displeased with the new Superintendent's actions. The union President no longer received a copy of the school board member's information packet prior to each meeting, and the board committee system, that had allowed easy teacher lobbying of individual members, was abandoned in favor of a 'committee of the whole' presided over by the Superintendent.

In 1979 the Superintendent went to the bargaining table with his agenda. He wanted to assert management control over the school schedule, over evaluation, and over curricular changes. He coupled his tough demands with an equally tough bargaining stance, offering packages in which management concessions on wage, salary, and working conditions were explicitly linked to labor concessions on contractual language and management control. Further, he suggested to management's chief negotiator (the school board President and an attorney) that he present a new package at each negotiating session on a take-it-or-leave-it basis. The union, which had been accustomed to negotiating over its agenda, was put in the unusual position of having to react to proposals made by others.

At first, union leaders did not take management's proposals seriously. They felt that management was playing games with negotiations, and this angered them. When the union finally realized that management was serious, it could find no way to negotiate its proposals. Management refused to 'open the packages' and negotiate their contents one item at a time, and the union was unable to come up with alternative packages.

After four months of bargaining, the union undertook what its leaders called a 'frustration strike'. With no hope of winning concessions from the school board, it could keep its members out for only three days before settling on what were essentially management's pre-strike terms. Despite the certainty of defeat, the union viewed the strike as necessary to reestablishing solidarity among teachers, who had so long gotten what they wanted without a fight. Even losing a fight was seen as having residual value.

However, the lesson in Industrial City is not that management opposed work rule clauses in the teacher contract and by so doing prevailed in a strike. The significance is that both parties, and management in particular, came to recognize that teacher unions have an influence on educational policy and to recognize that influence as part of the bargaining process rather than through an informal influence network. The key factor is that the union was recognized as a legitimate instrument of educational policy, not that labor and management disagreed over what the policy should be.

Generalizing From Industrial City

Although Industrial City is an unusual setting, we believe the experience of accommodative labor relations degenerating into political conflict over the propriety or efficiency of school operations is not unusual. We believe that Second Intergenerational Conflict is taking place, or will take place in other school districts, and that its dynamics will be similar to those operating in Industrial City, even though the specific issues and coalitions may be different. Evidence for these assertions comes from our own study sample as well as from other school districts. Of the eight case-study districts, two are entering the Second Intergenerational Conflict and one has moved through it into the Third Generation, which we have characterized as the era of negotiated policy. Of the sixty-four districts on which we have survey and interview data, five were classified as Second Intergenerational Conflict districts.

The dynamics of the Second Intergenerational Conflict seem generalizable because they follow precisely the same pattern as applies to districts going through the First Intergenerational Conflict. First, comes an increase in public dissatisfaction. In Industrial City, the community became disenchanted with the factionalism of the old school board. Thus, when new actors appeared on the political stage — candidates drawn from parts of the population that had not been represented before — they were quickly elected to the school board. Much the same thing was happening in Riverview, where the teachers were losing their once-powerful grip on the board, particularly when it came to defining the issues with which the school board should concern itself. These signs were evident in other districts as well, such as the one where the union President remarked:

> What's happened is a lot of younger people, professional people, have started having kids, their kids are in school, and this group has come in [to school board meetings.] It amounts to 10–12 people who want everything changed yesterday. We have chosen as a group not to get involved with them at all [I:9:T].

In other words, if these new people want to have their views known, they will have to organize politically.

Second, comes explicit criticism of the old order. In Industrial City, the new board members — even though they did not run as a political slate — coalesced around a single idea: the rediscovery of a general, common interest and the repudiation of special interests. Similar events were taking place in Riverview, with the addition that identified groups were supporting school board candidates. In political theory terms, this suggests that the aggregation of the polity had already begun.

The third element in the pattern is an overt battle in which the lines of political cleavage are redrawn. Once in office, the new Industrial City school board embraced a new idea about labor relations when it explicitly linked managerial policy with collective bargaining. Its open conflict with the teacher union represented a new alignment of interests rather than a power tussle along the old cleavage lines. The symbols of efficiency and propriety that played such a powerful role in Industrial City are emerging in other districts as well. No longer is labor peace enough. In the words of one respondent: 'Community pressures are to find peace without reference to price...but the trend is in the direction of peace on good terms' [I:15:S]. In a sense, Second Generation unionism is being asked to perform well beyond its original charter. It is being asked to respect the interests of the commonweal as well as to advance the interests of the teachers.

The Second Intergenerational Conflict As a Challenge to Unions and Management

Looking beyond our sample, we find substantial anecdotal evidence of rising dissatisfaction with the patterns of Second Generation unionism and of pressures to explicitly connect labor relations with school policy.

Of course, some of the criticism comes from people who just plain don't like teacher's unions. Others, such as Myron Lieberman, who once ran for the AFT presidency, have recanted their earlier beliefs and now conclude, 'all things considered, the conventional ways of resolving public-sector labor disputes prior to public-sector bargaining were better for our society'.[1] Other critics claim that unions are out of control, that they have damaged schools by asking for too much and by directing attention away from the fundamental questions surrounding education. As Grimshaw argues in his book about the Chicago Teachers' Union, 'not only has the mayor's office lost much of its ability to influence management but management is losing much of its ability to influence labor'.[2] The result, he argues, is a government which is neither powerful nor responsive. Embedded in this critique is a tacit expectation that unions *ought* to function as commonweal organizations displaying public-regarding behavior rather than the single-minded pursuit of self-interest. The critique is important because it legitimates political opposition to the current mode of labor relations — the current *idea of a teachers' union*.

Opposition grows partly from the politicization of school boards, the breakdown of the idea that schools were properly ruled by blue-ribbon elites as trustees for the entire community. Teachers have supported board candidates and applauded the breakdown of the club-like relationship between these board members and school administrators; but, as we have seen, politically interested school board members are also a threat to close relationships between unions and the school board.[3]

But it is primarily the movement toward school reform that convinces us that the Second Generation is not the last stage in the development of school labor relations. School reformers have taken center stage redefining the politics of education, and the impetus for changes in school operations and teaching work comes from them. Although virtually none of the reformers have succeeded in explicitly altering collective bargaining, any substantive reform involves existing relationships with unionized employees. The reformers have come to realize that educational policy cannot be removed from union contracts. Division of resources and establishment of work rules *is* educational policy.

Either unions or management can be politically cast as 'the problem'. In Industrial City, the initial unseating of school board members had nothing to do with the teacher union, but the new board came to focus on the union when it attempted to more overtly manage the district. In some cases, the teacher union itself is the prime mover in altering the basis of labor relations. Although none of our study districts exhibited this characteristic, the history of labor relations in other districts points to cases where unions initiated the changed relationship. In Toledo, Ohio, a bitter strike, and a change in management negotiators, paved the way for acceptance of a long-standing union negotiation demand that teachers be empowered to review their own performance. This change in the bargaining climate, in turn, led to a far reaching plan for peer review and assistance.

The pressure of reform constitutes a crisis for both labor and management. Each can be cast in the role of the spoiler, blocking desirable changes and pursuing narrow interests. But the crisis is particularly acute for unions. Reformers, then, like the school board in Industrial City, become the active agents suggesting that unions are standing in the way of educational excellence reforms.[4]

The structure of the Second Generation was specifically designed to prevent collective bargaining from having policy impacts, and (as suggested in chapter 6) most teachers' unions abandon their 'codetermination' stance and accept the industrial union adage that it is management's job to manage. The unions now find that the fundamental assumptions on which they built Second Generation labor relations are being called into question.

Other Images of the Third Generation

Although Industrial City was the only Third Generation district among the districts we studied, changes in the central idea of unionism in other districts around the country leave us with little doubt that the Third Generation of teacher unionism is emerging.

In 1981, the Toledo Federation of Teachers contractually agreed to establish peer review in a public school system thus instituting a form of evaluation in which teachers would assess the work of other teachers. Teacher judgments would be important in determining which novice teachers would be continued and which senior teachers had developed such serious problems that their continued employment should be challenged.[5] The agreement was wildly controversial at the time, and in many quarters remains so today. The idea of recasting unionism around the unique organizational roles of employed professionals was supported by Albert Shanker and the American Federation of Teachers.[6]

While less explicitly linked to changes in collective bargaining, the National Education Association has launched an ambitious school reform project in twenty-seven schools nationwide involving over 20,000 students and 2000 teachers. Entitled the NEA Mastery in Learning Project, it invokes many of tenets of effective schools research including school-level plans and research-based approaches to learning and teaching.[7]

Examples of these new relationships have begun to appear in the anecdotal literature on teacher unions:

1 In Rochester, the administration and union have agreed to a new career ladder plan for teachers, one that departs from the traditional seniority and college credits plan for teacher pay.

2 In Miami-Dade County, the union and school district are experimenting with shared decision making as a means to bring large-scale change to schools that have undergone rapid demographic change.

3 In Pittsburgh, the union has introduced a teacher professionalism project to change the nature of supervision and evaluation of teachers.

4 In Hammond, Indiana, union and management have developed a school site management system that gives increased authority to schools and teachers.

5 In Old Westbury, New York, teachers are involved in selection of their colleagues.

6 In Duluth, teachers are experimenting with Quality Circles as a means of problem solving.

7 In Petaluma, and five other California cities, teachers and unions are experimenting with a new form of broad-scope labor agreement called an Educational Policy Trust Agreement, which we describe in chapter 11.

Although these reforms are not of a single type, they share common characteristics. Each accepts and continues collective bargaining. At the same time, in some sense, each represents what Albert Fondy, President of the Pittsburgh Federation of Teachers, called 'the need to go beyond collective bargaining'.[8] These new labor relations practices appear to depart from three primary assumptions in Second Generation good-faith collective bargaining: the problem of public confidence in public education as an institution, the problem of making labor relations work toward producing effective school organizations, and the problem of consciously linking unionism and the definition of teaching work.

Institutional concern means understanding the link between public perception and continued support for public education as an institution. In Fondy's words, 'If we're going to have public (taxpayer) support, we have to obtain results that are satisfactory...'[9] Such statements are substantially different from the ancient admonition that teacher dedication will be recognized and rewarded. The unions maintain collective bargaining and lobbying as important functions, but they also know that institutional confidence is highly important to their success.

Notes

1 LIEBERMAN, M. (1980) *Public-Sector Bargaining*, Lexington, MA, Lexington Books, D.C. Heath, p. 162.
2 GRIMSHAW, W.J. (1979) *Union Rule in the Schools*, Lexington, MA, Lexington Books, D.C. Heath, p. 13.
3 BAER, D. (1979) 'The club's last days', *United Teacher*, 11, 13, December, pp. 4–5.
4 FINN JR., C.E. (1983) 'Teacher politics' *Commentary*, 75, February pp. 29–41 and p. 30; SCOTT, K. (1982) 'The case against collective bargaining in public education', *Government Union Review*, 3, pp. 16–25; ELAM, S.M. (1981) 'The National Education Association: Political powerhouse or paper tiger', *Phi Delta Kappan*, 63, pp. 169–74.
5 WATERS, C.M. and WYATT, T.L. (1985) 'Toledo's internship: The teachers' role in excellence', *Phi Delta Kappan*, 66, 5, January, pp. 365–8.
6 SHANKER, A. (1985) *The Making of a Profession*, expansion of a speech delivered to the representative assembly of New York State United Teachers, 27 April, Washington, D.C, American Federation of Teachers.
7 NATIONAL EDUCATION ASSOCIATION, (n.d.) *The Mastery in Learning Project*, Washington, D.C., NEA.
8 FONDY, A. (1987) *The Future of Public Education and the Teaching Profession in Pennsylvania*, Philadelphia, PA, Pennsylvania Federation of Teachers, p. 7.
9 *Ibid.*, p. 5.

8
The Second Generation and School Governance

This chapter, and the two that follow, examine the ways Second Generation, good-faith bargaining relationships impact education. Each of the three chapters offers a retrospective analysis of Second Generation impacts and a prospective essay that anticipates and examines issues and policy responses to the Third Generation. We emphasize Second Generation unionism because it represents the most common stage of development and because its ideas and practices are widely accepted.

Each of the three chapters is similarly constructed. Each looks at a problem commonly attributed to the onset of collective bargaining, but one that we feel the labor relations system has effectively solved. Then, each chapter examines a problem that remains unsolved, an unexpected consequence of Second Generation unionism that becomes one of the driving forces toward the Third Generation.

The Governance Question: Democracy and Public Confidence

Second Generation industrial unionism poses two fundamental problems for the governance of public schools: democratic control and the effective pursuit of public goals. The first of these problems is widely recognized, but poorly understood. It is commonly asserted that teacher unionism threatens democracy by undermining the sovereignty of local school boards. We believe this assertion to be incorrect.

There are three basic theories of democratic control in schools, and each embodies different indicators of whether school systems adequately protect individual rights while effectively expressing legitimate public interests. If one considers each of these three theories in isolation, one can easily conclude that Second Generation labor relations are antithetical to democracy in school districts. If one considers the three theories in combination over the ebb and flow of labor relations generations, however, one concludes that *labor relations have actively advanced school democracy*. Such is the argument in the first section of this chapter.

The second challenge to school governance posed by Second Generation labor relations is the problem of public confidence. Schools are not simply *political arenas* for the exercise of democracy. They are also *public agencies* through which (more or less democratic) educational policies are (more or less) adequately expressed. When the schools are viewed as public agencies, one must ask whether they forcefully and effectively embody public goals within their day-to-day operations, and whether the public perceives the schools to be well run and under control.[1] This problem is especially acute in the delivery of educational services because effectiveness depends so heavily upon the creation and maintenance of an appropriate cultural milieu or organizational climate within the schools. That this is a problem of school governance is forcefully underscored by the recent spate of national reports critical of the overall performance of the public schools. Clearly, the American polity doubts the ability of the public schools to deliver education effectively, and the unions along with the rest of the educational establishment have been tarred with this brush. We explore this problem in more detail later on in the chapter. Suffice it to say here that managerial control over technology and the bilateral negotiation of work rules — hallmarks of industrial unionism — do not provide an adequate basis for developing effective schools. Effectiveness requires professional autonomy and artistic spontaneity on the part of teachers, and it requires that teacher organizations take responsibility for, and engage actively in, solving educational problems. Linking unionism to school effectiveness is, we will argue, one of the greatest unsolved problems facing public education today.

Schools and the Three Theories of Democratic Control

By challenging the nature of the social order, collective bargaining joins other social forces in undermining the system of administrative domination and elected trustees introduced by the political reform movement in the first two decades of this century. In the process, critics charge, teachers have compromised the rudiments of public democracy. According to this view, collective bargaining distorts the political process by giving labor undue influence over policy, and thereby destroying the accountability of elected representatives to the voters.[2] For some, the new condition represents 'union rule' which Norton Long characterized as 'legitimating a degree of callous selfishness that surpassed that of the managerial elite of reform [government] and even the capacity of the machine'.[3]

We believe the contrary: that unions have served to create a functioning 'ecology of games' (to use another Norton Long phrase) in which the political players move on and off the field of contest depending on their own motivation and the excitement of the conflict.[4] Unionism has aided the political ecology. This conclusion is based on the generational nature of labor relations in education and on the relationship of the generational cycles of conflict and accommodation to the three dominant theories of democratic governance in school districts:

— Informed competition between established elites.
— Responsiveness to potent interests.
— Dissatisfaction and replacement of existing regimes.

The three theories offer different definitions of, and criteria for, democracy, but they are compatible, each accurately reflecting the governance of school districts during some part of the labor generational cycle. Each concerns itself with a different aspect of the political process. To a greater or lesser extent, all three theories derive from an open-systems perspective, where the environment or community enters the political process with demands or supports and thus alters the outputs of the system.[5] One can begin to understand the varying theories by referring to Easton's basic paradigm (figure 9). One first sees the familiar systems characteristics. In political theory terms, system inputs become articulations of interest, in terms of either demands and support or changes in levels of unfocused satisfaction or dissatisfaction. The technology or systems transformation process becomes the political process of interest aggregation within the bargaining and decision-making system. The articulation and aggregation of interests leads to system outputs, rules, laws, contracts, decisions. Each of the

Figure 9: Easton's basic political paradigm

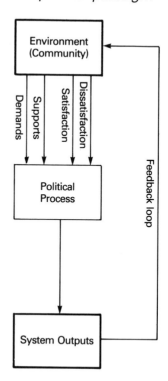

three theoretical perspectives is primarily concerned with a different part of the political system.

Informed Competition Theory

The most recent wave of governance reform literature, and the legacy of 'maximum feasible participation', are consistent with an *informed competition* view of school governance, which concerns itself with interest articulation achieved through open access to information. Under this conception, democracy requires an open flow of information, widespread knowledge of school issues, a lack of exclusionary barriers to participation, and a structure that promotes competition among the players. Such a democratic school system awards positions of authority to those who win the open competition of ideas. This conception of school governance is articulated in the work of David Minar and of Zeigler and Jennings.[6] The almost universal conclusion of those who have studied schools from this perspective is that they are not democratic. Rather, they are deliberately structured to exclude important population segments, and these exclusions have systematic biases so severe as to constitute a kind of the 'taxation without representation' charge.[7]

Given this conclusion, it is not surprising that most citizen-influenced reforms have aimed at facilitating participation of previously excluded groups. For instance, California's 'sunshine provisions' require that the topics of collective bargaining be presented at a public hearing for citizen comment. Similarly, Florida, through judicial decision, requires that bargaining be carried out in public session.[8] In a few isolated instances, direct, structurally legitimated access points for citizen input and participation have been provided.[9]

But generally, as one looks at the bargaining process in schools, one finds that the public access and information structures are underused even when they exist. A 'logic of participation' leads citizens away from direct participation in the bargaining process.[10] Compared with other arenas, bargaining does not appear permeable, efficient or effective to most citizens. In addition, labor and management frequently collude to keep access closed and information scarce, and the protractedness of educational negotiations discourages all but the most hardy citizen watchdogs. Citizens have learned other ways of exercising influence, ways consistent with the other two theories of governance: issue responsiveness and dissatisfaction theory.

Issue Responsiveness Theory

Issue responsiveness concerns itself chiefly with system outputs. Under this conception, a democratic school is one in which system outputs are fair, just, efficient allocations of resources, and hence legitimate ones. What is decided, rather than who participates, is the key: thus, direct participation in bargaining is relatively unimportant. Access to the decision structures is gained through penetration of the *agenda* rather than direct participation in the *arena* where decisions are made. In collective bargaining, this means that issues important to potent interest groups are carried into negotiations by the representatives of labor and management because those representatives understand that the interest group has expectations about the outcomes of negotiations and that the interest group's continuing support is important to the representative's own welfare.

According to responsiveness theory, the critical indicators of a functioning democracy are the existence of potent interest groups (not necessarily officially sanctioned ones), the presence of identifiable demands, and knowledge of the successful achievement of those demands. Interest groups are more concerned with the achievement of their demands than with *where* they are achieved. As long as the desired results are obtained, it makes little difference whether demands are obtained through collective bargaining or by some other means.

In educational politics, issue responsiveness theory is best represented by *The Polity of the School* edited by Frederick Wirt.[11] In labor relations research, Grimshaw's study of the Chicago Teachers' Union and its relationship with the Democratic Party organization is a prime example, as are the several studies involving analysis of contract outputs.[12]

Dissatisfaction Theory

According to dissatisfaction theory, democracy is found essentially in the periodic conflict that surrounds school politics. Flowing from the research of Laurence Iannaccone and Frank Lutz, this theory assumes that the polity has diffuse expectations about its schools and that most of the polity is inactive most of the time. When dissatisfaction mounts, it tends to be directed toward questioning the current elite's legitimacy rather than articulated into specific issues. Thus, most of the empirical work in this tradition has focused on the involuntary turnover of school board members through electoral defeat and the subsequent sacking of the superintendent and other appointed officials.[13]

As most conflict theories suggest, periods of high conflict do not continue indefinitely. Initially, the dissatisfied among the teachers, the community, or the school board promote conflict. Once the symbolic change in leadership or policy take place, however, the new elite moves quickly to routinize relations and contain conflict. Thus, decision-making is much more privatized during periods of low conflict than during periods of high conflict when the normally quiescent are attracted into the fray.[14]

Relationship of Governance Theories to Labor Generations

Each of the three governance theories accurately reflects how school governance works at some point in the conflict cycle which we call a labor relations generation. The indicators of democracy expected by each theory are present during part of each generation when there is an active democratizing force in school governance. However, dissatisfaction theory, which typifies governance during the intergenerational conflict periods, makes a unique contribution to our understanding of school democracy. At the critical moment in the conflict, the political process opens to embrace usually inactive citizens and parents. Their votes count at the critical moment when the new idea of labor relations is being defined and decided.

The fit between the three definitions of democracy and labor relations generations becomes obvious when the two are superimposed (figure 10). The Early Generational Period typifies the use of informed competition criteria for school democracy. Great attention is given to

Figure 10: Labor generations and democratic representation

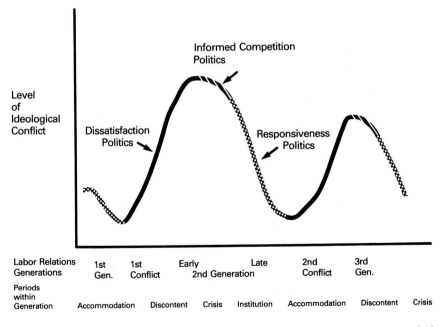

169

setting the rules under which labor relations will be undertaken, to deciding who the legitimate elites will be and how they will compete. Rules and structures are important, and vigorous efforts are made to define them. The study districts in this category were involved in debates over such matters as how to implement California's sunshine law, how to disseminate information to citizens, and who should have access to different aspects of bargaining. Teachers, administrators, and school board members were all embarked on a similar course, each trying to determine who among their ranks should be present and who had the right to present 'their' issues. The teacher unions we studied used elaborate devices to poll their members and elaborate means of choosing bargaining team members.

The informed competition theory is especially pertinent to Early Generation behavior because, like the mandate for the Early Phase, it concerns itself with the requirements for normalizing conflict, containing disagreements, resolving disputes, and reaching agreements. At the same time, the concept of informed competition creates boundaries around access. This is the case because informed competition is a system of representative democracy, and while the fair choice of representatives is important, so too is having representatives occupy positions of substance and authority.

As the Second Generation evolves, districts and unions regularize who may have access to negotiations; and all parties come to believe that conflict must be managed and that decisions are best made as routinely and as privately as possible. At this point, school governance is more accurately described as being responsive to established interest groups. Those who participate in bargaining do so because they are perceived to be 'good at what they do' rather than because they represent a particular faction or group within union or management. At the same time, sub-groups become acutely aware that, while they may not have direct access to the bargaining process, they do have a stake in its outcome. In the districts we studied, athletic coaches concerned with the size of their stipends and psychologists concerned with their case loads quickly discovered that only those with demonstrable political influence were able to affect the labor contract.

As responsiveness behavior spreads through the school district, the number of influential groups stabilizes. Individuals — including principals and school board members — are content to see their interests represented *by others* and less concerned with active, personal participation. The circle of collective bargaining elites narrows. In many cases, potential discontent is cooled out; management is carried out by official response agents (Tom Wolfe's 'flak catchers') or by agendas constructed so that only acceptable answers are allowed.[15] As conflict continues to abate, collective bargaining concerns itself with marginal adjustments to the current contract. Major changes are not sought except under extreme environmental pressure. Thus, in the 1970s as enrollments fell and employees had to be laid off, contracts were expanded to include reduction-in-force provisions which both labor and management deemed necessary.[16] More recently, there has been renewed interest in provisions attracting and socializing new teachers. Such expansion of the contract was not a revolutionary change, but rather an adjustment that made it easier to work within the existing social order.

Because it depends less on official sanctions and more on the resources and organizational ability of constituents, responsiveness activity tends to be more open to changes in participants than does informed competition. Potentially strong but unorthodox interests are often represented. But responsiveness politics also tends to become limiting and exclusionary, as well as organizationally costly to maintain. In settings with multiple interests, coalitions of interests form to achieve favorable settlements.[17] These coalitions, in addition to combining the strength of the partners, reduce the number of issues that can be addressed by eliminating those on which there is internal disagreement.

During the Late Phase of the Second Generation, the political activity surrounding collective bargaining diminishes even farther. Those within the established groups practice the politics of accommodation. Those on the outside have no say in the politics. Governance becomes the 'primary determinant of both the groups that enter the political process and the forms groups take when they do participate'.[18] At the bottom of the conflict curve, school labor relations politics hardly exist at all. Internal interests are legitimated, and schools operate as private governments.[19]

Dissatisfaction theory best explains the way governance operates during the intergenerational periods, when the old idea of labor relations is being challenged and the forces are gathering to promote the new one. The critical importance of the mechanisms of political conflict associated with dissatisfaction theory becomes apparent when one examines the sharp rise in conflict at the end of each generation.

Conflict rises much more quickly than it falls; and as conflict rises from its apolitical nadir, dissatisfaction activity comes into play immediately. In effect, dissatisfaction with the current elites increases because the mechanisms which support responsiveness and informed competition structures become rigid and lose their ability to function. The social exchange relationships on which they rest cease to operate. Exchange processes become fixed status relationships and no longer accommodate changes in the public values or in political influences. Status and position are defended as ends in themselves.

As the relationship between the parties becomes more firmly established, each party invests in the relationship in a number of ways: by collaborating to avoid or downplay conflict and by behaving in ways acceptable to the opposite party.[20] Often, one party will not press an advantage in bargaining to the hilt, knowing that the quality of the relationship may be more important than the specific terms of a contract. In Blau's terms, the relationship becomes one of social exchange: The parties do each other favors without explicit terms of repayment.[21]

Though often highly satisfactory and useful to the participants, these relationships are paradoxical in that social exchange establishes not only bonds of reciprocity, accommodation and obligation but also status differences.[22] In Second Generation labor relations, major status differences develop between the immediate parties to collective bargaining (school administrators and union leaders) on the one hand and those whose interests are supposedly represented in the process (school board members, rank and file teachers, and citizens in general) on the other. In such cases, a dependency relationship replaces normal social exchange.

The difference between a power-dependency relationship and social exchange is an important one. Reciprocity is the criterion by which social exchange is judged. Each party to the exchange asks whether the other has contributed in roughly equivalent ways. A power-dependency relationship is judged by the criterion of fair treatment.[23] The question asked of the ruling social order is not whether it gave as well as it got, but whether its treatment of the less influential was by some standard 'fair'. A social order judged to be fair elicits continued legitimacy and support. One judged to be unfair breeds, 'an opposition ideology... that further justifies and reinforces hostility against existing powers. It is out of such shared discontent that opposition movements develop'.[24]

In school labor relations, the norm of fair treatment is applied in each intergenerational period. In the First Intergenerational Period, teachers find it relatively easy to develop an opposition ideology based on their lack of a voice in their own work lives and the particularistic treatment they received at the hands of administrators. In the Second Intergenerational Period, we have seen the implied limitation placed on the pursuit of self-interest by teachers and administrators. There is a relatively narrow 'zone of tolerance' within which management and labor are allowed to operate according to the norms of social exchange. But those who are excluded from active participation in the process view the labor process and the operation of schools from the vantage of fair treatment.

Both the literature and our research offer some clues as to why the mutually supportive relationship between management and labor in the Late Second Generation is thought to be unfair. The school's political adjustment mechanisms appear to falter for two reasons. First, managers and labor leaders incorrectly interpret a quiet environment to mean that no problems exist. Because they live in a world where time and attention are scarce and where the opportunity cost of not attending to other duties is very high, they tend to discount any symptoms of disquietude, assuming that because there is no active opposition permanent stability has been achieved in labor relations.[25] Second, the current arrangement comes to be seen as so ideologically correct that outsiders are dismissed as 'malcontents, kooks, and social engineers' (in the words of one superintendent in our study). Status and position tend to rigidify. The ruling social order becomes 'so tenacious of its prerogatives that rather than part with any one of them it will often, by blind resistance, invite the loss of all of them.'[26]

When opposition cannot be smoothed, bought out, satisfied, or intimidated, opposition expands and conflict rises. Schattschneider was right: 'The best time to manage conflict is before it starts.'[27]

The Unique Role of the Public

The public's position is unique for two reasons. First, the public joins the conflict just as the issue of whether or not to redefine key labor relations concepts is brought out in the open. Second, because the public is positioned in the center of the political spectrum, it is naturally in a position to cast the deciding ballot.[28]

The pivotal importance of citizens in political conflict situations becomes clear when one examines the responses to our questionnaires about teacher organizations, administration and school boards. Figure 11 summarizes a discriminant function analysis of the questionnaires by role group. No other characteristic — race, sex, political identification, or age — discriminated among the 1082 respondents as well as did their role in the school setting. Teachers, union leaders, principals, superintendents and board members all stood in strong contrast to one another. But whatever these differences, citizens/parents stood in the middle as the crucial swing vote. Figure 11 shows the middle position of citizens/parents' in their perceptions of teacher organizations, school

Figure 11: Parents at the political fulcrum: Role group centroids from multiple discriminant function analyses

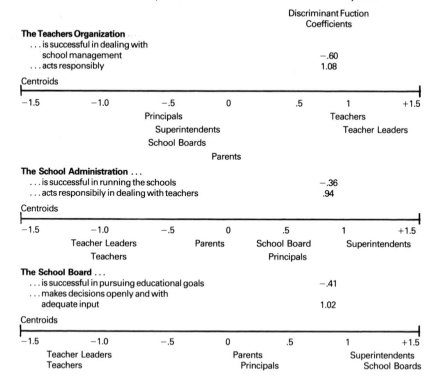

Discriminant Fuction Coefficients

The Teachers Organization
. . . is successful in dealing with school management   −.60
. . . acts responsibly   1.08

Centroids

−1.5	−1.0	−.5	0	.5	1	+1.5
		Principals			Teachers	
		Superintendents			Teacher Leaders	
		School Boards				
			Parents			

The School Administration . . .
. . . is successful in running the schools   −.36
. . . acts responsibily in dealing with teachers   .94

Centroids

−1.5	−1.0	−.5	0	.5	1	+1.5
	Teacher Leaders		Parents	School Board		Superintendents
	Teachers			Principals		

The School Board . . .
. . . is successful in pursuing educational goals   −.41
. . . makes decisions openly and with adequate input   1.02

Centroids

−1.5	−1.0	−.5	0	.5	1	+1.5
	Teacher Leaders			Parents		Superintendents
	Teachers			Principals		School Boards

administration and the school board. In each case, the citizen/parent role group centroid, or the average discriminant function score for each role group, stood between the organized teachers and their leaders and the school boards and superintendents.

For instance, with respect to perceptions of teacher unions, the questions that discriminated best among the six types of respondents were those having to do with success and responsibility. Teachers and union leaders tended to believe that unions were responsible but unsuccessful. Superintendents, principals, and board members believed unions to be successful but irresponsible. Parents/citizens were at a midpoint between the two poles. They were slightly closer to the management end of the axis, but a relatively small shift in attitude would have aligned them with teachers and union leaders.

With respect to perceptions of the school administration, the most discriminating questions, again, had to do with responsibility and success. School administrators believed themselves to be responsible but not particularly successful, whereas teachers and union leaders believed the converse. School board members were slightly closer to the administrators' view, whereas citizens were slightly closer to the teacher's view. Any slight change in the positions of either of these two most public of the role groups — school board members or citizens — would have shifted the weight of public opinion.

With respect to perceptions of school boards, a question about openness was the most discriminating. Teachers and union leaders agreed that school boards were highly secretive organizations, whereas superintendents and board members themselves felt that board decisions were made openly and with adequate input. Again, parents/citizens (this time joined with principals) found themselves on the middle ground.

The pivotal position of the public is underscored by Schatt-schneider in his admonition to 'watch the crowd' whenever a fight breaks out, because the public participates both in the spread and the control of social conflict.[29]

A Do-able Democracy

The unique position of parents and citizens, along with their apparent ability to organize around issues connected with labor relations, produces a crude yet functional democracy that is more robust than other conceptions of democratic control. A school democracy built on informed competition is extraordinarily difficult to sustain because the polity is seldom interested in sustained competition. But the structures of informed competition are important because they help to regularize conflict and enable the school district to proceed with daily operations. School governance built on responsiveness to interest groups is likely to be either unstable (if the interest groups are weak) or undemocratic (if the interest groups are strong enough to freeze out weaker competitors). But the same forces that limit access to decision making, also allow for the 'private government' necessary if higher-order professionalism is to develop — the latitude required for highly trained persons to undertake their work. In contrast, the only requirement of dissatisfaction theory is that the disenfranchised are able to mobilize periodically to 'throw the rascals out'. This democratic process is slow and imperfect. It may appear capricious and harsh on elected and appointed officials caught and frequently sacrificed in a web of conflict not entirely of their making. But taken on balance, the nesting of the three political modes operates to form a useful ecology of governance.[30]

Civic Culture and the Problem of Public Service

Successful school governance requires more than a do-able democracy. The episodic rise and fall of dissatisfaction and labor conflict, which produce an approximation of political equity, fail to address a second major governance problem: maintaining the productive capacity of educational institutions and directing them toward public goals. Unless the public believes that the schools are effective and that they are directed toward broadly advocated public goals, it will not give them stable support. So far, this problem has not been solved. A proper response lies in recreating a civic culture of education and legitimating teacher unions in support of this civic culture.

The Second Generation of labor relations legitimates teacher self-interest. With the advent of collective bargaining, teachers can speak for themselves rather than trusting others to recognize their needs for adequate salaries, decent working conditions, and a measure of industrial jurisprudence. But, the Second Generation does not legitimate teacher union responsibility for the health and welfare of schools as public institutions. Scope-of-bargaining restrictions keep unions at arm's length from school policies. Union proposals designed to cure the ills of public education — the UFT's 'For Better Schools' plan of the 1960s, union involvement in teacher centers in the 1970s, the NEA position on teacher certification in the 1980s — are met with suspicion and with the allegation that these proposals are motivated by little more than shallow and thinly veiled self-interest. School managers and trustees are quick to claim out that *only they* legitimately represent the public trust and that teachers forfeited their standing when they unionized.

Indeed, Second Generation teacher unions find it very difficult to rise above the self-interest of their members in order to address questions of the school's capacity to deliver services and achieve public goals. There are four reasons for this difficulty. First, unions have their own internal politics, which on occasion are as Byzantine and bloody as the politics of national parties. Holding together an organization of individuals who were first attracted by agitation and protest is no easy matter. Union leaders who espouse unpopular positions risk the taint of being 'soft on management' and their careers can be short ones. Second, agreements which satisfy all the factions within the union (or all the divisions within management) tend to be expensive and unwieldly. Bargaining theorists call this the problem of 'side payments'.[31] Third, union leaders tend to act in support of schools as institutions either so privately that their participation goes unnoticed or so conspicuously that their motives are questioned. Union leaders who counsel teachers to accept early retirement rather than face disciplinary dismissal (as happened in several of our study districts) dare not make this advice public. Those who advocate better schools and better teachers are labeled as unrealistic and incapable of grappling with the thorny problem of limited resources. Finally, union leaders have little access to arenas where they can advance the goals of education without appearing to sell out their own members. There are no institutionalized structures in which union leaders can shape and take responsibility for visions, strategies, plans, and commitments for a school district's future. For these four reasons, then Second Generation unions have difficulty joining the creation of a civic culture or helping to formulate a general definition of the common good.

Schools Need a Civic Culture

But is there anything wrong with an institutional setting in which unions represent the special interest of teachers and schools boards represent the general interests of the public? The answer to this question lies in understanding the tension between two very different roles of schools as public service organizations. Schools are commonweal organizations which exist to serve the general public: to socialize the young, perpetuate the large democracy, and educate workers. But schools are also client-service organizations designed to diagnose and prescribe programs that answer the particular needs of individual students.

In service organizations, the prime beneficiary is the client. The crucial problem of the organization centers on providing professional services, the competence or correctness of which the client is unqualified to judge. 'Hence, the client is vulnerable, subject to exploitation and dependent on the integrity of the professional for whom he has come for help.'[32] Employees in service organizations must steer a tight course between two dangers: They must not, out of concern for their own careers or status lose sight of the client's true needs, but at the same time they must avoid becoming 'captives' of the client, thereby losing the ability to render independent judgment.

Commonweal organizations serve not the client but the public at large. Thus, in the Internal Revenue Service or the United States Army, it is not the welfare of the taxpayer or the private soldier which comes first. As Blau and Scott put it:

> The issue posed by commonweal organizations is that of external democratic control — the public must possess the means of controlling the ends of these organizations. While external democratic control is essential, the internal structure of these organizations is expected to be bureaucratic, governed by the criterion of efficiency, and not democratic.[33]

It is not surprising, then, that commonweal organizations are subject to continuing cross-pressures for control and productivity. Those within the organization often come to question the need for external control. Like professional soldiers, professional educators come to believe that policy issues should be removed from civilian hands and given to those with technical competence. Because these organizations do not offer their employees the conspicuous rewards of self-aggrandizement associated with business firms (where owners/managers are the primary beneficiaries), they must pay special attention to the means for promoting extraordinary performance: bravery in the military, creativity in education or the arts. The selection and nurturing of employees takes on special significance.[34]

The conflict between the commonweal requirement for external control and the client-service requirement for professional autonomy cannot be resolved by ordinary bureaucratic means. If external controls structure client services in such a way that the service provider has no freedom to diagnose and prescribe for the needs of the clients, then the organization cannot perform its client-service function. If the professional service providers become so isolated from external control that they fail to reflect the basic values or direction of society, then the schools fail in their commonweal function.

Virtually all human service organizations face these two divergent requirements, and their histories attest to the tensions involved in trying to reconcile them. Even the military has difficulty reconciling the technical, knowledge-based decisions of professional soldiers with public attitudes toward war, peace, security and democracy. The result is a constant tension between military leaders and the civilian government. Similarly, medical care — which for sixty years was under the exclusive control of the profession itself — is coming increasingly under external control, chiefly as a result of soaring costs and the need to provide better services to the poor.

The most effective vehicle for mediating the tension between commonweal and client-service functions is the development of a strong civic culture. Organizational governance must, therefore, provide mechanisms by which a civic culture can emerge. The needed culture involved development of 'public regarding' attitudes among organizational members and broad acceptance of the view that organizational goals are more important than self- or group-interests. Civic cultures create a taken-for-granted 'public spirit' among leaders and an 'uncalculating affection' among citizens at large which cannot be derived from self interest.[35] Embracing a civic culture certainly involves curbing rampant self-interest, but it takes more than that. Leaders must be willing to sacrifice and to take risks with their careers, and followers must be able to consider the public as well as the private implications of professional decisions.

The historic instrument for conveying the civic culture is the trusteeship — the development of strong feelings of proprietary responsibility combined with a professional vision of the mission of an organization. Such a trusteeship took on literal meaning during the municipal reform movement. Reformed school boards were encouraged to act as trustees, to reflect the general will and seek the general good. Public support for the schools was nurtured by an expansive commitment to this redefined role. In recent years, the character of school boards, has changed again as the result of a growing perception, by both scholars and the public at large, that school board members are not really disinterested parties. The public has lost confidence in school board trusteeship as special interest groups succeed in electing overtly partisan board members. This loss is exacerbated when unionists run for the school board or teacher unions support candidates perceived to be representing their self-interest. To reverse this decline in public confidence, labor relations needs to develop mechanisms that allow for, even directly encourage, unions to express responsibility for the institutions of education — to articulate the civic culture and share in the trusteeship.

The political system will intervene if a civic culture does not adequately sustain feelings of trusteeship or a belief that the public is not being well served becomes widespread. But political action is an extremely weak mechanism for directing the flow of public service. Legislatures and public agencies can use only two types of not-very-satisfactory interventions. First, they can attempt to reform schools by remote control: that is, by explicating more specific rules and instituting stronger compliance mechanisms. This 'legislated learning' approach is apparent in the waves of reform which have buffeted the schools since World War II. As Wise reminds us, however, this strategy has limited effectiveness because it forces all action onto a procrustean bed of standard operating procedures that are generally insensitive to crucial variations in the needs of communities and children.[36]

The second type of political intervention available to the political system can best be termed 'disinvestment'. If a weak civic culture destroys public confidence in an institution's ability to deliver high quality services, the polity legitimizes alternative means of delivering the same services. This phenomenon, described by Hirschman, is represented in education by the enthusiasm for vouchers, tax credits and other public choice mechanisms for legitimating pursuit of the state's interest in education outside of the public schools.[37]

Over the long haul, neither legislated learning nor disinvestment in education can produce high quality schooling. The costs are too high and the effects on professional educators are too weak. Only the development of a robust civic culture can effectively link school governance to educational outcomes.

Notes

1 MEYER, J. and ROWAN B., (1978) 'The structure of education organizations' in MEYER M. and associates (Eds) *Environments and Organizations*, San Francisco, CA, Jossey-Bass, pp. 78–109.

2 WELLINGTON, H.H. and WINTER, JR., R.K. (1971) *The Unions and the Cities*, Washington, D.C, Brookings Institution, p. 328.

3 GRIMSHAW, W. (1979) *Union Rule in the Schools*, Lexington, MA, Lexington Books, D.C. Heath, p. xiii.

4 LONG, N. (1958) 'The local community as an ecology of games', *American Journal of Sociology* 64, 2, p. 251.

5 EASTON, D. (1956) *Systems Analysis in Political Life*, New York, Wiley; ALMOND, G.A. and BINGHAM POWELL, JR., G. (1966) *Comparative Politics: A Developmental Approach*, Boston, MA, Little, Brown.

6 MINAR, D.W. (1966) *Education Decision Making in Suburban Communities*, Evanston, IL, Northwestern University Cooperative Research Project 2440; ZEIGLER L.H. and JENNINGS, M.K. with PEAK, G.W. (1794) *Governing American Schools*, North Scituate, MA, Duxbury Press.

7 ZEIGLER, L.H. (1973) 'Creating responsive schools', *The Urban Review*, 6, 3, p. 41.

8 PISAPIA, J.R. (1980) '*Open bargaining: Florida style*', Morgantown, WV, West Virginia University.

9 WEINSTEIN, S. and MITCHELL, D.E. (eds) (1975) *Public Testimony on Public Schools*, Berkeley, CA, McCutchan; DAVIES, D. and ZERCHYKOV, R. (1978) *Citizen Participation in Education: Annotated bibliography* 2nd edition Boston, MA, Institute for Responsive Education; CHENG, C. (1976) 'Community representation in teacher collective bargaining: Problems and perspectives', *Harvard Educational Review*, 46, 1, pp. 153–74.

10 KERCHNER C.T. and MITCHELL, D.E. (1980) *The Dynamics of Public School Collective Bargaining and its Impacts on Governance, Administration and Teaching*, Final report to the National Institute of Education, Grant No. 79-0036, Washington, D.C., U.S. Department of Education, ERIC Document Service ED 221 925, pp. 5–22.

11 WIRT, M. (ed.), (1976) *The Polity and the School*, Berkeley, CA, McCutchan.

12 GRIMSHAW, W. (1979) *op cit.*

13 IANNACCONE, L. and LUTZ, F.W. (1970) *Politics, Power and Policy: The Governing of Local School Districts*, Columbus, OH, Charles Merrill; LUTZ, F.W. and IANNACCONE, L. (eds.), (1978) *Public Participation in Local School Districts: The Dissatisfaction Theory of Democracy*, Lexington MA, Lexington Press, D.C. Heath.

14 SCHATTSCHNEIDER, E.E. (1960) *The Semisovereign People: A Realist's View of the Democracy in America*, New York, Holt, Rinehart and Winston.

15 WOLFE, T. (1970) *Radical Chic and Mau-Mauing the Flack Catchers*, New York, Farrar; For a scholarly treatment of agenda making see: COBB, R.W. and ELDER, C.D. (1972) *Participation in American Politics*, Baltimore, MA, Johns Hopkins University Press.

16 McDonnell, L. and Pascal, A. (1979) *Organized Teachers in American Schools*, Santa Monica, CA, Rand.

17 CAPLOW, T. (1966) *Two Against One: Coalitions in Triads*, Englewood Cliffs, N.J., Prentice-Hall; BANFIELD, E.L. (1961) *Political Influence*, Glencoe, IL, Free Press.

18 WEERES, J.G. (1981) 'The management of political demand', unpublished manuscript, Claremont Graduate School.

19 LAKOFF, S.A. and RICH, D. (eds.) (1973) *Private Government: Introductory Readings*, Glenview, IL, Scott, Foresman.

20 MITCHELL, D., KERCHNER, C., ERCK, W. and PRYOR, G. (1981) 'The impact of collective bargaining on school management and policy', *American Journal of Education*, 89, 2, pp. 168–70; also see relationships to bargaining theory: WALTON, R.E. and McKERSIE, R.B. (1965) *A Behavioral Theory of Labor Negotiations, An Analysis of a Social Interaction System*, New York, McGraw-Hill.

21 BLAU, P. (1968) 'Social exchange' in SILLS, D.L. (Ed) *International Encyclopedia of the Social Sciences, Vol 7*, New York, Macmillan, pp. 452–7.

22 *Ibid.*, p. 455.

23 *Ibid.*, p. 456.

24 *Ibid.*, p. 457.

25 COHEN, M.D. and MARCH, J.G. (1974) *Leadership and Ambiguity: The American College President*. New York, McGraw-Hill. The relatively high opportunity cost associated with the psychology of management time allocations is treated in: MINTZBERG, H., (1974) *The Nature of Managerial Work*, New York, Harper and Row.

26 MacIVER, R.M. (1965) *The Web of Government*, rev. ed., New York, Free Press, p. 287.

27 SCHATTSCHNEIDER, E.E. (1960) *op cit*, p. 15.

28 LIPSET, S.M. (1963) *Political Man: The Social Basis of Politics*, Garden City, N.Y., Doubleday.

29 SCHATTSCHNEIDER, E.E. (1980) *op cit*, p. 3.

30 KERCHNER, C., MITCHELL, D., PRYOR, G. and ERCK, W. (1980) *The Logic of Citizen Participation in Public School Labor Relations*, IRE Report No. 3, Boston, MA, Institute for Responsive Education.

31 WALTON R.E. and McKERSIE, R.B. (1965) *op cit.*

32 BLAU, P.M. and SCOTT, R.W. (1962) *Formal Organizations*, San Francisco CA, Chandler, p. 51.

33 *Ibid.*, p. 55.

34 *Ibid.*, p. 56.

35 MANSFIELD, JR., H.C. (1976) 'The prestige of public employment', in CHICKERING, A. (Ed.) *Public Employee Unions: A Study of the Crisis in Public Sector Labor Relations*, San Francisco, Institute for Contemporary Studies, p. 48.

36 WISE, A. (1979) *Legislated Learning: The Bureaucratization of the American Classroom*, Berkeley and Los Angeles, University of California Press.

37 HIRSCHMAN, A.O. (1970) *Exit, Voice, and Loyalty: Responses to Decline in Firms, Organizations, and States*, Cambridge, MA, Harvard University Press.

9
Impact on School Organizations

During the Second Generation, school organizations are frequently preoccupied with managing conflict and maintaining stable operations — and understandably so. They enter the Second Generation fearing that conflict will not be containable and that continuing strife between union and school will seriously undermine service delivery. Labor-management conflict within schools is seen as a new demon, one whose presence is deeply troubling and whose exorcism requires elaborate and constant vigilance.

The schools are largely successful in controlling this demon. Administrators, and union leaders too, learn to manage conflicts, settle fights, and maintain their organizations in the face of collective bargaining, dispute resolution, and even occasional strikes. Good faith collective bargaining does not destroy management or hamper the routine operations of schools. As other authors have also pointed out, administrators develop a substantial repertoire of responses that allow them to cope and often flourish under stable, Second Generation labor relations.[1] However, the preoccupation of Second Generation labor relations with organizational maintenance problems deflects attention from organizational effectiveness and productivity. Except through informal means, which largely occur at the end of Second Generation, labor relations is thought to have very little to do with decisions that shape the way in which education is undertaken in schools or, indeed, the mix of curriculum and services that constitute schooling.

Even research into the impact of unionization is frequently interpreted according to organizational maintenance criteria. Strikes are studied to see whether they did or did not disrupt school operations.

Teacher salary increases were or were not proportionate to those received by other workers. Labor contracts did or did not intrude on school policy. No one asks, and therefore no one sees — how labor relations affect the fundamental character of school organizations or their productivity capacity. Attention to this aspect of labor relations remains the unsolved problem of Second Generation labor relations.

In this chapter, we look at the relationship between Second Generation unionism and the twin organizational functions of maintenance and productivity. First, we review the evidence about strikes, salary effects, and policy changes. We examine the rather singular focus of research on school maintenance and its lack of concern with educational productivity. Second, we explore the ways in which managing conflict and maintaining school operations have actually changed core organizational structures and functions in the schools. Changed authority patterns, decision-making processes, and teacher work orientations have had an overall rationalizing effect on school operations. We argue that this tendency to rely on control through bureaucratic rules interferes with the development of strong, productive organizational cultures.

Understanding Salaries, Strikes and Policies

Researchers have devoted considerable attention to the effects of unionization on teachers' salaries. Findings vary — depending on the author, the comparisons employed, and the time period of the study — that the 'union' effect on wages ranges from virtually zero to more than 20 per cent.[2] Examining the forty or so studies of wage impact leads one to conclude that there is a union wage effect in the range of 5 to 10 per cent. While this does not alter the overall economic status of teachers, it does represent an annual salary increment of $750 to $2500 for most teachers, a very handsome return on union dues. Wage effects of this magnitude are consistent with the lower end of the union-effect results found in private sector unions where effects in the order of 10 to 25 per cent are commonly found.[3]

Like many other workers, teachers suffered declining real incomes during the 1970–1980 decade, a loss of about 13.4 per cent.[4] They suffered larger declines than steel workers or autoworkers, and by the end of the decade teaching, when considered on a weekly salary basis, paid about the same as jobs in these elite blue collar industries. Thus, teaching retains its historic place at the bottom of white collar or professional salaries.

However, despite the differences in empirical findings and differences about statistical method, in the final analysis there is a strongly normative cast to studies of wage effects.[5] Ultimately, the authors edge toward questions of whether teachers *should* receive more money. Discussion of wage effects usually turns on questions of distributive equity, and much of the research has been driven by a quest to see how collective bargaining affects the price of government products for which demand is deemed to be relatively inelastic.

Seldom do these studies address the question of productivity effects.[6] In some respects this omission is understandable. Teacher productivity is difficult to conceptualize and even harder to measure. Among the few who have attempted to look at this question, Eberts and Stone conclude that productivity has decreased because teacher workdays are some 3 per cent shorter in districts with union contracts than those without.[7] However, the more usual conclusion is that, 'solid answers to these points of speculation must await the development of more effective measures of teacher productivity'.[8] But the failure is more deeply one of conception than measurement. Labor relations are not often regarded as involving productivity problems, at least these are not the concerns during the Second Generation. Productivity questions were virtually unraised in the Second Generation districts we studied. Changes in the configuration of staffing, which had significant effects on the curriculum, were negotiated without reference to these curricular changes. (In one district, the union later filed an unfair labor practices charge alleging that management had not informed the union that staffing changes would result from its settlement.) The idea that staff might be configured differently was never considered in any collective bargaining arrangement we witnessed or were told about. Thus, questions about making the schools more effective through differentiated staffing, new modes of teaching, or technological innovation were never raised. (The sole exception involved plans for early retirement in which unions and school districts negotiated agreements that would allow old/expensive/dispirited teachers to be replaced by new/cheaper/fresher ones.)

That practitioners and scholars pay so little attention to productivity is even more remarkable when one considers the extraordinary labor intensiveness of schooling. Any modification in assignments, hours, and specified duties is likely to affect school outputs. For example, over the last twenty years the pupil-teacher ratio has fallen from twenty-three to nineteen, and daily teacher student contact hours have fallen partly in response to teachers having won preparation periods and duty-free lunch periods.[9] Whether these and similar changes have altered teacher productivity in terms of cognitive outputs is not yet known. It should be added here that raising the productivity question does not imply that unionization has adversely affected school productivity. Recent studies of private-sector unionization suggest that the effect may be positive.[10]

Strikes are perhaps the second most frequently investigated labor relations effect. There have been scores of studies of strikes: their incidence, their prevention, their effects, and alternative means of dispute resolution. Through this body of literature, we find that walkouts are reasonably rare: Only about two of every 100 contract disputes ends in strike.[11] Strikes are of dubious economic value. Indeed, some scholars maintain that public employees achieve more through non-strike adjudicated settlements.[12] The impact of strikes is almost always calculated in terms of the maintenance of ongoing organizational functions. Studies report strike severity in terms of 'man-days' lost and according to whether schools were closed down or remained open. Keeping the schools open is often considered management's primary task during a strike: continued operation both strengthens management's hand in bargaining and allows management to minimize the disruption of services that most distress the public.

Relatively rarely do the practitioners (or scholars) contemplate the effects of negotiation impasses on school productivity. During strikes, editorialists weep and wail that children are being deprived of their education, but these assertions are little more than emotional rhetoric. Given the interruptions in school schedules — vacations, assemblies, in-service days, snow days, testing periods, field days, and cookie sales — the allegation that a three-day strike destroys the continuity of learning is difficult to swallow.

But the damage done to productivity by other kinds of disruptions is rarely calculated. While strikes are rare, long and festering disagreements are common. According to a study of California districts during the first full year of collective bargaining, school districts negotiated for an average of eleven months to settle their employee contracts.[13]

Several of our study districts had been involved in negotiations for more than a year, with a consequent breakdown in communications between administrators and teachers.

Strikes are measured in days, sometimes hours. But impasses, often associated with more modest forms of employee civil disobedience, can last for weeks or months. The incidents themselves may seem relatively harmless. To the casual observer, the refusal of teachers to attend back-to-school night is a rather pathetic protest — lame, tentative, wimpy. However, such incidents extended over time, take a heavy toll in terms of broken communications networks, psychological distancing, stress, discontent, and the minimization of work effect. In such circumstances, organized attention to school productivity questions becomes almost impossible. In school districts, such as Thresher, where virtually continuous negotiation impasse extends for years, long-term damage is done to the interpersonal communication network and the authority structure. Teachers may continue to perform their routine duties, but the organization in many respects ceases to function.

Efforts to establish a common culture take on the perverse characteristic of further dividing the organization. For example, in the Homestead district, which was just emerging into the Second Generation, the Superintendent had created a complex, sophisticated set of human interaction techniques to focus on goals and clarify roles. Rather than establish a single belief system under which the district could plan and move forward, the interaction technique provided another target for teacher dissatisfaction.

Second Generation labor relations are deliberately structured to keep policy matters separate from collective bargaining. Scope-of-bargaining restrictions assert that it is possible to distinguish between the conditions of teaching work and the policies which determine the content of schooling. And many commentators such as French and Nagel or Johnson assert that unionization has had only limited effect on school policy.[14] When we asked a well-known labor lawyer about the impact of unionism on school programs and policies, he responded with a trace of regret: 'Just as you wouldn't say that collective bargaining with auto workers has altered the product mix at General Motors very much, I don't think that you will see very much impact on the way schools work.' We have come to the conclusion that this observation is dramatically wrong.

Not only do labor relations change school policy, but those

changes are frequently unanticipated and unrecognized. Important changes in the way schools operate occur, to a surprising extent, as *accidental* by-products of a labor relations process in which negotiators focus their attention on conflict management and organizational maintenance rather than policy-making. Frequently, we found that leaders on both sides of the bargaining table had to stop and think carefully before they could respond to questions about overall program and policy impacts, while they could talk easily and in animated terms about their immediate bargaining strategies or about their legitimate interests. In Homestead, for instance, the contract settlement at the close of Superintendent Burroughs' tenure necessitated school closings and a substantial realignment of the curriculum particularly in teaching specialty areas. But at the time the deal was struck, it was handled almost entirely as a conflict management issue. During the months we tracked negotiations, the fact that educational policy was being made was never mentioned, in fact, one of the constant sources of teacher discomfort was that management's interpretation of the scope of bargaining was overly narrow.

Contract analyses show repeatedly that the scope of items covered in labor contracts expands over time. But most frequently the implication drawn is that teachers have breached the barrier between collective bargaining and policy thereby intruding on managerial or civic prerogatives. [15] But the question of whether the policies are good ones or not is seldom asked.

Changes in Organizational Structure and Function

In one sense, the inarticulateness of school personnel and union leaders about the impact of Second Generation unionism is surprising; in another sense; it is to be expected. The legal rationale for Second Generation unionism is that unionism is separate from educational policy, and the practical lesson of Second Generation practice is that public controversy can be reduced if all parties avoid conspicuous reference to unionism's policy impacts. Nonetheless, as we examined our field notes and interview records, we noted three categories of organizational impact:

— *Changes in the mode of managerial authority.* Because the changes in organizational structure brought about by

unionization — formalization, standardization, and cen-
tralization — emphasize curbs to managerial discretion,
increased attention is paid to manager's formal authority,
either through its conspicuous use or through development
of informal, school-site accommodations.
— *Changes in decision making* brought about by changes in the
agenda (the list of decisions to be made), the arena (the
forums in which decisions are made), and the actors (those
who participate in decisions). In addition, decisions become
increasingly hierarchically linked with one another in long
chains. Such changes give teachers a voice in decisions but
decrease the organization's ability to make quick affirmative
decisions.
— *Changes in work orientation or organizational culture* which
focus attention on worker rights rather than on organizational outputs.

Changes in Managerial Authority

It is often asserted that unionism is an assault on managerial authority,
but our data suggests that unionism is better understood as a flanking
movement that turns and shapes the force of management. Instead of
the frontal attacks on management, typical of the First Intergenerational
Conflict period, efforts are made to protect teachers' autonomy and
security by requiring that managers adhere to the rules of law, contract,
and what becomes defined as good practice. Managers often find that
the new rules work in their favor and proceed to use them aggressively.[16] In some respects, management authority increases: at least the
attention given to explicitly managing schools increases, as does the
recognition of school administrators as 'managerial'. At the same time,
management itself becomes rule-based.

In this situation, one would expect school-site managers to reflect
the comfortable relaxation and self-assurance generally found in
rule-bound bureaucracies. Such was not the case, however, among the
school principals we studied. Some appeared frustrated because the new
rules restrained their actions, some became aggressive in managing
through the rules, and some developed satisfactory ways of what they

called 'managing around the contract'. The latter technique of using informal accommodation and fractional bargaining increased markedly as schools moved into the Late Second Generation. Particularly, in a few districts with strong unions and well-trained building-level representatives, substantial school-site accommodation took place through union representatives. More frequently, the accommodative relationships were with teachers without regard to their union office or affiliation.

Changes in managerial authority take place in response to three distinct shifts in bureaucracy. First, relationships become more formal: that is, the details of relationships between individuals are made explicit in writing.[17] The labor contract itself formalizes — substituting a written and enforceable guarantee for informal understanding. Other aspects of formalization derive from the contract and the social relationships it establishes. In Industrial City, for instance, principals were required to notify teachers by memorandum of school assemblies and other deviations from the daily schedule. In Riverview, principals were required to provide written accounts to the central administration of any grievance or threatened grievance. (Labor relations are by no means the only formalizing influence. Federal and state categorical programs, testing requirements, and student due process all result in substantial increases in written rules, reporting requirements and other paperwork.)

Second Generation labor relations also involves increased standardization of employee treatment. Such standardization, is of course, the intended consequence of collective contracts: to end abusive treatment by managers and particularism and favoritism in the dispensation of rewards and punishments. But as a consequence, schools must give more attention to rationalizing their activities through planning, through considering contingencies when making or promulgating rules, and these requirements require even more elaborate rules.

Third, Second Generation labor relations increase centralized control. This change may, at first, seem surprising, especially to teachers who believed that unionization would increase their individual autonomy. But formalization and standardization enhance the organization's ability to enforce rules, and this is particularly so in the case of school central offices and site administrators. In one of our study districts, the Superintendent used contract administration to tighten his control over principals. He insisted on absolutely uniform personnel practices (and, in effect, on uniform curricular practices) in the eleven schools in the district. Grievances and complaints from the union gave him ample information about the extent to which principals were adhering to standard procedures, and within a few years he had removed eight incumbents, replacing them with others more amenable to his control.

In summary, unionization has organizational effects that push schools toward rationalization. In the language of the recent literature on organizational behavior, schools become more tightly coupled institutions. The organization extends its control (or potential for control) over behaviors it can specify and monitor. Fearing that it cannot control what is not specified, the organization also expands the web of rules and increases the intensity of its scrutiny.

Our experience suggests that labor relations rationalizes the couplings in two ways. It tightens the categorical couplings by making them more specific and enforceable. The category itself becomes a property right, and there is often vigorous enforcement of the right. Also, there are strong tendencies to increase the number of categories to be inspected because the political environment sends messages that it believes teachers bear watching.

These changes run counter to the history of schools as organizations in which substantial attention is paid to categories, such as whether the teacher has the right license, but hardly any attention is paid to the details of a teacher's performance. Loose coupling, it is argued, is not a manifestation of a sloppy organization, but a symbiotic relationship that allows schools to respond to demands on its system by making marginal adjustments in pupil treatment, client service levels, and teacher job description.[18] In this way schools as organizations and individual employees compensate for what is called a low technology — even the best laid plans, or the best thought-out lessons, frequently don't work or produce unexpected results that require change and adaption.

Changes in Decision Making

Second Generation unionism makes decisions more complex, just as it is supposed to. The press for collective bargaining began with an assertion that administrative decision making discriminated against teachers by unjustly distributing decisional rights. It is not surprising, then, that decision making in schools which practice good faith bargaining is more complex than it is in those which do not. We find decision making changed in several ways. First, the agenda — the list of decisions to be made — change. Second, the arenas — the forums in which decisions are made — changes with the introduction of negotiation and arbitration, arenas which did not exist before. Third, the actors or participants in decisions change. New participants include labor relations professionals, who bring with them rules, norms and standards of behavior acquired outside of school districts. Fourth, decisions become hierarchically linked. No decision is final; there is always somewhere else to go for an appeal or a more authoritative judgment. In short, it becomes more difficult to reach conclusions.

The agenda

Demands for attention frequently overload organizations, particularly public ones. Thus, understanding organizations requires observing the mechanisms they use to decide which problems will be attended to and which will be ignored. Agendas are set in two ways: by establishing a calendar which demands that attention be given to a particular problem at a specific time and by causing or threatening a disturbance, thereby preempting attention. [19].

Each decision takes place on its own calendar (for example, budgets are due in August, teacher reemployment letters by 15 March). Negotiations are triggered by the expiration of the old contract (or, in some states, by statutes that set a date for beginning negotiations) and so cannot be dismissed by the participants on the grounds that they have more important matters to attend to. Their only recourse is to begin bargaining, although they may agree to simplify negotiations or just go through the motions of bargaining. But to refuse to participate in bargaining when the schedule calls for it is to invite an unfair labor practice charge. Thus, it was not surprising that, in the study districts, we witnessed dutiful attention to bargaining even when neither party had anything to bargain. During the Homestead negotiations, both labor and management abruptly ended other meetings in order to rush to a bargaining session, although neither party was prepared to make a proposal or to entertain serious discussion. The union was undergoing internal reorganization, and its leaders' desks were piled high with paperwork. Management also faced serious work overload problems: indeed, its attorney-negotiator was so bogged down with other commitments that he momentarily forgot which school district he was bargaining for. For three hours we observed fifteen consenting adults working very hard to say nothing of substance to one another. And none of the participants thought their behavior odd!

Grievances and unfair labor practice proceedings also carry their own internal timetables: in addition, they preempt other events by threatening disturbance. Most grievance clauses and unfair labor practice processing rules require a response to an allegation within a specified number of days. Thus, managers must put aside their other work and give immediate attention to answering the allegation. Other disturbances can have similar effects. Teachers and others gain access to the agenda through oral protest (speaking at board meetings or staff meetings, or even conversing with important outsiders who visit the schools to monitor and evaluate), informational picketing, protest rallies, sit-ins, and the like. The disturbance itself may not be necessary: the threat itself may be sufficient. In fact, the threat may be more effective than the actual occurrence. A threat, if credible, is a renewable resource. Like a fir tree, if one threat is harvested, another can be grown in its place.

Arenas and actors

Changes in decision arenas and actors lead to two kinds of tension to which organizations must adapt. First, as new rules accumulate around each new decision arena, both new and old participants must make a concerted effort to learn and communicate them. Second, there is great tension over which arena will be used for which type of decision. Each party wants the decision moved to that arena where it has the best chance of getting the outcome it desires. Not surprisingly, union leaders prefer using collective bargaining as the decisional mode whereas managers prefer administrative decision-making. The tension between labor and management on this point manifests itself in the Early Second Generation as the scope-of-bargaining problem. Less recognized is the propensity of decisions to escape from the organizational bounds of school districts altogether. Grievances, of course, can go to outside arbitrators, in those districts which have binding arbitration. (The most recent available figures suggest that as many as 90 per cent of teacher labor contracts provide for binding arbitration of grievances.)[20] Tension over decisional arenas also manifests itself in a tendency to move decisions to legislative or administrative arenas when collective bar-gaining is not producing the desired results. That which cannot be achieved at the bargaining table often appears on the legislative agenda. At times, the choice between decisional arenas is conscious. As one union representative said, 'Why should we try to negotiate a seniority clause in 875 contracts, when we can go to Springfield [the state capital] and only pay once.'

Decisional chains

Decisional processes are not simply introduced; they are arranged into hierarchies. Decisions move from one arena to another, and the length of time required to reach a final decision increases. Perhaps the most vivid example of this kind of change comes from the Homestead district. Because of severely declining enrollments, the district was faced with the necessity of transferring some teachers to different schools or different job assignments. Union and management contrac-tually agreed to an assignment system whereby the most senior teachers would be alternated with those most recently hired (many of whom also happened to be minority-group members). The intent was to balance the staff at each school, thereby avoiding the creation of teacher ghettos (i.e., schools whose faculty consisted primarily of 'old' teachers or minority teachers).

Well-intentioned though it was, the transfer clause in the Home-stead contract proved impossible to administer. First, there was no clear-cut understanding about how seniority was to be determined: Did total length of service in the district count, or was the clause intended to cover only length of service at the individual school site? What was to happen in the case of broken service? Did the months of maternity leave count toward seniority? The problem was especially difficult for the least senior teachers. Since many of them began teaching on the very same day, how should they be differentiated? By the date when the administration sent them an offer of employment? When the board approved their contract? When they first applied for the position?

The chain of decisional elements grew grotesquely convoluted, first linking administrative decisions at the school site and at the central office, where hapless administrators tried to figure out some rational way of determining who was most and least senior. Then it became coupled with the grievance system, since every teacher selected for transfer filed a grievance. Ultimately it was alleged that unfair labor practices had been committed.

While the union reaped some benefit from all this fuss, it could not cause a decision to be reached once the conflict was engaged. A negotiated settlement, that might have redefined seniority, was impossible because the contract was already in place. The decision simply had to grind its way through the various hearings and appeals — a process that took several years.

The long chain of decision making is particularly pernicious when it comes to new initiatives or programs. As Pressman and Wildavsky point out, the probability of gaining a positive answer to an initiative is inversely related to the number of decision points involved.[21] As the number of decisions increases, the probability that all decisions will be positive decreases. Moreover, if the decisions are sequentially linked, the time needed to process a decision increases. Thus, the introduction of long decision chains constitutes an enormously conservative influence. Existing operations and processes are reinforced through rationalization, and decisional departures are difficult

Changes in Work Orientation

The twin imperatives of Second Generation unionism — the importance of the contractual agreement and the importance of due process — encourage teachers and administrators to interpret their problems as questions of rights rather than as possibilities for enhancing organizational efficacy. In this context, the union contract is a powerful document partly because it produces rights. Although contracts are negotiated for the whole collective bargaining unit, the rights they generate accrue largely to individual teachers. Contractual clauses for 'organizational security' and maintenance apply to the union as an organization and do not constitute the heart of the contract. To be enforceable, rights must be expressible in terms of property. A transfer clause gives the teacher an ownership right in a job at a particular school. If that right is violated, an arbitrator or a court will either require the school district to give the teacher the job to which he or she is entitled, or it will assess monetary damages, converting the right into money. In this context, questions of school outcomes are irrelevant. The question is not whether Ms. Jones is a better fifth grade teacher than Mr. Smyth, but whether she has a right to the position.

Even in the contract-making stage of labor relations, issues are expressed in terms of rights. If Ms. Jones and her colleagues say, 'we want to stay in our present schools and not be transferred', this assertion does not offer very attractive political symbols. But if Ms. Jones asserts that, because of her years of hard and dedicated service, she has gained a right to stay in the fifth grade at the Oak Street School, she has evoked symbols around which teachers can coalesce. Expressing a goal as a right elicits sympathy, wins converts, and shows determination. When Catholic lay teachers attempted to organize in the late 1970s, they wore buttons proclaiming 'Catholic Teachers Have Rights', in fact, they were organizing because they had so few rights.

Once a right has been asserted, or once a right is actually established in contract, compromise becomes retreat, a giving up of rights. For labor, constant vigilance over rights violations is part of the social saga of an uplift organization. For management, defending 'management reserved rights' means that any gains in teacher rights are losses to managers. When labor relations center on rights, they are conducted in accordance with what John Rawls calls 'pure procedural justice'.[22] It is assumed that the correct substantive outcome is unknowable and that one's rights are assured if proper procedures are adhered to — schedules, rules of evidence, choice of tribunals, access to information. Because rights are absolute and cannot be traded off, consideration of procedure takes precedence over consideration of the substantive outcome. Thus, in the case of Homestead, the sting of grievance and unfair labor practice allegations were decided without reference to the effects of teacher transfer on the substance of education in the district. The only allowable question was whether the teacher(s) had an accrued property right to their jobs. Clearly, either labor or management could have raised the educational efficacy question during bargaining itself, and the transfer clause could have been written differently. But here the definition of right and the definition of power merge. If labor had accepted managerial discretion over whom to transfer or to fire, a teacher's rights to due process would have been abrogated. To allow the union to make the choice on a case-by-case basis would have been an unthinkable concession on management's part. Joint consultation on a case-by-case basis would have threatened both parties.

The union's difficulty in being flexible is reinforced by the duty of fair representation by which a bargaining agent is obliged to defend members — and usually non-members who are part of the bargaining unit — against contractual violations. Unions also know that they must prove their worth to their members by displaying constant and resolute vigilance in defense of rights. Particularly early in the Second Generation, they must cultivate the image that 'your union is right there watching to see what comes out of the management rat hole'.

The Unsolved Problem of a Productive Culture

As we have seen, the effect of Second Generation unionism has been to strengthen the reliance of school organizations on bureaucratic controls. Consequently, Second Generation unionization exposes the limits on a bureaucracy's ability to guide a productive organization. Exposing the limits to bureaucracy helps establish the needs for schools and unions to establish productive organizational cultures so that individuals and groups of workers become more self-directed in their pursuit of legitimate organizational goals.

Bureaucracy flourishes as an ideal form of organization because of its ability to coordinate, routinize, and channel the joint actions of many individuals.[23] Bureaucracy cultivates expertise and encourages large-scale coordinated human effort. Since Max Weber, it has also become the ideal form of organizational control, the one with which we are most comfortable. Despite the pejorative connotations of the term, most of us are uneasy with organizations that do not conform to the classic requirements of a bureaucracy: An unclear line of authority or an incomplete job description does not fit with our concept of what's good or proper. But bureaucratic control has severe limits. Over the last fifty years, organizational research has explored the natural limits to bureaucratic control and identified the advantages of loosely structured, anarchistic, and seemingly absurd organizations. A generation ago, March and Simon suggested that the effort to control human work often has unanticipated side effects.[24] Maintenance of bureaucratic controls requires substantial overheads, a human capital investment in communications channels between individuals so that parts of the organization come to understand one another.[25] As Peters and Waterman note, 'To be narrowly rational is often to be negative.'[26]

Because rationality fears mistakes, it can lead to overcomplexity and inflexibility.[27]

The limits of bureaucracy are particularly apparent in complex or ambiguous work settings. When tasks are varied and difficult, the costs involved in monitoring behavior are particularly high and there is increased need for a professional culture.[28] Regulating transactions between employees and the organization is costly, and establishing equity among employees is difficult.

In schools, application of standard efficiency principles often goes awry, 'effectiveness declines, people become confused, and work doesn't get done'.[29] When principals respond to complaints of teacher ineffectiveness by making more frequent classroom observations, they are accused of harassment. Likewise, teachers are reluctant to criticize one another. Poor performance often persists because, as Weick puts it, 'inattention is justified as respect for professional autonomy'.[30] Attempts to tighten evaluation run into similar difficulties because teachers and administrators have little or no control over school inputs, and consequently the standards by which teaching should be judged are often open to debate. Due process requirements turn all expert judgments into rebuttable propositions. As Ouchi puts it, 'the rate of change, instability of employment, or ambiguity of performance evaluation may simply overwhelm all rational attempts'.[31] Even traditional manufacturing firms have begun to appreciate that the scientific management mode of production control has its limits. In these circumstances, it is not surprising that many organizations are considering alternative means of control. Conspicuous among these is the concept of organizational culture.

Partly as a result of the Japanese mystique, the power of organizational culture to guide and control complex undertakings has been rediscovered. The recent literature on effective schools and effective corporations celebrates the value of a central idea — a belief shared by all members of an organization — as a means to both motivate and direct extraordinary human effort.[32]

An organizational culture is that set of common understandings which anthropologists call 'thick' or shared social knowledge. It need not involve shared goals, although such is often the case. Rather, it involves shared norms and understandings of situations and their meanings.[33] Shared knowledge has the capacity to guide action, channel problems, and steer decisions without overt organizational controls. A culture is known by many names: purpose, calling, motto, mission, 'the definition of what business we are in'.[34] Shils calls it 'the center', the zone of symbols, values and beliefs which govern society and 'partakes of the nature of the sacred'.[35] Regardless of the name, culture operates as an unseen hand just as do economic or political profits in a market conception of an organization, or rules and authority in a bureaucracy.

Much of the attraction of cultural control rests in the fact that, while leaders who 'preserve the culture' are legitimate and given substantial latitude, direct intervention is seldom necessary. The people in the organization already know what to do. Such organizations become productive because the people in them know how to modify their behavior in response to circumstance without departing from the overall goals and purposes of the organization.

The literature on organizational cultures posits three conditions under which they tend to grow and flourish. The first condition is the presence of universally legitimated authority figures. The case histories of most organizations with strong cultures reveal a leader, frequently an autocrat, of epic proportions. The leader's values and philosophy are encapsulated in stories and myths and promulgated by experienced employees (sometimes called priests) who interpret their meaning to novices.[36] The second condition is environmental stability and the ability to buffer internal operations from the shocks of the external world.[37] The third condition is the lack of a strong competing culture. It is difficult to develop a strong culture in situations where there is an overt choice between two social realities, as for instance is the case between parents and children in immigrant families.[38]

It is difficult for Second Generation labor relations to aid the development of a strong organizational culture. First, Second Generation unionism is built on the presumption of internally competing organizational cultures — a management culture and a teacher culture. We know that labor leaders and managers cooperate with one another during the Second Generation, and we know that teachers are able to reconcile activism and good instruction. But the union's concern and involvement in a unified organizational culture is not a feature of Second Generation labor relations. Second, this lack of legitimation for the union's role in the organizational culture leads to a threat to cooperative labor relations. As we saw in the Riverview and Industrial

City cases, the close relationship between the union leadership and the superintendent became the object of school board opposition.

In conclusion, linking labor relations and school productivity remains an unsolved problem, one that was not anticipated when industrial unionism was applied to education. In Second Generation labor relations, teachers won a voice in decisions about the conditions of work but not a legitimate voice in decisions about the work itself. Unionism is conceptually and legally divorced from educational policy and management, and thus is supposedly void of implications for organizational effectiveness. Organizing the schools for effective operation is viewed as management's job, to be accomplished through aggressive rational planning and the wise and deliberate application of rules. Our experience leads us to doubt these assumptions.

Second Generation labor relations have few structures for addressing the organization's productivity problems. The narrowly constructed scope of bargaining makes it difficult for labor and management to consider substantive education questions except obliquely, as they arise under the guise of working conditions. And the current structuring of labor relations provides unions no incentives to care about or feel responsible for the outcomes of schooling. Management's attempts to control productivity by tightening the rule structure are often counterproductive: They make schools unpleasant places to work, more rule-bound and less situationally responsive.

Notes

1 JOHNSON, S.M. (1984) *Teachers' Unions in Schools*, Philadelphia, PA, Temple University Press.
2 For a review of these studies see: LIPSKY, D.B. (1982), 'The effect of collective bargaining on teacher pay: A review of the evidence', *Educational Administrative Quarterly*, 18, 1, Winter, pp. 14–42; FINCH, M. and NAGEL, T.W. (1984) 'Collective bargaining in the public schools: Reassessing labor policy in an era of reform', *Wisconsin Law Review*, 6, pp. 1573–670; KERCHNER, C.T (1986) 'Union-made teaching: The effects of labor relations on teaching work', *Review of Research in Education, Vol. 13,* Washington, D.C., American Educational Research Association.
3 LEWIS, H.G. (1963) *Unionism and Relative Wages in the United States*, Chicago, University of Chicago Press; ASHENFELTER, O. (1972) 'Racial discrimination and trade unionism', *Journal of Political Economy*, 80,

pp. 435–64; RYSCAVAGE, P.M. (1974) 'Measuring union-nonunion earnings differences', *Monthly Labor Review*, 97, 12, December, pp. 3–9.

4   LIPSKY, D.B. (1982) *op cit*, p. 15.

5   While differences in statistical method and conceptualization of the wage effect are not the primary focus of this chapter, they are quite important to understanding the overall union effect. For instance, the wage effect model can be constructed to consider individual differences, differences among school organizations, or differences among geographical regions. Implicit in these constructs is an assertion about how unions operate to gain wage effects. Chambers, for instance, is explicit about calculating the spillover effects on teacher wages that take place because of unionization in the region's labor force. See CHAMBERS, J. (1977) 'The impact of collective bargaining for teachers on resource allocation in public school districts', *Journal of Urban Economics*, 4, pp. 324–39; CHAMBERS, J. (1980) *The Impact of Bargaining and Bargaining Status on the Earnings of Public School Teachers: A Comparison in California and Missouri*, Stanford, CA, Stanford University, Institute for Finance and Governance, Report 80-B6.

6   LIPSKY, D.B. (1982) *op cit*, p. 31.

7   EBERTS, R.W. and STONE, J.A. (1984) *The Effect of Collective Bargaining on American Education*, Lexington, MA, Lexington Books, D.C. Heath.

8   CRESSWELL, A.M. and MURPHY, M.J. (1980) *Teachers, Unions and Collective Bargaining in Public Education*, Berkeley, CA, McCutchan Publishing, p. 462.

9   The hours that teachers work, including non-required hours have changed very little since 1960. See KERCHNER, C.T. (1986) *op cit*. However, comparisons of teachers in union and non-union districts undertaken by Eberts and Stone show substantial differences in the allocation of educational inputs. Their study, the most ambitious of this type, found unionization could explain little in the difference among student achievement scores. But, consistent with salary studies, unionized schools were about 15 per cent more expensive. See EBERTS, R.W. and STONE, J.A. (1984) *Unions and Public Schools*, Lexington, MA, Lexington Books, D.C. Heath, pp. 158–77.

10 BROWN, C. and MEDOFF, J.F. (1978) 'Trade unions in the production process', *Journal of Political Economy* 86, 3, June, pp. 355–78; FREEMAN, R. and MEDOFF, J.F. (1984) *What Do Unions Do?* New York, Basic Books.

11 In 1979, the year in which the most teacher strikes occurred, California's 1056 elementary and secondary school districts reported twenty-four strikes. Nationally, 174 strikes were reported in 1977 in approximately 10,000 unionized school districts. See Bureau of National Affairs, *Government Employment Relations Reporter*, p. 71:4095.

12 One study concluded that teachers gained only about $285 in wage concessions through a strike: DELANEY, J.T. (1983) 'Strikes, arbitration and teacher salaries: A behavioral analysis', *Industrial and Labor Relations Review*, 36, 3, April, pp. 431–46.

13 KERCHNER, C.T. (1979) 'Bargaining costs in public schools: A preliminary assessment', *California Public Employee Relations*, 41, 22.

14 FINCH, M. and NAGEL, T.W.(1984) *op cit.*

15 KERCHNER, C.T. (1986) *op cit.*

16 This effect was also found by JOHNSON, S.M. (1984) *op cit Teachers' Unions...*, and by KERCHNER, C.T. (1976) 'An exploration into the impacts of faculty unionism on community colleges and their presidents', unpublished doctoral dissertation, Northwestern University.

17 On consideration of bureaucracy as an organizational variable see PUGH, D.S., HICKSON, D.J., HINNINGS, C.R. and TURNER, C. (1968) 'Dimensions of organizational structure', *Administrative Science Quarterly*, 13, June, pp. 91–114.

18 WEICK, K.E. (1976) 'Educational organizations as loosely coupled systems', *Administrative Science Quarterly*, 21, 1, March, pp. 1–19.

19 MARCH, J.G. and OLSEN, J.P. (1976) *Ambiguity and Choice in Organizations*, Bergen, Norway, Universitetsforlaget.

20 Goldschmidt's contract analysis based on a nationwide sample showed 93 per cent of the contracts called for grievance arbitration. See: GOLDSCHMIDT, S.M., BOWERS, B., RILEY, M. and STUART, L.E. (1984) *The Extent and Nature of Educational Policy Bargaining*, Eugene, OR, Center for Educational Policy and Management, College of Education, University of Oregon, July. For a review of arbitration effects: FINCH, M. and NAGEL, T.W. *op cit*, pp. 1573–670.

21 PRESSMAN, J.L. and WILDAVSKY, A. (1979) *Implementation: How Great Expectations in Washington are Dashed in Oakland: or, Why It's Amazing that Federal Programs Work at All. This Being the Saga of the Economic Development Administration as Told to Two Sympathetic Observers Who Seek to Build Morals on a Foundation of Ruined Hopes*, Berkeley, CA, University of California Press.

22 RAWLS, J. (1973) *A Theory of Justice*, Cambridge, MA, Belknap Press of the Harvard University Press.

23 OUCHI, W.G. (1980) 'Markets, bureaucracies and clans', *Administrative Science Quarterly*, 25, 2, June, p. 134.

24 MARCH, J.G. and SIMON, H. (1968) *Organization*, New York, Wiley, p. 37.

25 ARROW, K.J. (1974) *The Limits of Organization*, New York, W.W. Norton, p. 55.

26 PETERS, T.J. and WATERMAN, R.H. JR., (1982) *In Search of Excellence*, New York, Harper and Row, p. 38.

27 *Ibid.*, p. 48.

28 For a review of this literature see JONES, G.R. (1983) 'Transaction costs, property rights, and organizational culture: An exchange perspective', *Administrative Science Quarterly*, 28, 3, September, p. 463.

29 WEICK, K.E. (1982) 'Administering education in loosely coupled schools', *Phi Delta Kappan*, 63, 10, June, p. 673.

30 *Ibid.*

31 OUCHI W.G. (1980) 'Markets, bureaucracies and clans', *Administrative Science Quarterly*, 25, 2, June, p. 140.

32 SMIRCICH, L. (1983) 'Concepts of culture and organizational analysis,' *Administrative Science Quarterly*, 28, 3, September, pp. 339–58. Cultural control need not preclude negotiation. See FINE, G.A. (1984) 'Negotiated orders and organizational cultures' in TURNER, R.H. (Ed) *Annual Review of Sociology*, 10, pp. 239–62.

33 Durkheim calls this concept 'organic solidarity'. DURKHEIM, E. (1964) *The Division of Labor in Modern Society*, New York, Free Press.

34 DRUCKER, P. (1974) *Management*, New York, Harper and Row, pp. 74–94.

35 SHILS, E.A. (1961) 'Center and periphery' in *The Logic of Personal Knowledge: Essays Presented to Michael Polanyi*, London, Routledge and Kegan Paul, p. 119.

36 DEAL, T. and KENNEDY, A. (1982) *Corporate Cultures*, Reading, MA, Addison-Wesley.

37 WILKINS, A.L. and OUCHI, W.G. (1983) 'Efficient cultures: Exploring the relationship between culture and organizational performance', *Administrative Science Quarterly*, 28, 3, September, p. 472.

38 *Ibid.*, p. 473.

10
The Impacts on Teaching Work

We believe that unionism has its greatest unseen effects, and its greatest potential, in shaping the substance of teaching work. In one respect, this conclusion is highly surprising. Although teachers had organized with the hope of making fundamental changes in the character of their work, the structures of Second Generation unionism were designed to affect the *conditions*, not the work, of teaching. But just as it is impossible to separate organizational policy from wages, hours and conditions of employment, it is impossible to separate *how teachers work* from *the kinds of workers* teachers are.

Understanding and demonstrating unionization's effects on teaching work is a complex matter, and relatively little attention had been given to this topic. The most common view is that unionization has not changed teaching very much. Administrators tend to assert that the 'real teachers', the ones who set the tone for a school, are not involved with the union. Union leaders tend to assert that bargaining restrictions and the administration's deaf ear keep them from having a substantial impact on teaching as an occupation. We think both assertions are false. Although there were sometimes separate union and non-union (or anti-union) social circles in schools we studied, during the critical turning points that established the character of each labor relations generation, teachers with an identification with the union were involved and dominant, regardless of bargaining restrictions.

Indeed, the bargaining restriction question is in itself somewhat of a red herring. As we argue in this chapter, even the narrowest constructions of collective bargaining involve organized teachers and management in policy-setting and in an unspoken bargain about what kinds of workers teachers are in that particular school district. A combination of factors — the contract itself, changes in the social relations of school districts, and labor politics — are changing teaching. In the following sections, we discuss teaching in terms of four idealized types of work — laboring work, craft work, professional work, and artistic work — and analyze the influences that Second Generation labor relations structures are having upon the conception of teaching.

The Dimensions of Teaching Work

The activities of teachers can be compared with those of other workers along two dimensions. First, every job has some system of 'task definition' which specifies the particular activities workers are expected to perform. Second, every job has some sort of 'oversight mechanism' for monitoring the performance of these tasks. By differentiating the four ideal types of work in terms of these dimensions, one obtains a framework for comparing the jobs of different workers.

There are two basic approaches to task definition: rationalization and adaptation. Under the first approach, specific tasks are pre-planned (either by managers or by the workers themselves) and then undertaken as a matter of routine enactment of standard operating procedures. Automobile assembly and building construction are examples of this approach. The adaptive approach to task definition applies to jobs requiring accommodation to unexpected or unpredictable elements within the work situation. In this case, pre-planning is impossible. Instead, the emphasis is on responding to conditions arising on the job, exercising proper judgment about what is needed, and maintaining intellectual and technical flexibility. Newspaper editors, firefighters, and emergency room doctors rely on this type of task definition.

Monitoring or overseeing work performance can be either direct or indirect. Some workers are subjected to direct oversight through close supervision (such as assembly line workers) or through stringent reporting requirements (such as police officers). For other workers (such as architects or accountants) oversight is indirect. Preparation and skill — that is, the ability to perform the work — are the prime considerations. In the first case, the work itself is inspected. In the second, the work often goes unexamined while the workers are certified or 'licensed' to perform the work on their own.

The criteria used to evaluate these two types of work are quite different. Licensed workers are expected to have at their disposal a set of learned techniques for performing needed tasks, and they are held accountable for the care and precision with which they apply them. Where work is inspected rather than licensed, however, a worker's cooperativeness, dedication, and overall level of effort are most important. If special skills or techniques are required, managers are expected to guide workers in their application through direct supervision and critical review.

As figure 12 indicates, these two dimensions — task definition and oversight mechanism — can be combined to create four distinctive work structures. 'Labor' (upper-left cell) is the term which best describes those work settings where tasks are rationally planned and oversight is undertaken by direct supervision. As used here, the word 'labor' has a special meaning. All jobs involve labor to the extent that they require an expenditure of effort to accomplish a task. In a broad sense, then, 'labor' describes any job requiring concentrated effort and attention. The Bureau of Labor Statistics uses the word 'laborer' to refer to any unskilled or semi-skilled worker. In this context, 'labor' connotes a low-level job, and it is somewhat a term of denigration.

OVERSIGHT AND MONITORING MECHANISMS

		Direct/ inspection Activity monitoring	Indirect/ licensure. Technique monitoring
TASK DEFINITION APPROACHES	Rationalized Preplanned programs Routinized	LABOR (loyalty/ insubordination as basis of evaluation)	CRAFT (precision/ incompetence as basis of evaluation)
	Adaptive Situation responsive Flexible	ART (sensitivity/ frivolousness as basis of evaluation)	PROFESSION (responsibility/ malpractice as basis of evaluation)

Figure 12: Task definition and oversight structures

While it is true that laboring jobs have limited skill, this sense of the term overlooks important structural and organizational differences between labor and other types of work. As we used the word here, 'labor' is distinguished from other types of work not by its association with low-level jobs but rather by the rationalized and preplanned character of the tasks and by direct inspection of how those tasks are performed. While low-level jobs (such as those of sanitation or assembly workers) are more frequently subjected to routinization and close supervision, there is no intrinsic reason why high-status jobs cannot also be so structured. In *Organization Man*, William H. Whyte describes the work we are calling labor being performed by people holding executive job titles but confronted with a social ethic which 'rationalizes the organization's demands for fealty and gives those who offer it wholeheartedly a sense of dedication in doing so'.[1]

Loyalty and insubordination are crucial concepts in evaluating laboring work. It is very important for laborers to give allegiance to the organization for which they work and to respond energetically and promptly to the directions of their superiors. This need for loyalty arises because laborers are not expected to take personal responsibility for the overall purposes toward which their efforts are being directed. As Frederick Taylor's *Principles of Scientific Management* makes abundantly clear, it is the manager, not the laborer, who must decide when, how, and for what purposes work effort should be directed.[2] Thus, the worst offense a laborer can commit is insubordination to a supervisor — not inadequate results. Laborers must do what they are told to do, when they are told to do it. If the result is inadequate, the fault lies with the manager, not the worker.

Craft workers (upper-right cell) are generally free from direct supervision but are held responsible for selecting and applying appropriate specialized techniques in order to realize the specific objectives of their work. Instead of being directly supervised, craft workers are licensed, certified, or otherwise explicitly identified as having special abilities. Managers (or clients in the case of craft workers who operate on a direct contract basis) establish the overall objectives of the work, but once craft specialists take an assignment, they are expected to carry it out without detailed instruction or close supervision. Because unskilled clients have difficulty recognizing incompetent or unscrupulous craft workers, licensure is a matter of public policy in many craft areas. Thus, when technical competence is crucial to adequate task performance, the watchful eye of the state is often substituted for the *caveat emptor* of the marketplace.

Craft work (typified by tool making, routine computer programming, and electronic instrument repair) is evaluated by its precision and competence. Craft workers are judged on how adequately they execute required tasks. While laborers are expected only to follow orders, craft workers are deemed incompetent if they are unable to recognize which techniques to use in performing particular tasks. Indeed, they may even risk insubordination to their superiors in order to apply the techniques of their craft competently.

Rationalization and planning are important to both labor and craft work structures. For laboring work, rationalization is bureaucratic and refers to *standardization* of procedures and the *specificity* of managerial directions. For craft work, however, rationalization is technical and refers to the *appropriateness* of the methods used. Laborers follow standard operating procedures because they represent management's authority. Craft workers follow standard procedures because they are technically correct.[3] As Parsons has noted, Weber's failure to grasp this distinction led him to an inadequate conception of modern bureaucracies, a conception that failed to incorporate properly craft and professional employees.[4]

Professional workers (lower-right cell), like craft workers, are expected to possess a set of specialized techniques. But professional work differs from craftsmanship in the way tasks are defined. While both craft and professional workers perform specialized tasks, professionals are expected to analyze or diagnose situational factors and to adapt their working strategies to the true needs (not just the expressed wishes) of their clients. A craft worker has to know whether a particular task *can* be performed and how to perform it. A professional must decide whether the task *should* be performed. As craft workers, surgeons must know how to operate; as professionals, they must know whether an operation is needed or ethically justified.

Responsibility and malpractice are the key elements in evaluating professional work. Professionals (for example, surgeons or architects) are expected to consider the implications of a particular course of action, resisting interference from superiors or outsiders and accepting personal responsibility for the outcome. Thus, while the worst criticism that can be leveled at a craft worker is incompetence, malpractice is the appropriate label for inadequate professional work. Malpractice differs from incompetence in two important ways. First, even if a task was executed competently, a professional worker is guilty of malpractice if it can be shown that the task was unnecessary or inappropriate to a particular case. Second, professional peers, rather than supervisors or other superiors, make judgments of malpractice.

Artistic work (lower-left cell) is characterized by adaptive task definition and direct monitoring. Although artistic work may require a high level of technical skill, the social interactions that artists undertake in their work are not premised on a common set of skills. Art is recognized in the products produced and by the quality of the artists' engagement in their work. When necessary for their work, artists are expected to rise above the limits of specific technique or established conventions and to develop novel, unconventional, or unexpected techniques. Like professional workers, artists are expected to be flexible and adaptive in defining their work responsibilities. Like laborers, however, artists are not licensed. Rather, their work is evaluated directly.

Actors and musicians are prototypical artists. Key concepts in the evaluation of their work are sensitivity and frivolity. Whereas the professional is required to be responsible, the craft worker to be competent, and the laborer to be loyal, the artist in an organizational setting is called upon to be sensitive to the need for integrity, creativity, and spontaneity. Artists are frequently granted considerable autonomy in the exercise of this artistic sensitivity. They cannot be accused of malpractice, but they can be charged with using their talent frivolously or refusing to enter fully into the creative process. Genuine art work requires dedicated and serious effort. Loyalty to pre-planned institutional programs, a basic requirement of laboring work, is often the enemy of great art.

The works of solitary artists (such as novelists or painters) are evaluated through inspection and critical review by individual consumers or by editors, juries, and reviewers in journals and newspapers. Organized artistic ventures, such as designing buildings or performing plays, are closer in form to teaching. Here, the creation of an artistic masterpiece depends upon adequate coordination or direction as well as sensitive review and critical evaluation.

The work structures shown in figure 12 are 'ideal types' in the sense in that Weber used that term.[5] *Real jobs always involve a mixture of labor, craft, art, and professional work activities.* Abstracting these four ideal types can help in interpreting teacher unionism. First, by applying these analytic distinctions to teaching work, one can see how labor relations policies affect teachers' job responsibilities and influence the supervision systems used by school administrators. Second, these distinctions help to clarify the personal stress and organizational tensions that arise when workers are confronted with multiple, and disparate, job responsibilities. For example, when teachers are assigned lunchroom duty or are asked to report student attendance to the school office, they are performing tasks which closely fit the ideal definition of labor. No special skills are presumed, no advanced training for this work is offered, and the work must be performed in strict accordance with preplanned guidelines. These tasks differ drastically from such craft or artistic tasks as planning curricula, leading discussions, and evaluating student achievement. If either teachers or their supervisors come to regard lunchroom duty and attendance taking as the model for all teaching work, the definition of other tasks will change substantially, as well as the structure of day-to-day working relationships. Similarly, if educators come to believe that all work activities are (or should be) essentially professional, craft, or artistic in character, pressures for organizational and job performance arrangements reflecting these assumptions will follow.

Second Generation unionism tends to support both rationalization (pre-planning and routinization of activities) and direct inspection (close monitoring of work performance). Rationalization represents the teachers' attempt to protect themselves. Direct inspection represents management's efforts to define and enforce its rights in response to unionization.

While craft, professional, and artistic conceptions are abundant in the literature on teaching work, the labor definition is most compatible with Second Generation unionism. Most of the school administrators in our study subscribed to a craft conception which encourages rationalization through improved techniques rather than standardization of practice. Traditionally, managers have believed that teacher training assures the development of needed skills and that certification attests to their mastery. Recently, however, widespread doubt about the efficacy of specific techniques, combined with a lack of confidence in teacher dedication, has encouraged managers to feel that school programs — not individual teachers' skills — are what counts. Nationwide concern about student achievement has created a suspicion that:

211

Incompetent teachers wind up in the classrooms because the state sets virtually no standard of performance. Most candidates become teachers after obtaining state certification, which simply means that the college student passed the required number of education courses at an accredited college or university.[6]

University training and teacher licensure were originally the keystones of a craft movement in teaching, replacing political patronage system which subordinated teaching skill to political party allegiance. Now, faced with rebellious teachers who openly assert the legitimacy of their own self-interests, school managers have lost confidence in the efficacy of these requirements. Direct inspection is a natural management strategy, and the redefinition of teaching as labor an inevitable result.

The Mechanisms for Rationalization and Inspection

Figure 13 summarizes the ways in which current labor relations practices in education support a laboring concept of teaching. As the figure indicates, contract language, changes in social relationships, and new political decision making mechanisms within the schools all contribute to the rationalization of teaching tasks and encourage increased inspection of teacher performance.

The Contract

As indicated in the first row of the figure, three aspects of the typical teacher contract encourage rationalization of work. First, by specifying hours and duties, contracts encourage the general industrial-society drift from 'mission-bounded' work to 'time-bounded' work. As Bernstein says:

> From the Olduvai Gorge to the spinning jenny, in both primitive and preindustrial societies, man's work was task-oriented. He picked nuts and berries until a sufficient number had been gathered for the meal; he hunted until the kill was made; he tended the cows until the milking was done; he worked from dawn to dusk in the harvest and hardly at all in the winter; and so on. He often measured time by the task. In the

THE LABOR PARADIGM SUPPORTED THROUGH

	Rationalization	Inspection
SUPPORT PROVIDED THROUGH CONTRACT LANGUAGE: (primary motivation)	1. Specifying hours and duties. 2. Separating regular and extra duties. 3. Elaborating procedural rules. (protecting teacher interests)	1. Creating grievançe processes. 2. Requiring standard practices. 3. Defining evaluation procedures. (enforcing management rights)
SUPPORT PROVIDED BY CHANGES IN THE SOCIAL SYSTEM: (changed principal work roles) (emergent teacher leader roles)	1. Dual organization system. 2. Homogenization of work roles. (manager) (policymaker)	1. Need to demonstrate power. 2. Intervention by labor pros. (supervisor) (advocate)
SUPPORT PROVIDED BY CHANGES IN THE POLITICAL SYSTEM: (dominated by)	1. Need for support coalitions. 2. Lobbying for remote control. (group solidarity building)	1. Breakdown in the "logic of confidence." 2. Evaluation-based politics. (winning elections)

Figure 13: How labor relations supports labor work structures

last two centuries, at first in Europe and by now in much of the rest of the world, work has become time-oriented. It has been divorced from the task. For those who are employed the amount of work to be performed is endless... Time is traded for money.[7]

Whereas the 'school day' has always been time-bounded, the teacher's day has been ambiguous. Classes begin and end at set hours, but the teacher has undefined duties that extend beyond those hours: grading papers, preparing lessons, and engaging in nonclass interactions with students and their parents. Through collective bargaining, however, teachers have asked that previously undefined hours and duty require-ments be specified. They demand explicit statements of when they are to be on campus and when they are to be available for after-school activities, meetings with parents, open houses and the like.

In addition to specifying hours and duties, contracts formalize the distinction between teachers' 'regular' and 'extra' duties. Regular duties are limited chiefly to classroom instruction, whereas extra duties cover most extracurricular and student supervision responsibilities. Contracts have also relieved many teachers of onerous lunchroom and playground supervision duties. By making this separation obvious, contracts dis-pose teachers to take a narrow view of their responsibility for outcomes and to concentrate on explicitly defined (i.e. rationalized) tasks.

Nor does contract language encourage teachers to take part in less rationalized, spontaneous, and extracurricular forms of teacher-student interaction. Moreover, where they are contractually specified, the stipends and other rewards offered for after-school and extracurricular work are so low that teachers frequently turn them down.

The third source of work rationalization is the propensity of negotiators to develop elaborate procedural rules covering all adjust-ments in job definitions and assignments. By expanding the require-ments for notification, consultation, and review of work assignments (through lay-off and transfer policies, curriculum planning councils, etc.), contracts effectively insure that every aspect of a teacher's job is planned and rationalized.

As figure 13 indicates, the primary motivation for using contract language to rationalize tasks comes from teachers who see rationaliza-tion as a mechanism for securing and protecting their interests. By contrast, inspection is a management concern. Three elements in the typical contract encourage increased inspection of the teacher's job performance.

First, arbitration proceedings require school site managers to show that their orders have a contractual basis and that they have enforced the same work rules for all employees. The threat of a grievance forces managers to attend to situations that they might have preferred to ignore. When a grievance is filed, managerial attention is quickly focused on the problem area involved and, particularly in smaller school districts, the Superintendent and the school board personally attend to the problem. In short, because grievances attract managerial attention, teaching work becomes more tightly inspected — inspected when a grievance is filed and inspected by site managers as a means of preventing future grievances.

Second, contract administration requires standardization of practice in all buildings and classrooms.[8] As principals come to accept their role as contract administrators, they also tend to adopt a narrower definition of management, confining their oversight to those work rules explicitly set forth in the contract.

Third, many contracts include evaluation clauses linking evaluation more closely to discipline and discharge and changing the definition of legitimate causes for dismissal. Instead of judgments by superiors of the teacher's technical competence or personal adequacy, such decisions are now based on factual assessments of whether the teacher did or did not follow the rules. For example, Cyril Lang, an English teacher in Rockville, Maryland, was suspended despite vigorous assistance from the NEA for misconduct and insubordination on the grounds that he had exposed tenth-graders to Aristotle's *Poetics* and Machiavelli's *The Prince*, books not on the approved reading list. To school officials, the issue was not the content of the books, but Lang's failure to follow the rules. As the school Superintendent said, 'I don't know whether Lang is right or wrong about the books, but in a public school system you have to have reasonable procedures to determine what is used and the Superintendent has to uphold them'.[9]

In the Lang case, a standard explicit to laboring work was applied to the evaluation of teachers. Had Lang been treated as a craft worker, the issue would have been whether the children learned, not whether orders and procedures had been followed. Had he been viewed as an artist, critics might have questioned his assigning Aristotle and Machiavelli, but again the issue would have been the improvement of instruction, not employee discipline. Had he been viewed as a professional, judgments about his choice of course material would have been left to other English teachers (as professionals).

Evaluation abuses, in the form of capricious or irrelevant standards, have long been a rallying point for teachers and among the prime causes for teachers unionization. In interview after interview, teacher leaders told us they had been converted to militancy after seeing one of their co-workers 'screwed by the system'. The union response to these abuses has been to insist on narrow standards and explicit procedural due process. These procedural standards, in and of themselves, have become an important value for teachers.

Increased external pressure has encouraged some union leaders to be more open to the idea of inspection. As AFT President Albert Shanker put it, current pressures for educational vouchers and tuition tax credits require union leaders to:

> turn to the members and say, 'Look, you may not like evaluations, you may not like testing, you may not like to do things that will involve some discomfort... But unless we in the public schools respond in a very strong and obvious way, a way which is visible to the public, a way that turns around the present weaknesses and balance; then at the end of the decade there is going to be no such thing as public education left in this country'.[10]

The Social Organization

As shown in the second row of figure 13, changes in the social organization of schools have also contributed to the rationalization and closer inspection of teaching work. In some respects, these changes are more dramatic than the changes resulting from written contracts. As a national teacher organization staff member told us, 'Schools changed a lot when senior teachers shifted from bringing up the younger ones into line with what principals wanted to adopting the ideology that any grievant is right'.

Most school districts now contain two distinct social organizations that compete for the loyalty and cooperation of teachers. The administrative organization, led by the Superintendent, wants teachers to embrace and pursue district goals. The teacher organization, led by the union President or the staff executive, wants teachers to challenge the legitimacy of management directives, where necessary, and perhaps even to withdraw services. These two social systems are integrated largely by rationalization; that is, the powers of each system are circumscribed, the importance of formal 'official' interpretations of all rules and practices is emphasized. As a result, principals experience increasing pressure to treat all teachers alike, and teachers experience peer pressure for uniform response to rules. These pressures intensify whenever labor tensions are high.

While competition for teacher loyalty encourages rationalization, each social system's need to demonstrate its vitality and power leads to closer inspection. Administrators must show that they are willing and able to monitor and enforce the rules governing teacher behavior. At the same time, although they often do not recognize it, teacher organizations need to call attention to the behavior of their members. In their efforts to prove that they are serious in their demands for improved working conditions, teachers go out of their way to attract attention to their work. In one district we studied, teachers opted for 'teachless Wednesdays', on which they met with their classes but did not teach lessons. The principals found themselves spending a great deal of time in the classroom, monitoring teacher performance and futilely trying to make sure that instruction was taking place. When less dramatic demonstrations of power are needed, teacher organizations will often publicly remind their members to 'work to rule': that is, to do only explicitly mandated tasks.

Grievances are frequently used to demonstrate the power of the teacher organization, a process that has a socializing effect on both teachers and administrators. For many teachers, the grievance process is their first expression of militancy. School principals respond to a grievance by giving immediate attention to the specific problem and by labeling as 'suspicious' any teacher who does not side with us in the 'us-or-them' power struggle.

Strong grievance clauses also enable teachers to exercise their power through what Kuhn calls 'fractional bargaining': modifying contractual rules through direct informal negotiations with middle managers. Since virtually any complaint can be linked to health and safety violations or to unilateral changes in working conditions — items that are nearly always grievable — teachers can easily threaten a grievance in order to get the principal's attention.[11]

Another force contributing to the rationalization of teaching work is the surprisingly strong pressure to homogenize teacher job definitions. Both teachers and administrators generally come to believe that unionism requires identical working conditions for all teachers. Teachers tend to feel that any administrative effort to differentiate work rules is merely an attempt to control them rather than to improve education. Moreover, the political structure of teacher organizations and the dynamics of collective bargaining make the homogenization of teacher work roles attractive. During contract negotiations, the demands of specialist teachers may be put forward in initial proposals but are rarely embodied in completed contracts. As noted earlier, specialist teachers generally lack political influence because they are relatively few in numbers and tend to feel that they have already moved out of the classroom proper to embark on new careers. Moreover, 'regular classroom teachers' often suspect that specialists have less demanding jobs, perform non-essential tasks, and are protected by law from economic risks. School managers also find it politically unsound to support special work rules for specialist teachers, since any offer to accommodate the needs of specialists is immediately seized on by teacher negotiators as an indication that management 'has something to give'. Thus, specialists are seldom able to win contractual concessions and often find their programmatic desires traded off as 'frills' when finances become tight.

Labor professionals contribute substantially to both the rationalization and the close inspection of teaching work. Bringing with them the ethos of private-sector labor relations, they assume that workers are motivated primarily by salary incentives and that they need direct supervision in order to work productively. Such a view encourages the belief that close inspection and performance evaluation are the primary vehicles for controlling educational outcomes.

The overall impact of these various changes in the school's social system can be summarized in terms of changes in the roles of principals and teacher union leaders. For school principals, unionization has meant giving greater attention to two concepts that are now enjoying a vogue in professional and scholarly circles: *management* and *supervision*. Widespread use of 'management by objectives' (MBO) techniques and recent enthusiasm over 'clinical-supervision' and 'instructional leadership' are only the most obvious indicators of this new emphasis on the principal as manager and supervisor. As managers, principals are expected to help rationalize the teaching process. As supervisors they are asked to increase the scope and intensity of oversight. Data from a study of 1500 school board members offer further evidence that principals face new role expectations. Asked for their opinions of the effects of collective bargaining, 63 per cent of the board members believed that it forced school districts to adopt more effective management and budgeting practices, 64 per cent thought it called for administrators to be better informed about school operations, and 78 per cent said that it required principals to take a more aggressive role in planning, goal setting, and the like.[12]

Teacher union leaders have emerged as important educational policy-makers and advocates for fellow teachers. As policy-makers, they help to rationalize the system through salary setting, curriculum planning, and day-to-day management of tensions and problems. As advocates, teacher leaders stimulate inspection by challenging the *status quo*, thereby drawing attention to teacher activities that would otherwise go unnoticed.

The Political System

Public-sector labor relations depend more upon political than economic factors. If a satisfactory contract settlement in education is to be achieved, each side must be able to attract and hold the support of politically active citizens. The same dynamic applies in school board elections, where the outcome determines the overall direction for labor relations and other school policies.

The importance of forming political coalitions with citizens is enhanced by the weakening of what Meyer and Rowan have called the 'logic of confidence'.[13] They argue that schools have traditionally operated on the basis of 'ritual' classification rather than close inspection of work performance. For example, special requirements for certifying mathematics teachers are scrupulously followed; but once they are certified, almost no attention is paid to what they actually do. Traditionally, students are also screened and tested before they are placed in a grade level but routinely passed from one grade to another. However, these ritual classifications can be sustained only if:

> Parties bring to each other the taken-for-granted, good-faith assumption that the other is, in fact, carrying out his or her defined activity. The community and the board have confidence in the Superintendent, who has confidence in the Principal, who has confidence in the teachers. None of these people can say what the other does or produces, but the plausibility of their activity requires that they have confidence in each other.[14]

By formalizing conflict, unionization weakens this logic of confidence and renders suspect the dedication and loyalty of teachers. Consequently, once negotiations are institutionalized, interest in inspecting the work of teachers increases. School managers are fond of saying that teacher unionization robs them of their ability to manage. But this assertion is wrong. The politics of unionization forces school managers to act more like managers than ever before. They must plan programs more carefully, look more closely at how teachers execute these plans, and give a more detailed accounting of both to school board members. Unionization has made it more difficult, however, for school administrators to socialize teachers, to create internal cohesion at the school site, and to rely on mutual confidence.

Two other aspects of school politics interact with labor relations to foster a laboring conception of teaching work. One is the emergence of teacher organizations as lobbyists and major political contributors at the state and federal levels. In appealing to state and federal policy-makers for support, teachers have endorsed the belief that education can be rationalized and controlled through program structures, funding categories and procedural regulations. Taken by itself, this belief would tend to support the craft rather than the labor paradigm. It must, however, be considered in conjunction with a second factor: a wide-spread demand for accountability and assessment underlying the 'politics of evaluation' which has dominated most recent state and federal initiatives.[15] Teacher power has interacted with evaluation and achievement politics to create a climate in which state and federal policy frequently encourages compliance rather than excellence, maintenance of effort rather than appropriateness of service, and adherence to guidelines rather than response to needs. Teacher union involvement in politics carries with it the potential for backlash and increased pressures to rationalize teaching work.

Toward a Professional Work Culture

As educators, our instincts and training have led us to apply the word 'professional' to teaching. For the last eighty years, teachers have aspired to join the increasingly large group of workers who claim professional character and hope for professional status. Educators became true believers, and even Etzioni's phrase 'semi-profession' seemed an unacceptable compromise.[16] In this context, speaking of teachers as laborers is an outright affront. But leaving behind the normative conception of occupational status, one must ask why one conceptualization of teaching is to be preferred over another. Not all jobs *should be professional*. It has been argued, for instance, that police officers should never be true professionals, that the obligation to respect civil rights is far too restrictive and the requirement to obey commands are far too severe to allow professionalism to control the occupation.[17] In saying that Second Generation labor relations forwarded the laboring aspects of work, we are not suggesting that unionism degraded teaching from some former exalted position as a profession or priestly art. It simply recognized and codified the extent to which teaching is being treated as a rationalized and inspected activity. As we have noted, it was a form of worker organization that matched the organization of schools and school districts.

In one respect, finding a relationship between unionism and teaching work is encouraging, since it suggests that unions are a much more powerful and important force than has heretofore been recognized. That unions are shaping the nature of teaching work reminds us afresh that teaching is a socially constructed reality. Teaching may have some innate characteristics that flow from the technology of teacher-student interaction, but teaching work is in large part a human creation, the product of human organizations and their political systems. This means that educators have choices. They can create different kinds of teaching if they want to. It suggests that the traditional union concern for 'the quality of work life' need not be limited to trivial details: making minor decisions, and resolving work disputes. The term 'quality of work life' can mean constructing the work itself.

Our finding also means that the current conceptualization of unionism is incomplete. Unionism as we now know it speaks largely to the laboring aspects of teaching work. These are essential, but they are not enough. As our reading of history reminds us, teacher unionism has been motivated by grand ideals and high hopes for substantive changes in teaching work. So far, however, these aspirations have largely gone unrealized. The system of labor relations as a whole — not just the unions — has not come to grips with the set of policy decisions necessary to forge unionism into the instrument for bringing about desired changes in teaching work.

Empowering Different Worker Organizations

Historically, the debate over labor policy has centered around the strength of unions: the extent to which collective bargaining should shift power into the hands of teacher organizations. Relatively little attention has been given to the *nature* of the powers given workers. Yet it is the types of powers that unions have acquired — not their acquiring too much or too little power — that explains the role of contemporary labor policy in redefining teacher work. Some understanding of how specific policies contribute to shaping an occupation is necessary if unions are to become intentional agents in shaping teaching work as a craft, an art, or a profession.

As figure 14 indicates, various labor relations policies and practices generally provide worker organizations with specific powers in four broad arenas. They give unions: (i) a voice in defining workers' job responsibilities; (ii) control over worker access to employment in specific jobs; (iii) power over union membership; and (iv) mechanisms for strengthening workers' influence over the work itself. By deciding on a specific mix of these powers, policy-makers can significantly influence the degree to which work in any industry is structured as a labor, a craft, a profession or an art.

As illustrated in the lefthand column of figure 14, the laboring

WORK STRUCTURE TO BE SUPPORTED

	LABOR	CRAFT	PROFESSION	ART
WORKER ORGANIZATIONS EMPHASIZE:	Bargaining with management	Organizing workers	Certifying practitioners	Evaluating products
WHEN THEY ARE EMPOWERED TO:				
1. Define work based on:	Working conditions	Task definition	Public policy	Product distribution
2. Control worker access to:	Terms of employment	The guild	Client treatment	Specific jobs
3. Define membership based on:	Employment	Apprenticeship	Examination and license	Recognition of talent
4. Give workers control by:	Limiting management rights	Expanding autonomy	High social status	Product ownership

—————MORE CONTROL OVER THE WORK ITSELF—————→
←————MORE CONTROL OVER PRODUCTION PROCESSES————

Figure 14: Labor relations policy strategies for empowering teacher organizations

paradigm is supported when unions are organized around plants, firms, or specific public agencies (such as school districts). The laboring aspects of work are emphasized when unions: (i) define working conditions for all employees in a firm or plant through good faith bargaining of contracts; (ii) prohibit managers from negotiating separately with individual employees; (iii) through the right of agency shop, give job access only to those workers who contribute to the union; and (iv) support individual workers by appealing managerial decisions through the processing of grievances.

These four principles lie at the core of what we know as industrial unionism. Collective bargaining of 'wages, hours and conditions of employment' has become almost synonymous with unionism. Other means of representation tend to be disregarded. Although the concept of collective solidarity has been carefully shorn of the social class implications that dominate unionism in other countries, the idea of industrial unionism is to satisfy group rather than individual interests. Salaries, for instance, are nearly always expressed as rates for a job classification, not as minimums. Employment by a particular organization becomes the primary criterion for union membership. A worker who is not represented by a collective bargaining contract has virtually no incentive to join an industrial union. Indeed, in the economically-rational-man sense, individual employees have little incentive to join. Thus, industrial unions (like all large organizations) must depend on coercive effects of peer pressure, agency shop, or union shop to compel membership. Industrial unionism action respects the principle of union reaction to managerial decision — management acts, unions grieve. The role of the workers and the union is to seek justice within the confines of bureaucracy.

Although one may not be accustomed to thinking of teachers as laborers, the elements of laboring work in teaching — and thus the appropriateness of industrial unionism as a means of representing teachers — are easy to recognize. Clearly, the school district is the primary organization for teaching. Employment contracts, tenure rights, seniority, and pay grades are all school-district-specific. In addition, teachers are often judged by the laboring standards of faithful and loyal fulfillment of organizational routines. The question to be addressed in deciding what kind of unionism we want is the extent to which teaching work should be defined as preplanned and inspected work. If we favor a highly centralized and preplanned curriculum, then we need to strengthen the identification of teachers as laborers and to reduce opportunities for individual deviation and inventiveness.

Craft Unions

To understand the relevance of the particular mix of powers associated with industrial unionism, one must compare that mix with the mix that characterizes other types of worker organization. For example, the primary problem confronting craft unions is that of defining, controlling, and integrating workers into a strong organization. Once craft workers are adequately organized (and so long as the craft is vital to production), they find it is fairly easy to press their demands on managers. The historical problem for craft unions is the difficulty involved in controlling access to the craft as was demonstrated in the 1981 air traffic controllers' strike. Because the Federal Aviation Administration, rather than the union, certified controllers, it was able to find and train an adequate supply of replacements who had little allegiance to the union and who were willing to cross picket lines. To strengthen their position, craft unions have to secure the cooperation and support of virtually all practitioners of the craft. They cannot rely, as industrial unions do, on organizing around the firm.

To solve their organizational problems and to deal successfully with employees, craft unions must have the power to: (i) define specific tasks for union members, through negotiating of task assignments; (ii) control workers' access to the union or guild independent of their employment by any particular firm; through operation of a hiring hall or other means of employment; (iii) establish the criteria for membership in the union, through control of apprenticeship or other certification mechanisms; and (iv) expand workers' autonomy by keeping non-union workers from performing craft tasks and by limiting supervisors' rights to direct the work.

Teaching has many elements of craft. Teacher education programs are constructed around a body of techniques that novices are supposed to master, and state certification standards demand that candidates demonstrate specific skills and competencies. However, teachers have not been organized as a craft. Their specialty organizations (music, mathematics, special education) are generally weak, and they clearly do not control access to work in a specialty. Because teaching is so thoroughly corporatized, craft is also a logistically difficult form of unionization. Because employment is assumed to be long term within a district, rather than project-based, the concept of a hiring hall or craft-certified clearinghouse for employment is not feasible. Concerted action in defense of the craft, such as a strike over the hiring of teachers with noncraft 'emergency' credentials would be difficult to muster. If labor relations policy were to be used to develop the craft aspects of teaching, it would legitimate unions to become more fully involved in setting standards, developing examinations for teachers, and overseeing teacher specialties. It would also legitimate the involvement of teacher unions setting standards for and participating in teacher training programs.

Professional Organizations

Professional unions engage primarily in certifying or licensing practitioners and setting the standards of practice. Generally speaking, organizations which function as professional unions (including the American Medical Association) are more concerned with controlling the legal system which grants them specific rights and protections than with collective bargaining. This is the case partly because professionals traditionally have been self-employed and therefore need statutory rather than contractual protections. However, the distinctive characteristic of professional work is not self-employment but the legal autonomy to set work standards coupled with the responsibility for fulfilling them. To this end, professional organizations must have the power to: (i) use statutory policies that empower workers to set standard operating procedures and to establish the means for punishing those who do not follow them; (ii) control access to the treatment of clients by making it illegal to practice the profession without a license; (iii) make membership in the profession dependent upon an extended period of rigorous training and formal examination; and (iv) increase workers' autonomy by assuring that high social status accrues to members of the profession.

Obviously, the power of professional organizations is sustained by their prestige and status. However, public policy-makers greatly influence occupational prestige by establishing professional licenses, funding training programs, defining standards of performance, and relying on members of the profession to develop and enforce these standards. Teaching as an occupation has adopted many of these professional mechanisms, but it has not placed them in the hands of those who actually teach. Professionalization of unionism would address this difference.

Artist Organizations

The power of artist unions are focused primarily on the evaluation of art products rather than on bargaining, organizing, or certifying members. By equating union membership with creativity, artist unions are able to establish minimum pay scales and to give individual artists a starting point for personal contract negotiations. Artistic worker organizations are supported in the pursuit of these interests if they are empowered to: (i) control the distribution and use of their products through royalties, copyrights, residuals, and so forth; (ii) limit workers' access to certain jobs by requiring producers to hire only union members; (iii) define artistic talent by granting union membership only to individuals whose work has won public recognition (for example, limiting membership in the Writers Guild to those who have had a manuscript accepted); and (iv) empowering individual workers to negotiate the value or ownership of their artistic creations.

As the arrows in figure 14 indicate, the four types of worker organization lie along a continuum. At one extreme are the labor organizations, seeking to control working conditions in firms where their members work. At the other extreme are the artist unions, seeking to gain control over the work itself. Craft and professional worker organizations occupy the middle ground. Craft workers want unilateral control over the exercise of craft techniques, but they collectively negotiate other aspects of their work. Professional workers insist on controlling both the particular techniques which they use and decisions about when and how those techniques should be applied.

The extent to which teaching work will be structured as labor, craft, profession or art depends to some degree on the particular mix of powers given to teacher unions. But it also depends on factors beyond the control of unions. The destruction of craft unions in railroads and newspaper typography, for example, resulted from technological developments. These unions became powerless (and their workers redundant) because their craft skills were no longer necessary to production. Granting specific powers to worker organizations can encourage, but cannot command, the adoption of any specific work structure. What is important in this context is that we recognize the need to align labor relations policies with policies on school finance, curriculum, leadership, and school operations. Labor relations policies will assist in shaping whatever form of work is desired if they are fundamentally consonant with the work technology, the social system, and the organization. If the labor relations system is designed around one conceptualization of work, while the technology, polity and organization favor another conceptualization of work, then unions can only frustrate rather than advance change.

Conclusion: The Reprise of Professionalism

The unsolved problem of Second Generation unionism, discussed over the last three chapters, are all directly related to constructing public school teaching as an authentic profession.

Professionalism attacks the unaddressed problems of a civic culture, of a productive organization, and of a work definition that is well suited to the actual requirements of teaching work. Of the four ideal types of work, only professionalism carries with it a public or civic responsibility toward the *institution* of education. Only professionals are *expected* to act in the public interest, to create a calculus that balances self- and civic-interest. This aspect of profession is most often observed in its breach, for instance when a doctor or lawyer acts in ways that are conspicuously self-serving.

The tension between economic service delivery and serving children will never be resolved within the political system. Only professionalism is capable of developing the necessary balance between client and commonweal interests in order that schools may be simultaneously caring and productive places. Likewise, professionalism is capable of resolving tension between the normative systems of professionals and of those of the control hierarchy.

Finally, professional work characteristics are the only ones that adequately respond to the complexity and ambiguity inherent in classrooms. For eighty years efforts at establishing a simple technology of teaching have failed, and attempts to assure quality by external examination appear artificial. Teaching needs to be structured in such a way that its art and craft are emphasized. Craft places the work technology in the hands of the workers and makes them responsible for its standards and execution. Art requires engagement rather than ritual performance. Both these characteristics are embodied in the idea of a profession. Whereas public policy cannot legislate commitment, it can structure the conditions that are likely to bring it about.

While there is no assurance that professionalizing teaching will solve school problems, it at least attacks the most important ones, and in the process professionalization opens up tantalizing vistas of what might be.

Notes

1 WHYTE, W.H. (1956) *The Organization Man*, New York, Simon and Schuster, p. 6.
2 TAYLOR, F.W. (1911) *Principles of Scientific Management*, New York, Harper.
3 GOULDNER, A. (1954) *Patterns of Industrial Bureaucracy*, New York, Free Press, pp. 223–4.
4 PARSONS, T. (1957) *The Social System*, Glencoe, IL, The Free Press.
5 WEBER, M. (1947) *The Theory of Social and Economic Organization* trans. by A.M. Henderson and Talcott Parsons, New York, Oxford University Press.
6 *New York Times*, 3 July 1979, Section C, p. 4.
7 BERNSTEIN, I. (1977) 'Time and work', in *Proceedings of the 25th Annual Winter Meeting*, Madison, WI, Industrial Relations Research Association, p. 3.
8 GONDER, P.O. (1981) *Collective Bargaining Problems and Solutions*, Arlington, VA, American Association of School Administrators, p. 41.
9 'How To Protect Tender Minds', *Time*, 116, 24, 1 December 1980, p. 77.
10 Albert Shanker interview, Burlingame, CA, 1981.
11 KUHN, J. (1961) *Bargaining in Grievance Settlement*, New York, Columbia University Press.
12 GONDER, P.O. (1981) *op cit*, p. 12.
13 MEYER, J.W. and ROWAN, B. (1978) 'The structure of educational organizations' in MEYER, M.W. and associates (Eds) *Environments and Organizations*, San Francisco, CA, Jossey-Bass, p. 79–109.
14 *Ibid.*, p. 101–2.
15 HOUSE, E. (1974) *The Politics of Educational Evaluation*, Berkeley, CA, McCutchan Publishing Co.

16 ETZIONI, A. (1969) *The Semi-Professionals and Their Organizations: Teachers, Nurses, Social Workers*, New York, Free Press.
17 FEUILLE, P. and JURIS, H.A. (n.d.) *Police Professionalism and Police Unions*, Evanston, IL, Northwestern University Graduate School of Management.

11
Professional Unionism in the Third Generation

We believe that the Third Generation of teacher unionism is rapidly approaching. Passage into what we have called the Era of Negotiated Policy will signal a realization that unions inevitably affect educational policy and an acceptance that schools need to manage through their teacher organizations rather than around them. Pressure for change is already present, embodied in the critique of American public schooling and in the various attempts to reform it. The reform issues, which have been raised nationally and in each state are also found in the politics of each school district. These issues color school board elections, superintendent selections, union presidency campaigns, and collective bargaining itself.

Because many of the reforms are visionary and, in the words of one of the reports, have 'not assumed that any present organizational or legal structure will necessarily continue', movement toward the Third Generation will be controversial and conflictual, just as was the passage into the Second Generation of good-faith bargaining.[1] But the controversies will not center on whether teachers should organize or whether they should bargain collectively. Those fights have been fought and settled in the two previous labor relations generations. Attempts to refight old wars plunge labor and management into prolonged trench warfare, and such battles are fruitless, as our studies in the Thresher district and elsewhere show. The battle that begins the Third Generation is about how unions can help solve educational problems, not whether they will continue to exist.

Pressure toward the Third Generation does not arise out of an explicit union or management failure, but rather because the labor

230

relations system jointly created by labor and management reveals important unsolved problems in public education. As we have suggested in the three previous chapters, these unsolved problems involve establishing confidence in public education as an institution and developing a strong, productive organizational culture. At the core, however, we believe that the fundamental choices surrounding Third Generation teacher unionism have to do with how teaching work is structured. As we have shown Second Generation labor relations borrows heavily from the assumptions of industrial unionism and, at least implicitly, from the assumptions of industrial manufacture. Unionism reacted to a view of organizations as quasi-machines and rallied workers around the abuses of that mode of organization. The deeply-rooted issue in the current round of school reform is whether reform is to be about building a better machine, perfecting industrialism in the schools, or whether it is to be about organizing teaching around craft, art and profession. The existing relationships between teachers and managers and the assumptions of Second Generation labor relations are challenged by each of the major reform proposals: teacher control and responsibility for entry standards, career advancement opportunities involving differentiation among teachers, evaluation of teachers by their peers, and lead teachers with substantial responsibility for school sites. Proposals such as these make an issue of whether it is possible to support public school teaching as an authentically professional mode of work and to create schools as work places for professions. Teacher unions face the same issues.

The Need for Reform

As teacher unionism followed across the United States in the 1960s, industrial unionism was adopted largely by default. It had become *the* dominant model in the American private sector, and more than a generation of statutes, case law, and professional practice produced strong norms about what constituted 'good labor relations'.

The institutionalization of industrial unionism in the United States involved broadening the organizational appeal and power of labor by focusing unionism on the whole firm rather than the individual occupation. In return for a role in setting wages, hours, and working conditions, unions accepted the principle that 'management acts and unions grieve', placing policy initiative and job definition in the hands of management. This ideology, expressed in the form of a narrow scope of bargaining, has been transferred to the public sector; it is clearly part of the Second Generation ideology that 'the shortest contract is the best one'.

The structures of industrial unionism evoke what is known in industry as 'job control unionism'. A worker is assigned to a highly articulated and sharply delimited job and surrounded by complexes of specific rules, customs, and precedents concerning how the work is to be done and what obligations the worker has to the employer. The atomization of work is structurally enforced through strict lines of demarcation between bargaining unit jobs, supervisory jobs, and jobs in other bargaining units. Wage rate and seniority systems structure careers and reinforce current production processes, since each change in production entails a threat to current or projected income, which has taken on the character of an accrued property right. In this context, 'industrial democracy is reduced to a particular form of industrial jurisprudence in which work and disciplinary standards are clearly defined and fairly administered, and disputes over the application of rules and customs are impartially adjudicated'.[2] As suggested in previous chapters, both the strengths and the weaknesses of industrial unionism stem from its tendency to concentrate on governance and organization-level problems. Even as it gives workers increased organizational power and effective political parity, it deprives them of meaningful involvement in the conceptualization of their jobs and reduces their responsibility for the quality of their work performance. Thus, industrial unionism has not resulted in the kind of personal satisfaction and job enrichment that many union leaders (and many rank-and-file workers) envisioned.

The challenge to labor relations in education is to develop a unionism idea that focuses on the problems of teacher job definition and addresses issues of school organization and governance in the context of teaching work. The new unionism must give first priority to formulating appropriate teacher job definitions and supporting the development of a productive work culture. Such a conception may appropriately be called 'Professional Unionism' since it combines the essential elements of a professional work structure with the organizational and governance features of a unionized public agency.

As was pointed out earlier (chapter 10), professions are distinguished by their rigorous self-enforced certification procedures coupled with their responsiveness in defining and performing the work to be done. The extraordinary autonomy granted to the profession and flexibility expected of individual practitioners reflects society's belief that the professional worker's skills will be applied to the benefit of clients and society. Professional unionism recognizes the inherent complexity of teaching work, including its artistic and craft elements.

The remainder of this chapter explores the meaning of professional unionism for the public schools. We propose professional unionism as a solution to the critical problems of job definition, organizational culture, and school productivity described earlier. We argue that in order for teacher organizations to adopt a professional union model, three basic elements in the legal and organizational framework of labor relations must be changed: the scope of bargaining, the nature of negotiated agreements, and the definition of bargaining units. As the argument unfolds, we will note that some of the critical elements of professional unionism are already in place in various school districts. What remains is that these diverse and generally creative approaches to labor relations be integrated into a comprehensive new model and that their implications for reshaping the legal framework of labor relations be fully analyzed.

Solving the Problems of Industrial Unionism

The essential ideas behind professional unionism can best be understood by reviewing the problems associated with the implementation of the industrial union model, beginning with its distortion of teacher work roles.

The Problem of Work Role Definition

The most pressing problems created by industrial unionism arise because it equates work with laboring work. That is, it sharply distinguishes between the conception and organization of work on the one hand and the execution of specific tasks on the other. Work conception is defined as a management prerogative. Execution is assigned to the workers, and thus the conditions and payment for work become the primary object of collective negotiation. This model requires that jobs be 'unambiguously defined' and that changes in job definition and work assignments be 'sharply limited'. Otherwise it would be 'meaningless to attach specific wages and employment rights to each job'. Moreover, the 'governing rules and customs' used to control adjudication of labor-management conflicts would become 'too ambiguous to be administered through the grievance system'.[3]

To implement industrial unionism's conception of work, at least three conditions must be met. First, managers must have sufficient skill, time and access to the work place to supervise each worker's task performance. Without high-quality close supervision, managers are powerless to enforce work rules. Employee discipline is impossible, because realistic and equitable standards of performance cannot be established. When laboring workers are not closely supervised, they tend to redefine their own jobs but without the rigor or dedication of craft, artistic or professional workers.

Second, tasks must be defined wholly by management, either through direct orders or through thoroughly standardized and repetitive procedures. In other words, workers are held responsible either for 'faithful compliance' or for 'piecework' execution of specific tasks. Moreover, the rewards for laboring work are assumed to be extrinsic (i.e., wages and fringe benefits) not the result of enjoyment or self-expression found in the work. Only in these circumstances is it possible to strike explicit bargains over how much work is to be traded for what wages under what working conditions.

Third, the laboring conception of work inherent in industrial unionism requires that the quality of the work be minimally affected by the individual worker's level of emotional involvement. The industrial model assumes that disagreements between labor and management are endemic to the work place and that work responsibilities can be defined and task performance be monitored without resolving the emotions aroused by these disagreements. Thus, according to this view, management's choice of technique, rather than a worker's engagement or disengagement, determines the quality of the product. Formalized rules and objective third-party adjudication are intended to substitute for shared beliefs and common understandings. Fair play, not mutuality of interest, is the guiding principle of labor-management relations under the industrial union model.

Unfortunately, teaching work meets none of these three conditions. Administrators do not have the skill, the time, or the access to classrooms necessary for the close supervision routinely exercised over laboring work. To be sure, some serious efforts are being made to increase oversight, but in our judgment, even the most ambitious of these schemes falls far short of the supervision levels found in most labor-intensive work settings. Nor is closer supervision necessarily desirable. High-quality teaching is, we suspect, more likely to be disrupted than reinforced by the sort of intensive managerial scrutiny typical of work places that closely fit the industrial model.

Teaching effectiveness does not depend on the faithful execution of predefined techniques or specific orders. No set of rules yet devised comes close to covering the complex contingencies which teachers face every day.

Good teaching is not possible without emotional involvement. Burnout is feared and engagement applauded because everyone recognizes that technique alone is not sufficient. The technique that worked on Monday may fail on Tuesday. Thus, great teaching requires that teachers cultivate the capacity for 'doublemindedness', the ability to internalize and respond to the environment while simultaneously moving forward toward a teaching objective.

Not only does teaching work not fit the requirements of supervised labor, but teacher union leaders never intended that this model be adopted. On the contrary, most of the union leaders with whom we spoke insist that good-faith collective bargaining was intended to safeguard teachers from management scrutiny and interference. Under the protection of strong labor contracts teachers would have the autonomy to exercise their professional judgment and to control the nature of their work as well as the quality of its execution. However, industrial unionism does not support the professional work roles sought by teacher leaders. Instead, it creates a situation in which managers try to separate the union from any active involvement in educational planning and decision making and to use labor relations primarily to legitimate task assignment and to control the performance. This process prevents Second Generation labor relations from ever producing the kind of work roles and job definition responsibilities intended by the pioneers of teacher unionism.

Whatever the final outcome, Third Generation labor relations will need to recognize that teachers must be involved in conceptualizing and planning their work as well as in building a system for assuring fair and equitable supervision of their performance. This means that the professional unionism of the Third Generation must provide for the negotiation of teacher job definitions and work roles as well as rules governing task assignment and performance criteria.

To this end, the contract-negotiating process will have to be restructured. The subjects covered will have to include the purposes and character of educational programs as well as the nature of teacher assignments and the procedures to be used in evaluation. Only if the nature of negotiated agreements are themselves altered will this be possible. Teacher work role definitions cannot be reduced to rules; they must also include statements of purpose and affirmations of responsibility that go well beyond the confines of a predefined task structure. Such a transformation of the negotiating process will require a redefinition of the organizational relationship between teacher unions and school systems. If roles are to be negotiated, organizational relationships will have to include the development of cultural norms as well as routinized procedures. We turn to this problem in the next section.

The Organizational Culture Problem

At the organizational level, Second Generation industrial unionism vigorously attacks the abuses of work place bureaucracy but tends to overlook the importance of a productive work culture. Unionism has been able to achieve a measure of fairness and equity for teachers by enforcing formalized and standardized rules and procedures. It is assumed that management will be responsible for directing the educational process. Such an approach might work in occupations where tasks can be fully preplanned and labor-management tensions are mostly over job rights and work rules. These conditions are not present in schools, however.

Effective teaching requires flexible, adaptive responses to classroom contingencies that can never be fully described or anticipated. The fundamental tension between teachers and managers involves educational judgments that can only obliquely be subjected to the grievance process. In the struggle over rules and procedures to prevent abuse of individual rights, unionists and school officials alike have failed to organize teachers into the integrated workforce necessary for high quality education.

To develop integrated and cooperative work groups, more is required than the detailed specification of working conditions or of individual rights and responsibilities. Integrated work groups exist only in the context of shared values and mutual planning. Because it does not support the development of a work place culture or an integrated teaching work group, the industrial model threatens the long-term health of the schools and with it their potential for high teaching performance.

Schools need well-developed organizational cultures because, as their history demonstrates, bureaucratic techniques do not adequately support instruction. Even the literature on effective schools, which is currently the most bureaucratic and 'formula-based' approach to school improvement, makes it abundantly clear that productivity depends on organizational cultures, not on the elaboration and strict enforcement of detailed work rules.[4] Industrial unionism as we have seen, assumes that faithful performance of work routines will produce efficient and satisfactory educational outcomes.

Second Generation industrial unionism places a great premium on conflict management. Indeed, so fundamental is the expectation of conflict that its absence arouses anxiety and uncertainty among both union leaders and school managers, who fear that they will be seen as having 'gone soft'. Both sides invest heavily in contingency planning and in the development of skills for limiting conflict and reducing the chances that it will seriously disrupt work. But the major vehicle for conflict management within industrial unionism is *formalization* — of rules, of contract language, even of social relationships. This formalization is the enemy of the shared understanding needed to create an organizational culture.

We are not suggesting that the tension between industrial unionism and an appropriate work culture in the school was intended by either the teacher leaders or the school managers who were responsible for developing Second Generation labor relations in today's schools. On the contrary, dedicated leaders on both sides regularly voice their disappointment over the corrosive and potentially alienating tensions that threaten the quality of working relationships in the schools. A remarkably large number of early teacher organizers we interviewed agonized aloud that unionization has not produced the kind of unified profession they had envisioned, and they recognize the problem as a serious threat to effective school organizations (though they often blame recalcitrant managers or school board members for the problem).

The problem, as we see it, is that the mechanisms of industrial unionism cannot generate strong and productive organizational cultures. A new pattern of relationships between teacher unions and school organizations needs to be developed.

We believe that teacher unions should be able to negotiate policy, not just rules and working conditions. If teachers are to behave as organized professionals, they must have some means of formulating and giving organizational authority to their collective professional judgments. They must be able to express their ideas about the proper goals of education, the most promising plans for pursuing agreed upon goals, and the most appropriate strategies for handling educational problems. Moreover, teacher organizations need to create more integrated work groups within the school, groups that share much more than common work rules and grievance mechanisms. They need to be organized around shared educational goals and integrated school programs.

This need to restructure the relationship between teachers and district organizations raises anew the problem of school governance. How can political legitimacy be given to teacher organizations whose authority touches every aspect of school planning and policy? What authority will school boards and school managers have? How can the public interest be brought to bear on the educational system? In short, how will the twin political problems of appropriate representation of interests and maintenance of high productivity be simultaneously addressed? If a broad ranging professional unionism replaces the narrowly structured good faith bargaining requirements of today's industrial unionism, what will guarantee the survival of democratic control over the schools? We turn to these questions as we review why industrial unionism has failed to deal with the basic governance question of public confidence in school productivity.

The Problem of Public Confidence

At the governance level, industrial unionism tackles forthrightly problems of political power and representation but overlooks the political importance of public confidence in the productivity of any agency supported by tax funds. In private-sector industries, this lopsided attention to the politics of representation is understandable. Private-sector governance flows from ownership, and American unions have generally not followed the path of their European counterparts in seeking representation in the corporate board room.[5] When employee interests are expressed outside of collective bargaining, they are generally channeled through governmental policy where unions have been particularly active proponents of safety legislation, minimum wages and tariff and trade restriction laws. But the central assumption undergirding industrial unionism is that productivity and public confidence are assured through market choices.

Such a view might work in the public schools if marketing processes played a major role in the delivery of educational services, if school operations were effectively tied to government regulatory and finance decisions, and if education was a consumer service whose quality is of immediate interest only to those who receive it. But none of these conditions is present in public education. Educational services are not generally marketed to a clientele whose choices are translated into direct judgments about the quality of school services. In the private sector it can be argued that, whenever excessive self-interest on the part of workers leads to shoddy goods or excessive prices, demand for their services disappears and they are punished for their avarice. Whereas market forces clearly influence the environment in which education takes place, the market is the wrong metaphor for discussing political control over educational service delivery. Though the political system must legitimate education's worth, this process has little to do with anyone's ability to identify its cash value. Education is supported by the belief systems of our *political culture*, rather than by a balance sheet in the *political economy*.

Public concern over union activities and declines in educational quality have little to do with an actual assessment of increased cost or an objective evaluation of the work done by teachers. Rather, the problem lies in a political reaction to unionism. The legitimation of teacher economic self-interest at the bargaining table has aroused public suspicion that teachers no longer speak for the public interest of schools or represent the real needs of children. The polity has come to doubt the legend we saw on a picket sign: 'Teachers Want What Kids Need.'

A cultural interpretation of this problem underscores the possibility that insisting on representation without accepting responsibility for school productivity may seriously damage the 'logic of confidence' which for more than 100 years has supported informal teacher control over educational content and school practices.[6] Because educational quality is measured in cultural rather than economic terms, industrial unionism appears at odds with the assertion that teachers are organized in the public interest as well as in their own interest and that teaching ought be accorded professional standing. Appearances of unvarnished self-interest make it difficult for the public to accept teaching as a 'moral occupation'.

Faced with this perception, the political system has responded by simultaneously trying to disinvest in public education and to over-regulate its operations. Educational vouchers and tuition tax credits are touted as vehicles for the creation of a true consumer market for education that would curb inefficient practices and excessive expenses. In addition, planning and program decisions moved from the hands of local educators and were given to state-level policymakers. The broad array of actions proposed and taken in this arena are collectively referred to as 'legislated learning'.[7]

The solutions are worse than the problem, however. The problems of mass public education will not be solved by making public schools the educators of last resort for the unmotivated and unchosen. Nor will an avalanche of programs, regulations and carrot-and-stick funding schemes produce engagement in the classroom.

Instead, both teachers and the public need to respond to the vision of professionalized teacher work roles. They all need to recognize that educational productivity springs from dedicated action by teachers who insist upon taking responsibility for the quality of their work, and whose judgments about when and how to do their work must be carefully conceived and widely honored.

The Legal Foundations of Professional Unionism

To support the shift from industrial to professional unionism, broad changes are needed in the way we think about labor relations and in the laws that structure labor relations. To be effective, these changes must first become operative in the minds of educators; teacher organizations and school district leaders must change how they think about labor relations problems and processes. These changes in belief should be followed by changes in the law. While statutory changes are not essential and cannot guarantee desired results, present labor laws do not help the situation. In a general sense, they undergird the ethos of industrial unionism and support the wrong-headed and self-defeating processes we have been describing. In a more specific sense, they make the adoption of a new idea of unionism legally suspect.

Current labor law enshrines two assumptions that impede professional unionism. One assumption is that there must be a clear distinction between employees and managers. If one follows the logic of the Yeshiva University case, employee participation in the governance process voids their eligibility to organize as a union.[8] In one case the National Labor Relations Board went so far as to rule that any faculty member who served on a university committee was a 'manager' and thus ineligible for membership in a bargaining unit.[9] While these private-sector university cases, which fall under federal jurisdiction, represent an extreme, the state laws that govern public school teachers have failed to recognize unions as an agent of professional interest.

In addition to differentiating employees and managers, labor law tends to assume that the interests of labor and management are antithetical. Section 8(a)(2) of the National Labor Relations Act makes it an unfair labor practice 'to dominate or interfere with the formation or administration of any labor organization'. Its author, Senator Robert Wagner, saw employer domination of unions as 'the greatest obstacle to collective bargaining'.[10] Early NLRB decisions held that 'virtually any employee group interaction with management' was a violation of this section.[11]

Over the years, this interpretation has been relaxed, and the notion of labor-management cooperation increasingly accepted. But the legal cloud has not disappeared entirely. Under one interpretation, Quality of Worklife programs and most other forms of employee-management interaction are not legally protected labor relations activities.[12] This interpretation suggests that activities outside of the traditional collective bargaining activities are not 'union' activities. Thus, in their recent decisions the NLRB and the courts appear to be narrowing the definition of a labor organization.[13]

Taken as a whole, the statutes cast a shadow on the relationship between organized professionalism and unionization for teachers. While some argue that the logical step is to repeal collective bargaining rights, we advocate reform building on the strengths of current teacher organizations. A teaching profession requires strong, independent teacher organizations — organizations able to express teachers' educational judgments aggressively and to negotiate agreements that combine professional judgments with vital public and political interests to produce effective school programs and policies.

Existing teacher unions have two characteristics absolutely essential to the development of the professional unionism we envision: strength and independence. They must be strong so they can be held accountable for formulating and articulating sound professional judgments about the planning and conduct of school programs. As the literature on educational change abundantly demonstrates, vigorous teacher involvement in school improvement is essential if a change is to be adopted. Thus, changes in teacher methods or strategies, in curricular coverage, or in the interrelation between parts of the curriculum have been among the least successful educational reforms. Many of the federal categorical programs aimed at these reforms have disappeared 'without a trace'.[14] Unions must be independent to allow a professional culture — the silent pressure of opinion and traditions — to develop within school organizations without being dominated by them. Just as house unions and sweetheart contracts proved too weak to protect industrial workers from abuse, domesticated professional organizations cannot effect a proper balance between professional judgment, organizational convenience, and political expediency. Existing teacher unions have shown their independence, but it was not always thus. In its pre-collective bargaining days, the NEA was anything but independent of administrative domination. Early AFT locals were frequently ineffectual. And the other traditional teacher groups — subject matter organizations in English, music, mathematics — have always been either wards of the universities or too small and weak to enforce any real standards.

Our studies, and those of other researchers, have revealed several nascent examples of teacher unions that have adopted critical features of the professional unionism we have in mind. They have done so largely through thoughtful and dedicated leadership of individual teachers and the understanding support of enlightened school board members and administrators. Generalizing from their experience, we have identified the basic elements of a new unionism, which we propose here as a meaningful and realistic response to the problems confronting public education. As we envision it, professional unionism follows the pragmatic tradition of the American labor movement: solving the pressing 'problems of today', rather than building a utopian but unrealizable model for a future that never arrives.

The Changes We Propose

We propose three basic changes in the legal and ideological framework for public school labor relations: the scope of bargaining, the nature of negotiated agreements, and the determination of membership in teacher bargaining units. Before describing each element in detail, we want to emphasize that they are fundamentally interrelated. Changing any one of the elements without adopting commensurate changes in the others is not likely to produce the results we have in mind. While the need for multiple simultaneous changes makes the shift from industrial to professional unionism especially difficult, piecemeal change will almost certainly disrupt the delicate balance required to make unionism function as well as it does now.

The Scope of Bargaining

The first major change proposed is a dramatic expansion in the scope of negotiations that take place between teachers and school managers. With its focus on worker protection and its rejection of responsibility for organizational productivity, Second Generation labor relations policy easily embraced the principle that the scope of bargaining should be closely circumscribed. But because it includes worker judgments in the definition of work roles, professional work does not easily fit into this scheme. Professional workers should be encouraged to discuss all aspects of their job responsibilities, not just salaries and work rules.

Second Generation bargaining embodies the legal fiction that bargaining can be separated from policy. For professional workers, this proposition is not only factually wrong but also inappropriate as a basis for planning and executing their work. Faith in the statutory separation of policy from bargaining is misplaced; the scope of bargaining expands through judicial interpretation, administrative decision, and the natural inclination of both parties to solve problems as they arise. Thus, Second

Generation labor relations are characterized by 'accidental policymaking'. The recognition that labor relations inherently generate school policy is one of the causes of the political revolt that we have labeled the Second Intergenerational Conflict.

If professional unionism is to integrate labor relations and school policy in a beneficial way, it must address important and legitimate questions and must discourage, expose, and punish those who trivialize the process or try to use it for illegitimate purposes. When it comes to school politics and labor relations, these are not abstract issues. School politics can easily be distorted to serve political expediency or organizational convenience. Union leaders often allege that school board members are using their offices for particularistic or partisan purposes; whereas, the teachers are seeking 'what's good for education'. (In exceptional cases, including one in our study districts, the school board's particularistic purposes led to charges of criminal corruption.) And school board members often accuse the union of unvarnished greed and narrow self interest, while proclaiming their own dedication as 'elected public servants'.

The question, then, is what kinds of interests should be legitimated, and how can the tensions between them be regulated? In discussing the problems of school governance in chapter 8, we recognized the tension inherent in high-level public service institutions: providing services to clients and implementing the wishes of the general public or commonweal. Client service is supported by giving employees responsibility for making judgments about what services are appropriate for their clients and broad latitude and independence in making and implementing those decisions. Commonweal interests are best supported through strong external control over service organizations. External control helps insure that the political will is followed rather than that of the employees. The armed forces are the archtypical commonweal organization. In the United States, great care is taken to ensure that the military officers from the chiefs of staff to lieutenant colonels are responsive to the Congress and to the civilian secretaries of each armed service rather than free to rely on their own judgment about when and where to fight a war. Violation of this principle invites national scandal.

Historically, public school unionism has treated the tension between client service and commonweal interests in different ways at different times. During the First Generation, it was assumed that teachers and administrators alike would alter client services to meet the commonweal interests of the community. The phrase 'neutral professional competence' described the idealized role of school employees, who were to direct their professional judgments toward the ends chosen by legislatures and school boards. During the Second Generation, school boards continued to act as the repository of commonweal authority. It was assumed that teachers as an organized collective (union) had legitimate self-interests but that client service interests were to be expressed individually or through other channels. The structures of professional unionism that we propose for the Third Generation are intended to legitimate both client service professionalism and commonweal public service interests of teachers and to create an arena where the tensions between them can be resolved.

The problem is to create an arena in which legitimate professional client service and commonweal political interests can be served and illegitimate interests can be discouraged. There are, of course, numerous ways of structuring school boards and other public bodies so that the public interest rises over political expediency. The history of school politics reform is filled with examples: non-partisan election, public agendas, and open meeting laws. Labor law also incorporates structures designed to curb worker self-interest and organizational convenience. In some states, initial proposals of labor and management must be made public. In many states, strike alternatives, such as fact finding, are designed to expose proposed settlements to public scrutiny.

But these mechanisms have done little to encourage unions and management to address those areas of educational policy and practice that are the *joint* concern of both the commonweal and the professional. In fact, as indicated earlier, both the statutes and the organizational structures of unions and management militate against substantive engagement in the resolution of educational policy issues. It is precisely this engagement professional unionism is designed to encourage.

Introducing Policy Trust Agreements

Expanded professional negotiations between teachers and school managers need forms of agreement in addition to conventional collective bargaining contracts. It does little good to discuss educational goals or to decide how teacher professional judgments are to be balanced with political and organizational needs if the results of these deliberations are forced into the straightjacket of formal rules and grievable contract clauses. The problem is at once simple and profound. Labor contracts are intended to govern behavior, not to express the concepts, plans or intentions of those who negotiate them. They are formulated with the express intent of reducing flexibility and uncertainty so that there will be fewer opportunities for mistreatment or abuse of workers. From the standpoint of organizational policy and planning, labor contracts are at best neutral and more frequently negative documents. They specify the conditions under which workers are expected to work, but they do not define the goals or programmatic frameworks for organizing their efforts. And there are good reasons why this is so.

The rights established by a labor contract must apply to all of the individual cases to which they refer. Thus, they must be framed and written in ways that clearly establish the obligations of each party to the other, removing whenever possible elements of uncertainty and questions of individual intent. Good labor contracts cannot define the goals of work or the purposes of the employing organization, and they are not good at expressing the wishes or desires of either party. Organizational policies, not labor contracts, are the appropriate vehicles for establishing collective goals and plans. Because policies do not create individual property rights or managerial prerogatives, policies can be more expansive expressions of collective beliefs and desires. Policies guide, but do not explicitly specify work activities. Even if a policy is followed only 90 per cent of the time, it is probably doing a powerful job of shaping the performance of an organization and the people in it. In contrast, if a labor contract is followed only 90 per cent of the time, it is likely to cause enormous tension and disruption. One would be ill-advised to include in a labor contract any clause which makes work obligations dependent on contingencies that are difficult to foresee clearly or describe explicitly.

Labor contracts do not, of course, fully express the working agreements that are reached in most organizations. Even in industrial settings, collective bargaining contracts have always been an incomplete reflection of the relationship between employers and employees. Contracts are what Selznick calls 'an incomplete law of association'. They embody only a part of the diffuse and complex relationship that has evolved legally and socially, from the relationships between masters and servants.[15]

As we reflected on our data, we realized that in virtually every case in which unions and management had explicitly and intentionally tried to solve educational problems they did so outside of the contract. When asked, the parties explained that they chose not to use the contract because the situations were ambiguous. They understood that a problem existed and that they wanted to solve it, but they were not at all sure of a solution. Agreements other than the collective bargaining contract provided them the flexibility they wanted. In the words of one union leader, 'they were ways to approach the problem when you don't know what you're doing'.

In the development of professional unions, as we envision them, contracts will continue to exist, but they will work in parallel with a new form of agreement which we call an Education Policy Trust Agreement. These agreements are designed to allow labor and management to negotiate and reach accord on organizational goals and policies. They will enable the parties to discuss such central education issues as curriculum development, instructional goals, the assignment of students or teachers, the substance of evaluation, and the bases for discipline and discharge of unprofessional teachers. The negotiations leading to Education Policy Trust Agreements will provide an effective mechanism for balancing teachers' professional judgments with the public service and organizational effectiveness criteria critical to school system performance and support.

The name of the new form of agreement suggests its content and function:

— **Educational.** Trust agreements are intended to deal with a broad range of educational matters: What are student achievement goals? How should scarce resources be allocated among competing educational missions? What freedoms and what flexibility should teachers expect? What level of care and dedication should the schools and the students expect?
— **Policy.** The new agreements are intended to move well beyond work rules and terms of employment. As we have repeatedly argued, professional teachers must deal with school policy matters. They must help to shape the general goals and the overall intent of the school, not just propose formal work rules.

— **Trust.** These agreements are trust agreements in both the most common senses of the term. Formally they are related to the trust instruments used to control the use of property. Organizationally they involve each side's holding 'in trust' the judgments, desires and wishes of the other.

— **Agreement.** The set of educational policies that constitute the trust are explicitly negotiated agreements between organized teachers and school management, similar in this way to labor contracts. The agreements would have legal standing and could be adjudicated either through court review or through procedures developed by the parties.

Though similar to other more familiar forms of agreements, Educational Policy Trust Agreements also have some marked differences. Trust agreements would serve functions similar to the informal 'sidebar' agreements that are sometimes part of labor contract negotiations. Under industrial unionism procedures, labor and management negotiation often wish to address problems that they feel should not be reduced to contract language. In the most informal of these cases, the parties reach 'handshake' agreements. At a more formal level, a 'letter of understanding' is sometimes drawn up, or the school district agrees to make changes in specific educational policies. Educational Policy Trust Agreements capture the important contributions this practice makes to the incorporation of teacher judgments into organizational plans and programs. In addition, they have a finite life, expiring on a given date and thereby creating occasions for reconsideration. Unlike contract expiration, however, there is no presumption that a new agreement would arise. The trust agreement would work more like the 'sunset' clauses of certain laws — automatically lapsing unless reenacted.

Educational Policy Trust Agreements resemble ordinary private trust agreements like those found in wills or like 'blind trusts' which public officials use to manage their assets while in office. These trusts are legal documents that both empower and instruct those responsible for executing them. Preparing a will (establishing a testamentary trust) or establishing a trust while still alive (an *inter vivos* trust) allows one to express one's goals and to authorize a trustee to make certain decisions about how to pursue those goals.

Trustees are empowered to buy and sell from a portfolio of securities and are expected to exercise sound professional judgment in maintaining or disbursing the assets. Trustees are also responsible for following the instructions included in the trust. If a trust sets up a fund for the education of one's grandchildren, for example, it might give the trustees broad discretionary power to decide what kinds of education and what kinds of educational expenses qualify. Are only tuition and living expenses allowed? Does only undergraduate education qualify? Can the trust fund be used to support study abroad? Or summer vacations? The key to a successful trust is the establishment of a proper balance between precision of intent and flexibility of action.

The proposed Educational Policy Trust Agreement differs from private trusts in that its content is created by the joint agreement of teachers and managers. Both teacher unions and school boards are expected to treat the policies contained in the trust agreement just as they now treat board policies. They are expected to follow the policies in their daily decisions and activities, and they would expect others to follow them, too. When deviations occur, representatives of labor and management meet to determine whether the deviations break with the intent of the agreement or are necessary to implement its spirit. In this situation, the differences between an Educational Policy Trust Agreement and a contract become apparent. The question asked is not whether specific clauses or rules had been violated, and, if so, what redress should be made. Rather, the question is whether the deviation is reasonable, given the general intent of the parties, and whether the good of the school organizations or the public interest is better served by enforcing or by modifying the agreement. The process either reaffirms the existing agreement or results in the development of alternative actions to be taken in future decisions of this type.

Trust agreements have strong parallels with conventional labor contracts and some equally strong differences, as figure 15 shows. Contracts contain compensation and work rule clauses that both define and structure teaching tasks. These clauses convey property rights to individual teachers (such as the right to be classified at a particular pay grade) and organizational rights (such as released time for officers) to the union. Trust agreements establish intentions, goals that specify the purposes for pursuing a particular program or project about which the union and management are negotiating. Trust agreements also contain resource statements specifying the sources of time, money and allocation of authority to be used in support of the agreed upon goals. For example, if the parties agreed to develop a new literature-based writing

Contracts	Policy Trust Agreements
1 WORK RULES	1 WORK GOALS
☐ Required activities	☐ Purposes
☐ Individual rights	☐ Criteria for progress
☐ Collective rights	☐ Resources of time, money, authority to be held in trust
-and-	-and-
2 GRIEVANCE PROCEDURES DEVELOPED TO:	2 EXECUTION PROCEDURES DEVELOPED TO:
☐ Create procedures for dispute resolution	☐ Assign authority for implementation
☐ Assign authority to adjudicate disagreements	☐ Create authority to resolve implementation disputes.

Figure 15: Educational policy trusts agreements compared with conventional collective contracts

program, they might specify that part of the district's training funds would be used for the effort, that inservice education days would be devoted to the program, and that teachers would devote time to meet, plan and test the new program.

In addition to substantive rules, contracts contain procedural requirements for their administration. It is usually assumed that management is the active party in contract administration in that it will run the schools in such a way that observes its contractual obligations. Labor's responsibility is to be vigilant and to grieve contract violations representing teacher's substantive and procedural due process rights. In conversational shorthand: management acts; labor grieves. Trust agreements do not automatically assume that management will implement the agreement. A trust agreement might empower a group of teachers to plan an outdoor education project or assign responsibility for evaluation to a joint union-management board. They have the facility to create organizational structures which match newly-articulated joint goals.

As in the case of contracts, trust agreements need a means of resolving disagreements. But the issues in a dispute would be quite

250

different. The question is not whether an individual did or did not live up to the letter of the agreement, but whether the implementers of the Trust Agreements were making progress toward agreed upon goals. It is assumed that the beneficiaries of a Trust Agreements are the clients and community, not the individuals involved, and thus the remedy is to fix the program rather than indemnify the staff.

Trust agreements are amenable to a wide variety of dispute resolution techniques. At the informal level, labor and management could meet either on a case-by-case basis or periodically to consider policy deviations before they reached crisis proportions. Third-party conciliation could also be used on this basis.

If a time comes when repeated deviations from the Educational Policy Trust Agreement indicate that it is completely unworkable or that bad faith by one of the parties is undermining its integrity, either party can appeal to an adjudicatory body. Rather than litigation through the courts, however, we suggest that appeals be made to a permanent umpire named in advance by the two parties. Such arrangements are sometimes used in private sector labor relations as an alternative to rights arbitration. Their relative simplicity and continuity is appealing. The permanent umpire would be someone familiar with the school district in question, someone known to union and management, someone who can trace the effects of decisions on the operations of the school organization.

While both labor and management take risks in approaching Educational Policy Trust Agreements, they also have powerful alternatives if the trusts do not work out as planned. First, the agreement has a finite life. The parties can simply let its unworkable provisions expire. Second, either party has alternatives about where to turn for subsequent agreements. If teachers feel that managerial actions are based on organizational convenience, political expediency, or personal bad faith, they can seek to have the terms of the agreement transformed into contract language of the sort now used to protect individual workers from abuse. If management feels that labor has used the trust agreement to further inappropriate self-interests or to obstruct proper operation of the schools, it can reject future agreements and treat teachers as non-professionals.

Our interest in negotiated policy springs from our field research where we found several examples of teachers and school districts engaged in negotiating educational policy. In the framework suggested above, we have tried to refine and extend some of these practices. At least a quarter of the Second Generation districts we studied engaged in some form of informal negotiation over items that were not put in the contract. Sometimes these resulted in 'letters of agreement' or oral agreements that were later ratified as administrative or school board policy. In two districts we found more explicit policy negotiations. In one Illinois school district (where teachers had not affiliated with either national union) the school board set aside one section of its board policy document for the expression of jointly developed policies. The section opens with the statement: 'Under ordinary circumstances no provisions in this will be changed without full consultation with the teacher organization.' While this statement does not have the legal standing we are proposing for Educational Policy Trust Agreements, it was universally perceived to be morally and politically binding on both parties. In another district where labor negotiations were in progress, the negotiators agreed to incorporate the teachers' desires regarding duty assignment into the contract provided the union agreed to a phrase specifying that this portion of the contract could not be subjected to the grievance process. While weakening the agreement more than we would have liked, this approach had the result we are seeking: it made the policy interests and judgments of teachers an active part of the negotiating process.

Since we first wrote about Educational Policy Trust Agreements for the California Commission on the Teaching Profession, we have had the opportunity to pilot-test the idea in districts represented by California Federation of Teachers locals. While these projects are still incomplete, it is already apparent that unions and districts can use the Trust Agreement format to develop very substantive agendas for negotiation. Districts and unions are discussing the substance of teacher evaluation, including how an evaluation program can encompass the artful and intuitive qualities of teaching as well as its routines and techniques. In one section of an agreement already concluded, teachers and administrators in Petaluma, California, have agreed to jointly run an in service education program that replaces 'outside experts' with an ongoing program of teacher-run workshops and continuing assistance.

A number of other districts and unions not included in our field investigations have entered into agreements that have substantively redefined the scope of labor relations. In Toledo, Ohio, the teacher union has negotiated a peer review system that covers both new teachers and experienced teachers who are in trouble. The plan, begun in 1981, has won the support of both union and management.[16] Other expanded working relationships have been developed in Miami, Rochester and Pittsburgh.

The Problem of Unit Determination

The third major change needed to provide an appropriate legal and organizational framework for professional unionism is to redefine what is an appropriate bargaining unit. The law of unit determination recognizes a *community of interest* among workers as a primary criterion for grouping workers into a common unit. A community of interest has come to mean that workers with similar job titles and work assignments in the same organization belong to the same unit. Almost universally, all teachers in a school district are placed in a single bargaining unit, regardless of the size of the district. Depending on the locality, specialists and support personnel, such as psychologists and counselors, either are included in the teacher's bargaining unit or form their own district-wide bargaining units. Teachers' aides are almost always in different bargaining units, as are secretaries, nurses, and similar support personnel. Principals and assistants are virtually never in the same bargaining unit as teachers. In many locales, they are barred from bargaining altogether.

The 'community of interest' concept is a good one that would take on a much richer meaning in professional unionism than it now has. Logically, the organization that has the ability to raise and allocate funds ought to be the locus of wage and salary bargaining. Thus, organizing unions around school districts will continue to be both pragmatic and necessary. However, school districts are gradually taking on different organizational and fiscal functions than those they have historically fulfilled, and these changes have substantial implication for labor relations. Changes in taxing and budgeting practices in many states are eliminating the fiscal independence of local districts, making them a less and less important basis for determining bargaining units. Administratively large school districts are decentralizing, small ones are combining service units, and schools are contracting with outside venders rather than employees to the extent that it is sometimes difficult to tell who the real employer is.

But regardless of where wages are bargained, professional union-ism recognizes that employees have multiple and complex interests. This implies both district and sub-district agreements. Multilevel bargaining could be used, with master contracts dealing with district-wide concerns (such as staffing patterns and teacher recruitment) and smaller bargaining units dealing with problems specific to each aspect of education (such as textbook adoption or school site program develop-ment). Variations on this mechanism are, of course, already employed in steel, autos and other industries. Some subjects of Educational Policy Trust Agreements should logically be undertaken with employee groups that share common policy interests and thus need to plan jointly the educational services for which they are responsible. These units should comprise the smallest groups needed to carry out what might be called a complete technical process — something larger than face-to-face work groups but generally smaller than a large school district.

The composition of these functional work groups might vary substantially from place to place. The size, the geography, and even the educational philosophy of a school district could play an important part in unit determination. For example, an individual school site with a distinctive academic mission, such as an elite high school of science or the arts, might form its own bargaining unit because such a school comes close to being self-contained. The same might hold for a geographically isolated school. Conversely, in a school district that emphasizes academic articulation from grade school through high school, the bargaining units might consist of teachers from a high school and several elementary feeder schools.

The types of employees covered might also vary according to the work technology and level of work integration in the district. Where teachers are essentially in 'private practice', a teachers-only bargaining unit is appropriate. Where education is delivered by work teams whose members have different titles, however, it would be appropriate to include all of the members in the bargaining unit. In schools where the Principal plays the historic role of 'principal teacher', authentically one of first among equals, the bargaining units would appropriately include them. But where teachers' work is clearly differentiated from admin-istrators' work, principals would not share the requisite community of interest. Forming bargaining units according to an authentic com-munity of interest eliminates the dual structures found in most schools today in which an administrative hierarchy is used to set policy and labor relations structure is used to define wages and working conditions.

Creating functionally integrated professional bargaining units would allow fuller development of program improvement concepts and more effective work planning processes. Concepts such as Quality Circles or project task forces, which have been used extensively by corporations, could be implemented more easily if they coincided with bargaining unit structures.

In combination with school-site budgeting, smaller bargaining units would also give teachers more freedom to experiment with new teaching technologies, particularly those involving differentiated staffing, the use of specialists, and the integration of computers. If bargaining units were organized around functional work units, it would be easier to negotiate freedom from narrow statutory bonds, experimental use of alternative incentive systems, and conscious substitutions of one resource for another.

Conclusion: Toward Professional Unionism

Over the course of this book we have described how the idea of unionism changes. We have shown how teachers and school managers conceive successive ideas of employee relations, fight to establish those ideas as a commonly understood generation of labor relations, and structure labor practices to support and implement the basic ideal. We do not know whether Professional Unionism will become the central organizing idea for the Third Generation or whether some alternative will be adopted, but it is already apparent that public education is under great pressure to redefine itself in ways that ultimately redefine teaching. Our demographics, our politics, and our economics all require we create schools whose primary characteristics are flexibility in the face of a changing social environment and adaptability to different client needs. These qualities have not historically been associated with complex public bureaucracies or the conception of teaching work as implementing someone else's curriculum plans.

Professional unionism becomes a compelling object of reform when one gains the conviction, as we have, that the key to reforming education is recognizing and supporting teaching as a profession and rethinking schools as work places for employed professionals. Our

255

reasons for this are both highly pragmatic and highly idealistic. We want teaching to be psychologically satisfying, morally driven work, and we are also convinced that teacher professionalism is 'what works' for schools. Creating conditions that empower teachers to diagnose problems, and placing responsibility to come to grips with those problems will create a more potent organizational response than yet another pedagogical magic pill or an additional layer of educational middle managers.

For Professional Unionism to be compelling to union leaders and managers, they have to be convinced that industrial bureaucracy has reached its limits in education, that change is necessary and possible, and that rethinking unionism is a requirement for reworking teaching. People are beginning to be convinced. Both national teacher unions are rethinking their futures and the role of unions in reforming teaching.[17] Consistent with our ideas about generational change, old taboos are being broken and radical ideas advocated and adopted. People are changing their beliefs and betting their careers that their beliefs can become persuasive.

Notes

1 CALIFORNIA ROUND TABLE ON EDUCATIONAL OPPORTUNITY (1985) *Teaching: Making it an Effective and Attractive Profession*, Sacramento, CA, CRTEO, p. 2.

2 KOCHAN, T. A. and PIORE, M. J. (1984) 'Will the new industrial relations last? Implications for the American labor movement', *The Annals of the American Academy of Political and Social Science*, 473, May, p. 179.

3 *Ibid.*, pp. 179–80.

4 BROOKOVER, W.E. *et. al.* (1982) *Creating Effective Schools*, Holmes Beach, FLA, Learning Publications, Inc.

5 KASSALOW, E.M. (1984) 'The future of American unionism: A comparative perspective', *The Annals of the American Academy of Political and Social Science*, 473, May, pp. 52–63; KORNBLUH, H. (1984) 'Workplace democracy and quality of work life: Problems and prospects', *The Annals of the American Academy of Political and Social Science*, 473, May, pp. 88–95; WIRTH, A.B. (1983) *Productive Work in Schools and Industry*, Lanham, MD, University Press of America; Garbarino, J.W. (1984) 'Unionism without unions: The new industrial relations', *Industrial Relations*, 23, 1, winter, pp. 40–51.

6 MEYER, J. and ROWAN, B. (1978), 'The structure of educational organiza-

tions' in MEYER, M. and associates (Eds) *Environments and Organizations*, San Francisco, CA, Jossey-Bass.

7   WISE, A. (1979) *Legislated Learning: The Bureaucratization of the American Classroom*, Berkeley, University of California Press.

8   444 U.S. 672 (1980).

9   'Yeshiva Case: One Year Later' *Newsletter of the National Center for Collective Bargaining in Higher Education* 9, 2, April/May 1981.

10   78 *Congressional Record*, p. 3443, (1934.)

11   FULMER, W.E. and COLEMAN, JR. J.J., (1984) 'Do quality-of-work-life programs violate section 8(a)(2)?', *Labor Law Journal*, 35, 11, November, p. 677.

12   SOCKELL, D. (1984) 'The legality of employee-participation programs in unionized firms', *Industrial and Labor Relations Review*, 37, 4, July, p. 554.

13   SCHMIDMAN, J. and KELLER, K. (1984) 'Employee participation plans as section 8(a)(2) violations', *Labor Law Journal*, 11, 12, December, p. 779.

14   KIRST, M. (1983) 'Teaching and federal categorical programs' in SHULMAN, L. and SYKES, G. (Eds) *Handbook of Teaching and Policy*, New York, Longmans, p. 441.

15   SELZNICK, P. (1980) *Law, Society, and Industrial Justice*, New Brunswick, N.J., Transaction Books, p. 52.

16   WATERS, C. M. and WYATT, T. L. (1985) 'Toledo's internship: The teachers' role in excellence', *Phi Delta Kappan*, 66, 5, January, pp. 365–8.

17   *Education Week*, 4, 20, 2 February 1985, 1.

APPENDIX A: Questionnaire

QUESTIONNAIRE OF THE IMPACTS OF COLLECTIVE BARGAINING IN SCHOOL DISTRICTS

This survey is an important part of research being conducted into the impacts of collective bargaining on school districts, parents, students, teachers and school administrators.

The research is financed by the National Institute of Education and is being accomplished by researchers from the Claremont Graduate School, the University of California and the University of Illinois.

Your response to the survey will be kept completely confidential. You will not be identified in any way, nor will your community or your school district. The code number below merely allows us to tabulate this response with others received from the same school district.

Please return the completed survey in the envelope provided to:

Dr. Charles T. Kerchner
Labor Relations Research Project
Claremont Graduate School
Claremont, California 91711

School District Code _____

Thank you for agreeing to help.

This survey concerns the effects of teachers' organizations and collective bargaining on schools and how they operate. Each question in the survey asks for your feelings and perceptions about different aspects of employee-relations and school operations.

Answer each question by circling the response that best reflects your feelings about the question. Answer with your first impression. There are no right or wrong answers.

Please answer *all* the questions. Most questions are in the same general form as the question below.

SAMPLE QUESTION

Schools in the United States are basically well run.

1. Strongly Disagree
2. Largely Disagree
3. Disagree Somewhat
4. Mixed Feelings
5. Agree Somewhat
6. Largely Agree
7. Strongly Agree

-1----2----3----4----5----6----7

If you strongly agreed that the schools in the U.S. were well run, you would circle the number 7; if you felt that they were not at all well run, you would circle the number 1.

If you felt that schools were best characterized as being somewhere between these extremes, you would circle the number that best represented your feelings. For instance, if you felt that the schools were well run in most cases, you would circle 6, to largely agree with the statement.

A. THE TEACHERS' ORGANIZATION

In this section we are concerned with the teachers' organization — whether it is called a union or an association — and your perceptions of it.

1. Strongly Disagree
2. Largely Disagree
3. Disagree Somewhat
4. Mixed Feelings
5. Agree Somewhat

The teacher's organization...
6. Largely Agree
7. Strongly Agree

A1 ... is strong and well organized. -1----2----3----4----5----6----7-

A2 ... is successful in dealing with school management. -1----2----3----4----5----6----7-

A3 ... has competent leadership. -1----2----3----4----5----6----7-

A4 ...acts responsibly. -1----2----3----4----5----6----7-

A5 ...actively tries to influence school board policies. -1----2----3----4----5----6----7-

A6 ...supports political candidates. -1----2----3----4----5----6----7-

A7 ...tries to influence the state legislature. -1----2----3----4----5----6----7-

A8 ...is successful in rallying community support. -1----2----3----4----5----6----7-

A9 ...tries to influence parents. -1----2----3----4----5----6----7-

A10 ...is quite likely to go out on strike. -1----2----3----4----5----6----7-

B. THE SCHOOL ADMINISTRATION

These questions concern the overall management or administration of the schools.

1. Strongly Disagree
2. Largely Disagree
3. Disagree Somewhat
4. Mixed Feelings
5. Agree Somewhat
6. Largely Agree
7. Strongly Agree

The administration of this school district. . .

B1 ...is successful in running the schools.

-1----2----3----4----5----6----7-

B2 ...is made up of highly competent individuals.

-1----2----3----4----5----6----7-

B3 ...acts responsibly in dealing with teachers.

-1----2----3----4----5----6----7-

B4 ...emphasizes the development of innovative programs.

-1----2----3----4----5----6----7-

B5 ...pre-occupied with maintaining and supporting existing programs.

-1----2----3----4----5----6----7-

B6 ...has taken steps to tighten accountability and performance standards for teachers, other employees and students.

-1----2----3----4----5----6----7-

B7 ...is actively achieving student achievement through program evaluation and reorganization.

-1----2----3----4----5----6----7-

C. THE SCHOOL BOARD

The third set of questions has to do with the school board in your district.

1. Strongly Disagree
2. Largely Disagree
3. Disagree Somewhat
4. Mixed Feelings
5. Agree Somewhat
6. Largely Agree
7. Strongly Agree

The school board in this district...

C1 ...is well organized and efficient.

-1----2----3----4----5----6----7-

C2 ...is successful in pursuing educational goals.

-1----2----3----4----5----6----7-

C3 ...has competent members who understand educational problems.

-1----2----3----4----5----6----7-

C4 ...acts responsibly and in the best interests of the school district.

-1----2----3----4----5----6----7-

C5 ...is in close contact with a broad cross section of citizens.

-1----2----3----4----5----6----7-

C6 ...is characterized by high conflict, loud debates, and split votes on important issues.

-1----2----3----4----5----6----7-

C7 ...has been the focus of political opposition (including defeats of incumbent board members in contested elections or recall elections).

-1----2----3----4----5----6----7-

C8 ...makes all important policy decisions openly and with adequate input from all interested parties.

-1----2----3----4----5----6----7-

C9 ...is pre-occupied with collective bargaining issues or
problems.   -1----2----3----4----5----6----7-

C10 ...accepts as legitimate the
rights of teachers to bar-
gain collectively.   -1----2----3----4----5----6----7-

C11 ...is satisfied with the
current relationship it has
with teachers.   -1----2----3----4----5----6----7-

D. OPINIONS ABOUT SCHOOLS

In this section we are concerned with your own views about education
and employee organizations.

1. Strongly Disagree
2. Largely Disagree
3. Disagree Somewhat
4. Mixed Feelings
5. Agree Somewhat

As a rule, I believe that   6. Largely Agree
the public schools should...   7. Strongly Agree

D1 ...emphasize a thorough
grounding in fundamental
skills.   -1----2----3----4----5----6----7-

D2ˊ ...support a broad range of
socially and culturally
enriching activities.   -1----2----3----4----5----6----7-

D3 ...provide a full schedule
of sports, drama and other
extra-curricular activities. -1----2----3----4----5----6----7-

D4 ...emphasize vocational
education.   -1----2----3----4----5----6----7-

D5 ...provide very high level
academic training   -1----2----3----4----5----6----7-

E. ABOUT YOURSELF

It would be helpful to know a bit about you personally. These responses are optional and will be used for the purposes of statistical tabulations only.

1. Strongly Disagree
2. Largely Disagree
3. Disagree Somewhat
4. Mixed Feelings
5. Agree Somewhat
6. Largely Agree
7. Strongly Agree

E1 Generally speaking, I consider myself a political conservative.

-1----2----3----4----5----6----7-

E2 Generally speaking, I consider myself favorably disposed toward labor unions.

-1----2----3----4----5----6----7-

E3 What is your relationship to the school district coded on the front cover of this questionnaire? (Please circle *all* the responses that apply.)

a. Parent of child in district
b. School principal or assistant
c. School board member
d. Central office administrator
e. Classroom teacher
f. Leader in teacher organization

g. Active in parent-teacher group
h. Member of a school site council or advisory committee
i. An interested citizen
j. Active in a school monitoring organization such as the taxpayer's association or the League of Women Voters
k. Other _____

_____

E4 Your sex (Male) (Female)

E5 Your approximate age (Under 30) (30–45) (46–65) (over 65)

E6 Your ethnic background (Black) (Hispanic) (White) (Asian) (Other)
E7 Your approximate family income (0–$15,000) ($15–$25,000) ($25–$50,000)   (Above $50,000)
E8 Your occupation _____
E9 Are you a member of a labor organization? (Yes) (No)

F. COMMENTS

We would appreciate it if you would take the time to tell us about any other factors that explain the impact of teacher organizations in your school district, or help us to understand that process.

_____
_____
_____
_____
_____
_____
_____
_____
_____
_____
_____

Appendix B: Discriminant Analysis of Survey Data

As indicated in chapter 4, multiple discriminant analysis (MDA) is the basic statistical technique we used to examine the extent to which ideas about unions, school administrations and school boards are influenced by the changing nature of labor relations in school districts. While MDA is a standard analytical tool available in all major social science statistical packages, it is not widely used. Since many readers may not have encountered this technique previously, this appendix offers a brief review of how MDA works and how it was used to interpret our survey data. Readers interested in a fuller discussion of the technique may consult any good textbook on multivariate techniques. (We used the form of discriminant analysis incorporated into the Statistical Package for the Social Sciences. See *SPSS–X User's Guide, 2nd ed.*, Chicago, McGraw-Hill, 1986).

As a statistical technique, Multiple Discriminant Analysis distinguishes between the attributes of groups within a sample, in our case, the attitudes of respondents to our questionnaire. MDA assesses whether individuals who belong to the same group (on the basis of some identifiable characteristic or experience) tend to give similar responses to specific survey questions. Although the mathematics involved are complicated, the process is conceptually straightforward.

First, respondents are assigned to groups on the basis of some measured characteristic, a *criterion* that applies to all respondents. In our application we used two criterion variables. One involved a questionnaire response assessing school board acceptance of the teacher union's legitimacy, and the other involved the level of conflict within the school district. As described in chapter 7, the mean scores on these responses were used to place each district in one of five generational phases — First Generation, First Intergenerational Conflict Period, Early Second Generation, Late Second Generation or Second Intergenerational Conflict Period. The district's generational category was applied to each respondent from that district and used to divide the 1038 respondents into five groups.

Next, the *discriminating* or predictor variables are identified. These may be any set of variables on which one has measurements for all respondents. In our study, we hypothesized that individuals belonging to the same labor relations generation would hold similar values about unions, school boards and administrations, and thus we undertook a discriminant analysis about attitudes toward each of the three.

MDA calculates the average or mean score on each discriminating variable for each of the identified groups in the sample. The power of any particular variable to distinguish between groups depends on the extent to which members of the same group give similar answers and the extent to which members of other groups give different answers. An ideal discriminating variable would be one on which all members of a particular group give the same answer while no member of any other group gave that answer. For example, if all respondents in the nine districts undergoing the First Intergenerational Conflict circled 'strongly agree' for the statement: 'The teacher organization in my district acts responsibly', and if no members of any other group of districts give this extreme score, the response could be used to perfectly predict membership in the First Intergenerational Conflict group.

Of course, perfect discrimination is almost never found, but we generally find some difference in the mean or average scores for the various respondent groups. Moreover, by asking several questions we are often able to identify differences between groups that can be recognized only if we look for response patterns rather than large differences on individual questions. The mathematical question asked by an MDA statistical program is whether the mean score differences on a set of discriminating questions are large enough (and the associated variability among the individuals small enough) to justify concluding that the individuals in each group gave significantly different responses to various questions. Where several groups and a number of questionnaire responses are being analyzed, MDA examines the possibility of more than one important pattern of separation among the groups. It is frequently the case that two groups give rather similar responses to items that sharply differentiate them from the remaining groups. However, these two groups may diverge on a different subset of questions which are not particularly powerful at differentiating between other groups. When this happens, MDA reports more than one significant 'discriminant function' or weighted array of questions for predicting group membership from the discriminating variables.

In our study, we found that respondents from Early and Late Second Generation districts differed from each other in ways unrelated to their divergence from respondents in districts undergoing inter-generational conflict. In such situations, MDA provided us with two significant discriminate functions. For instance, with regard to opinions about teacher unions, Early and Late Second Generation groups were not widely separated in the first discriminate function, which reported reactions to the success and responsibility of unions. But the two respondent groups appear radically different on the second discriminant function that contains questions about organizational as distinct from external political activity.

In reporting results, MDA provides four types of information: (i) a reliability estimate; (ii) a power estimate; (iii) discriminant function coefficients; and (iv) group centroid scores. The *reliability* measure is usually reported as a Chi-squared statistic with its associated degrees of freedom and probability of chance occurrence estimates. The Chi-squared statistic is an estimate of the possibility that the differences among group responses could be the result of chance factors associated with drawing a small random sample rather than surveying everyone in the population. As indicated in chapter 4, discrimination among the generational phase groups in our sample is extremely reliable. In each case, the probability that differences as large as those found between the different groups could have arisen by chance was substantially less than one in one thousand (a p value of less than ·001).

The second important piece of information reported by the MDA statistical program is an assessment of the *power* of the discriminant analysis. Statistical power is a measure of the extent of difference among the groups identified in the analysis. This is usually reported in terms of a multiple correlation coefficient — a number that measures the extent to which the discriminant function produced by the analysis can be relied upon to identify the members of each group. The best way to interpret the multiple correlation coefficient (Multiple R) is to think of it as a measure of the extent to which an individual's response to questions can be predicted by knowing the categorizing or criterion variable. In our case, the Multiple Rs provide a guide to the strength of labor relations generations in predicting attitudes about unions, school boards and administrations. The larger the Multiple R, the better the prediction will be.

The third important bit of information provided in MDA is an assessment of how much each of the questionnaire items contributes to the overall *power* of the discriminant function. This assessment is provided by discriminant function coefficients, which are analogous to factor loadings in statistical factor analysis or beta weights in multiple regression analysis. The size of the discriminant function associated with each item is directly proportional to the importance of that item in differentiating among various groups. The more a questionnaire item approaches the idea of eliciting a unique answer from each sample group, the larger its coefficient. The most powerful items in terms of their ability to discriminate between groups are frequently used to explain substantive differences between the groups. For example, differences in opinion on questions about 'union responsibility' and 'union success' were critical in discriminating between the generational groups. They were also consistent with our field data regarding the apparent 'reasonableness' with which teacher leaders are depicted during the First Intergenerational Conflict Period. For any given discriminant function, the items that have no discriminating power (because group members disagree about how to respond or because all groups give similar answers to the question) will produce discriminant functions coefficients approaching zero. Generally, as is the case here, these are not reported.

The fourth important piece of information contained in a discriminant analysis report is a set of group '*centroids*'. Centroid scores represent the average score for all members of the group on all items being analyzed multiplied by their discriminant function coefficients. If one thinks of each respondent as represented by a dot in space, the centroid is the point at the geometric center of the swarm of group dots. The difference between group centroids is a measure of the substantive differences between the groups. Where several groups are being analyzed, they are used to identify groups having relatively similar responses from those with very different orientations.

Index